The Language of Vision

OTHER WORKS BY JAMAKE HIGHWATER

FICTION

Mick Jagger: The Singer Not the Song
Anpao
Journey to the Sky
The Sun, He Dies
Legend Days
The Ceremony of Innocence
I Wear the Morning Star
Eyes of Darkness
Kill Hole
Dark Legend

POETRY

Moonsong Lullaby
Songs for the Seasons

NONFICTION

Rock and Other Four Letter Words
Songs from the Earth: Native American Painting
Ritual of the Wind: Indian Ceremonies and Music
Dance: Rituals of Experience
The Sweet Grass Lives On: 50 Indian Artists
The Primal Mind
Arts of the Indian Americas
Native Land, Sagas of American Civilizations
Shadow Show: An Autobiographical Insinuation
Myth and Sexuality

The Language
of Vision

Meditations on

Myth and Metaphor

Jamake Highwater

Grove Press
New York

Published simultaneously in Canada
Printed in the United States of America
FIRST PAPERBACK EDITION

Library of Congress Cataloging-in-Publication Data

Highwater, Jamake.
The language of vision: meditations on myth and
metaphor / Jamake Highwater.—1st ed.
1. Major arcana (Tarot). 2. Myth in art. 3. Metaphor in art.
4. Semiotics and the arts. I. Title.
BF1879.T2H34   1994   93-38667
ISBN 0-8021-3346-0 (pbk.)

Design by Laura Hough

Grove Press
841 Broadway
New York, NY 10003

2 4 6 8 10 9 7 5 3

FOR RUTH

Lost in the storm of our years
Reborn in the springs of memory
With love and pain and timeless wonder.

This is in the end the only kind of courage that is required of us: the courage to face the strangest, most unusual, most inexplicable experiences that can meet us. The fact that people have in this sense been cowardly has done infinite harm to life; the experiences that are called "apparitions," the whole so-called "world of spirit," death, all these things that are so closely related to us, have through our daily defensiveness been so entirely eliminated from life that the senses with which we might have been able to grasp them have atrophied.

Rainer Maria Rilke

Contents

Contents

I.

The Fool

Labyrinth of Dreams

We have not even to risk the adventure alone, for the heroes of all time have gone before us. The labyrinth is thoroughly known. We have only to follow the thread of the hero path, and where we had thought to find an abomination, we shall find a god. And where we had thought to slay another, we shall slay ourselves. Where we had thought to travel outward, we come to the center of our own existence. And where we had thought to be alone, we will be with all the world.

Joseph Campbell (1990)

You awaken from a dream. You are anxious and frightened. You try to shake off the fantastic grip of the dream, but, somehow, you cannot focus on the "real world." The sense of urgency and fear continues to haunt you. Summoning all your verbal skills, you approach a friend hesitantly, and then you stammer: "I had this dream."

"A dream . . ." your friend echoes uncomfortably.

"That's right. It was a dream."

"Ahuh . . ."

You push on, despite your friend's apparent disinterest. "I was in a room," you falter. "Well . . . not exactly a room. More like a cave. Or maybe it was a bird cage."

"Sure . . . a bird cage," your friend mutters, with a vacant expression.

"Anyway, you came in. Well . . . not exactly you. More like your mother. Or could it have been the dog?"

Now your friend smiles impatiently and tries to change the subject.

You sigh and feel thoroughly confounded. What confounds you is not your friend's impatience, but your realization that the language upon which you are completely dependent for expressing your thoughts and feelings is incapable of conveying something you experienced vividly but cannot put into words.

Faced by such a baffling situation, most of us distort and alter the experience so we can put it into words. We change the dream so it makes sense in the only language we have available to us. And as a result of our efforts to make sense of what seems to be nonsense, a powerful and visionary experience is lost in the use of a few precise but prosaic words: "I was in a room and you came in . . ."

The dream has been reduced to a commonplace. And, sadly, the visionary experience has become a banality.

3

It seems to me that much of what passes as "reality"—what we innocently call history and reportage—is nothing more or less than our dreams turned into banalities. Most of us are content with such a practical fiction. But there are also people who refuse to abandon their dreams. Instead, they change the language we use to describe our experiences. And they do this as an act of passion, driven by the hope of somehow capturing the illusive power of their visions.

Painters do just that when they abandon or rethink conventional concepts of visual representation. Composers reimagine the sounds and the forms they use to make music. Choreographers reinvent the human body. Writers destroy the ordinary language of daily life and use words "poetically"—as metaphors capable of describing the indescribable.

This book is about the vastly different ways that such artists have found their way through the labyrinth of dreams. It is concerned with the mythic trail that countless visionaries have left in the winding maze; a trail that helps us find our way through the vast interior of ourselves. What those visionaries have left for us is a dim and somnambulistic glow. A fragile beacon that beckons us into the shadows. A world of sounds, words, images, and movements invented by those who have gone into the labyrinth before us. By those who have ventured to the center, where ideas become acts. Where myths are transformed into rituals. By those who have risked a journey into the cavern of the heart, where art is born and where we dream ourselves into existence.

This book is about the relationship of art, myth, and metaphor—those intuitive and imaginal effervescences of the mind that coax us into the infinite darkness of things unknown and unnamed. Mythic tales that transform the unreal into a new reality. Metaphors born out of the dreamtime that mysteriously change the ineffable into something that is finally spoken. And, by such ancient acts of the imagination, the mythic and metaphoric elements of art are capable of changing forever the way we see ourselves and the way we see our societies.

*   *   *

According to legends, if the twenty-two cards of the Tarot Major Arcana were placed in a precise arrangement, allowing them to be "read" both horizontally and vertically, then they would reveal their secrets. The exact nature of those "secrets" has been the subject of a great deal of speculation and debate since the time of Dante, when Tarot cards first appeared in Europe. For many scholars, the cards have an alchemical power: "a genuine Gnostic document of the soul's initiation into higher consciousness" (Roberts).* For others, the cards are a means of prophecy, something akin to "fortune telling." Some regard the Tarot cards as psychic mirrors that provide vivid reflections of the unconscious mind, an access to the nonfactual and the nonspecific. There are also those, like nineteenth-century Romantics, who exaggerated their antagonism for the pragmatic world by insisting that the Tarot cards were both empirical and mystic, an oxymoron that envisioned "reality" as unreal and, at the same time, insisted that mystic experiences were "real." Thus the Romantic point of view saw the messages gleaned from the Tarot cards as statements of fact, much as today's religious fundamentalists concretize all their great religious myths and insist that those myths are historical facts.

For me the Tarot are not tools of divination. Nor are they phantasmagorias. They are not historical facts or oracular messages disguised as picture cards. Rather, the Tarot cards are eclipses of utilitarian logic, in whose penumbra we imagine that we see ourselves. The Tarot cards are evocations of the human psyche that are spread before us and that coax us to "read" their colorful faces both in terms of the *horizontal* nature of the commonplace world

---

*Attribution for all materials quoted in this book may be found in the bibliography under the author's name. If there is more than one book or article listed for a given author, then the date of publication of the work from which a quotation is drawn is listed after the name of the author each time it appears in the text: e.g., (Campbell 1986).

and the *vertical* nature of that other world, which plunges downward and rises upward into the labyrinth of dreams.

Among the picture cards of the Tarot deck, one of the most fascinating figures is called "The Fool." He is depicted as a young man carrying a small bundle on his shoulder. He walks with the aid of a staff while a dog tears at his trouser leg. It is generally agreed that the Fool represents the beginning of an adventure, when endless opportunities beckon him to experiences of unlimited possibility. The Fool also represents folly and irrationality, intuition and extravagance. Thus the Fool seemed to be an ideal symbol for the opening chapter of this book. And because of my fascination with the allusions of the picture cards of the Tarot deck, I have built each of the twenty-two chapters of *The Language of Vision* upon the symbolism of the Tarot's twenty-two Major Arcana, with the hope of exploring the "messages" evoked by the cards as they are laid out in horizontal and vertical patterns, and with the hope of implying the impact that the symbolism of the Tarot cards has upon our lives as they are endlessly shuffled and reshuffled through all the senseless circles of time.

II.

The Emperor

Chimera of Reality

See, when I paint, it is an experience that, at its best, is transcending reality. When it is working, you completely go into another place, you're tapping into things that are totally universal, completely beyond your ego and your own self. That's what it's all about.

Keith Haring

"The Emperor" of the Tarot cards, who lends his name to this chapter, signifies male authority and world power. He represents the domination of reason and stoicism over intuition and passion. The Emperor also denotes stability and pragmatism, order and clarity. Obviously, he is not an advocate of impressionism or expressionism. He believes that reality is no more and no less than exactly what he perceives the world to be as it stands before him. He is not fond of poetry and intellectual abstractions. Nor is he likely to approve of sentience and expressiveness. He is the father figure of the Tarot cards, and, as such, he connotes all the various attitudes and values of a patriarch ruling over a patriarchy.

Joseph Campbell (1990) said that "art is the clothing of a revelation." But the Emperor is intimidated by revelations, because they bring him face to face with both himself and the unknown. Revelation is an unexpected experience, and the Emperor does not relish encounters with the unexpected. So he is unable to have the revelation that is born of an experience of art. He puts barriers between himself and experience. This can be done by ideologues, by bureaucrats, or it can be done by people who expect of art what they have already gotten from art, rather than allowing themselves to expect the unexpected. People like the Emperor, who approach art with preconceptions, whether political or moral, effectively deprive themselves of the experience of art.

Art doesn't want to be familiar. It wants to astonish us. Or, in some cases, to enrage us. It wants to move us. To touch us. Not accommodate us, not make us comfortable. To have an experience you have to allow yourself to be part of the experience or it does not happen. You cannot just sit there passively, like someone watching a sitcom on television in which emotional trivia is repeated endlessly. Unless the Emperor is jarred out of his fear and complacency by experience, he is not going to have an artistic experience. But the Emperor doesn't like to be jarred. He likes things to be nice.

Joseph Campbell was profoundly aware of the relationships among revelation, art, and experience. He said that people often talk about trying to discover "the meaning of life," whereas what they are really after is "an *experience* of life" (italics added; 1990). The revelation clothed as art is an instance of that experience of life. But the Emperor has no interest in the experience. As Oscar Wilde said: If such prosaic people were given the chance to choose between going to heaven or hearing a lecture about heaven, they would go to the lecture.

The Emperor believes that facts inform us. He believes that if he attends a lecture about a painting or a sonata or a poem, he will *understand* the mysterious language that he imagines he encounters when confronted by works of art. The Emperor wants to *understand* art; he does not want to *experience* it. Unlike the dauntless, mythic medieval hero on a quest, who lets the reins lie slack on the horse's neck as he ventures into the darkest part of the forest, the Emperor anxiously tugs at them, fearful of being carried away. He dreads the impetuousness of the horse, for the mythic horse often represents the measureless force of nature. And so the fainthearted Emperor insists upon retaining rational control of the beast.

The revelation that is called art tells us: "Yield to nature. Experience the astonishment of the unknown. Let nature take you on its journey." But the Emperor counters: "Correct nature! Cage and leash and domesticate it! Do not let it lead you into the unknown!"

Today the Emperor can no longer resist his encounter with the overwhelming sense of "improbability" that has become the keynote of late twentieth century physics. In confusion and dread he has come to the end of all the familiar paths. The pavement has run out. The durable landmarks of civilization have vanished. And he is in Kansas no longer.

In January 1982 I watched with some surprise as the Emperor came face to face with the twentieth century. It happened at Big Sur, a spectacular town perched at the edge of the rugged coastline of northern California. The Emperor's name was Dr. Roger Guillemen, a Nobel laureate in the field of biology, and he had come to Big Sur to meet Joseph Campbell.

In one of several conversations, Campbell told Dr. Guillemen: "The problem of science is to give you an image of the universe, what it's like, what it actually is like. And this changes from decade to decade. No scientist says, 'I've found truth.' There's a working hypothesis, and the next season we have another structure."

Dr. Guillemen blinked with skepticism, saying: "Mmmmm. I would qualify that. Enormously. *Enormously!*"

All of us sitting at the conference table laughed. But Campbell was not amused. Without a moment's delay, he retorted: "Okay, they think they've found truth! So, the problem of mythology is to relate that found truth to the actual living of a life."

Someone attempted to make less of the distinction between the function of science and mythology, suggesting that what prediction is to science, prophecy is to mythology.

Dr. Guillemen: "But in the predicted power of mythology, how statistical is it? Will it really happen when the prediction is made?"

At this point, I took up the battle. "The question," I said, "has nothing to do with the whole basis of mythology. The empirical question that you ask is a completely valid one, but mythology serves the ineffable, serves the unfathomable, serves the very things that we cannot deal with in terms of science. If we could deal with our entire experience in terms of the empirical or in terms of the practical, then there would be no reason for any of this discussion" (Campbell, Cousineau 1990).

The Emperor was not convinced. Nor would he probably be convinced by the argument of one of the most noted scientific philosophers of the last forty years, F. S. C. Northrop (1966): "The point to be noted here is not that empirical knowledge of this traditional Western type is not the most excellent knowledge of its kind, but merely that it is *only one type* of knowledge." There is an equally important and significant kind of knowledge that Northrop championed. It is visionary experience—the mythic point of view, which provides genuine experience in its own right. And it is specifically this allusive and alternative kind of experience and knowledge that finds its existence in myth and metaphor and art.

But this alternative point of view is still alien to people who believe that anything *meaningful* must necessarily lend itself to expression in commonplace language. Ironically, the very opposite may be true.

According to a delightful apocryphal tale, a young journalist approached the great American dancer Isadora Duncan after a concert and asked if she would explain the meaning of her dances. "I want to write about your performance," he explained, "but I'm not quite certain what I saw."

Duncan smiled politely and said, "But if I could tell you the meaning of my dances, young man, I would have no reason to perform them."

Art, then, is not an elaborate subterfuge aimed at confusing people untrained in the arts. It is not something of dubious significance because its "meaning" cannot be easily or coherently expressed in prosaic terms and empirical facts. Art has no interest in facts. And nothing makes this point better than a commentary given by television journalist Bill Moyers at a dinner honoring Joseph Campbell.

Moyers said that he and Campbell had been invited to a distant place called the Garden of Eden to investigate the tragedy of a man and a woman who were about to be evicted. According to Moyers, he and Campbell interviewed the victims and did a great deal of research. "And," Moyers modestly but insightfully concluded, "after a lot of hard work, I realized that I had gotten all the *facts,* but Joseph Campbell had gotten the *story."*

Art is about the story. It is not about the facts. And to tell the story, to paint it or write it or dance it or compose it, the artist must grasp its mythic dimensions: its subtle shape and its "virtual meaning," which, as Suzanne Langer has explained (1957), is

12

"anything that exists only for perception, and plays no ordinary, passive part in nature as common objects do." Art is that kind of virtual entity. "It is not unreal; where it confronts you," she wrote, "you really perceive it, you don't just dream or imagine that you do." The image in a mirror is a virtual image. A rainbow is a virtual object. "It seems to stand on the earth or in the clouds, but it really 'stands' nowhere; it is only visible, not tangible."

The Emperor has grave problems with such ideas. To him these explanations seem to be intentionally baffling. They seem to intensify his suspicion that the arts are secret languages that only the initiated comprehend; whereas, to the contrary, there is nothing as profoundly and communally human as those things we call art. Art connects us to that narrow aspect of nature we naively call "human nature." It allows us to escape the merciless bounds that we in the Western world call "identity."

"The imagination is that which is least human in [human-kind]. . . . It wrenches us away from ourselves and plunges us into ecstasy; it puts us into secret communion with the powers of nature. 'Who speaks to me, with my own voice?' From ourselves comes a marvelous stranger called art" (Dufrenne).

The mythic dimension of art is its capacity to wrench us away from ourselves. But the Emperor finds such a notion both strange and disagreeable. After all, he contends, isn't it the central aim of each of us in the Western world to forge a clear identity? What is left if there is no "self"? And isn't it just that clear identity that radiates in all great works of art?

Not according to artists like Keith Haring, who declared that, to the contrary, when art is working, "you completely go into another place, you're tapping into things that are totally universal, completely beyond your ego and your own self."

The only egoistic trick needed by artists is knowing how to get out of their own way. How to lose oneself by deeply submerging *into* oneself.

Again, the Emperor has problems with these concepts. They seem to contradict several of his basic beliefs; beliefs so entrenched in his mentality that they have become aspects of the language he speaks.

The invention of the individual is a relatively recent cultural event, one which is reflected in the languages we began to speak just before and after the dissolution of the Roman world. Art, too, was not individuated for countless centuries. A great portion of world art was anonymous and seemingly "unauthored" until the Renaissance, when the artist gradually arose from the ranks of all other artisans and was given a special, but curiously subordinate, role in European culture.

If art is not the outpouring of an immense ego but arises from a primal and mythic source—"Who speaks to me with my own voice?"—and if art is about the story and not about the facts, then how do artists manage to turn ineffable experience into movements, words, images, and objects?

As I have already pointed out, they do it, in part, by inventing new languages. By creating metaphors that *allude* to meaning but do not *denote* meaning. By saying precisely what they mean as imprecisely as possible.

If such a creative process sounds like humbug, perhaps another concept of Joseph Campbell's will help to make my point.

Campbell and I had many disagreements. Whereas he wished to explore the ways in which all of us are the same, I wanted to explore the ways in which all of us are different. Campbell was quite literal in his approach to Jung's ideas about a collective unconscious, which envision a profound level of human consciousness which is transcendent and universal. On the other hand, I favor the celebration of differences between cultures and individuals, and I, therefore, have a far more figurative view of Jung's theories.

But for all our intellectual differences and animated debates, Campbell and I strongly agreed that the modern artist is best understood as the protagonist in what he called the "hero's journey" (1949).

Mythic heroes venture beyond the limits of the commonplace world (a process Campbell called "the Departure"), where they experience some kind of revelation (which Campbell called "the Initiation"), which they then transform into expressive myths (called "the Return"), so people who have not ventured beyond the world may share the hero's revelation.

As Campbell often mentioned, among primal people the role of the mythic hero was usually assumed by mystics, shamans, and saints. But in today's secular Western world it is the artist who has assumed the role of mythmaker. And it is in that unique role that the artist finds it necessary to create metaphoric forms of expression that are capable of dealing with the ineffable—the revelation.

As I have pointed out, these metaphors *allude* to meaning but do not *denote* meaning. They provide artists with the capacity to say precisely what they mean as imprecisely as possible, which is the only way they can express the inexpressible. Such ambiguity is the very essence of metaphors. And as such, metaphoric expression is a process of figurative expression that is not easily grasped by the literal-minded Emperor.

In the last years of his life Joseph Campbell agreed to undertake a national promotional tour. It was a fascinating and astounding experience for the eighty-some-year-old Campbell, who likened the mad trip to the adventures of Alice through the looking glass. "I am not mad!" protested Alice. "You would not be here if you were not mad!" retorted the Cheshire Cat.

In one of several cities he visited Campbell came face to face with the Emperor: a young radio journalist who decided to confront Campbell, though he knew virtually nothing about his vast body of work. The result was an amusing story that Campbell loved to tell again and again. The interview was "live," and about five minutes before the end of the program, the interviewer asked Campbell why a man of his education and experience would spend a lifetime studying fairy tales and myths.

Campbell was shocked. "Myths are very important," he insisted.

"They're just lies," the interviewer exclaimed. "Mere nonsense."

"Mere nonsense?" Campbell hissed. "They are metaphors

that allow us to know things we otherwise could never know. Do you know what a metaphor is?" Campbell demanded.

"Of course," the interviewer answered.

"Well, then give me an example of one!" Campbell commanded, carried away by the authority of his forty years of dealing with slothful college students.

After hedging for a moment, the interviewer said: "The man ran like a deer. That's a metaphor!"

"No," Campbell was quick to correct, "that's a simile."

"Then, what's a metaphor?" urged the exasperated radio interviewer, who knew that time was quickly running out.

Campbell smiled triumphantly and said, "A metaphor is this: the man is a deer."

"That's a lie!" shouted the interviewer.

"No," Campbell said with a knowing grin, "it's a metaphor."

At just that moment, the time allotted for the interview was over, and Campbell walked out with a lavish smile on his face.

According to Campbell the radio journalist was crushed. But I suspect that the Emperor still did not understand the power of myths or metaphors.

III.

The Falling Tower

Death of the Sacred

If our life lacks a constant magic it is because we choose to observe our acts and lose ourselves in consideration of their imagined form and meaning, instead of being impelled by their force.

Antonin Artaud

The Tarot card called "The Falling Tower" is customarily depicted as a stone tower that is struck by lightning emanating from the sun. Two figures fall from the tower. The card has been variously interpreted to mean change and disorder; the breakdown of old beliefs and the loss of stability. For these reasons, the Falling Tower serves as an ideal basis for the discussion of the series of historic events that brought about the transformation of art from an act of revelation in the service of the sacred to a purely secular activity, often in the service of an aristocracy. As we shall see, many of the difficulties we experience when dealing with art and many of the problems we have in comprehending the social significance and social function of art derive from this radical shift of art as a sacred activity to art as artifact—the product of a marginal and secular activity.

Throughout prehistory and everywhere in the primal world art has been an integral part of life. For reasons we shall eventually explore, contemporary industrial societies usually view art as the idle product of a leisure class, an ornamentation, a product of taste, privilege, and affectation. In fact, we live in the only civilization that sees art as peripheral, that has little or no grasp of the value of art, and is uncertain what artists actually do or why they bother to do it. In essence, we have little or no use for the arts, and this is mirrored, especially in America, by the fact that the media rarely if ever deal with subjects that have any connection with the arts unless, of course, a painting is auctioned for an immense amount of money or a choreographer beats his wife or a photographer makes pictures that shock the sensibility of people who seem to have little sensibility. This is the predicament of our mercantile mentality and the result, as we shall see, of the transition from church to aristocratic domination of the arts, which took place just prior to the rise of the merchant princes and the new middle class.

This predicament of the arts is a sad devaluation of human

expressiveness by societies that have gradually separated their sentient needs from the utilitarian necessities of daily life. But history does not readily uphold the mercantile antagonism to art, which has made it into something "difficult and serious" and beyond the grasp of the "man" on the street. Nor does history support the American notion that the arts are so extraneous and so removed from the central issues of society that only people who are characterized as emotional, impractical, and socially insignificant take any interest in art. Such people, in the parlance of the Emperor, are women and effeminate men.

Although the modern arts seem to lack a utilitarian relationship to society, they have been used for self-aggrandizement by a pretentious and often conservative elite, which clings to the idea that art has something to do with aristocracy—the very aristocracy that was destroyed by those same burghers who now opt for all things aristocratic. Their motto is: "Let them eat art!" Their emulation of church and aristocratic art patronage has both positive and negative aspects, but it also mirrors the historical chain of events that led art from its central and sacred role in society to its present predicament as a handmaiden of an elite that often cares more for the prestige of associating with the arts than the merits of art itself. This predicament reminds me of a conversation I had with Julius Rudel, then director of the New York City Opera. I asked him why there wasn't an opera season in New York in the summer. After a long pause, he said: "Probably because it's too hot to wear a fur coat."

Originally art was a staple of humankind—never the plaything of a social class. Art can enforce class distinctions, but it does so unwillingly. In fact, art has quite the opposite relation to society, insofar as it can function for any economic, intellectual, or social group. In fact, art is so urgent, so utterly linked with the pulse of life and feeling in human beings, that it becomes the singular basis of survival when every other aspect of civilization fails: in concentration camps, among the brutalized and dispossessed, the mad and the too mighty. Like hunger and sex, art is a disposition of the human cells—a marvelous fiction of the brain that re-creates itself as mind. Art is consistent with every aspect of every day in the life of every people. It even expresses a nation's self-contempt when it recognizes its failures and frustrations.

The dwellers of caves in the early morning of this human world built scaffolds in the dark interiors of their rock caverns, and with pigments made from ground roots and bark and minerals they painted an amazing world upon their ceilings by the meager light of tiny oil lamps. They were creating "art" before art existed, spending their time making paintings when the Emperor would say that they should have been out finding food and facing the tremendous improbability of their survival.

But art is essential to life. It is not superfluous.

Art is a way of *seeing*, and what we see in art helps to define what we mean by the word "reality." Not everyone sees the same things, though the dominant, industrial societies usually presume that their "realistic" or "illusionist" visions represent the sole truth about the world. But each culture, and often individuals within the same culture, understand reality uniquely.

The complex process by which an artist transforms the act of seeing into images and rituals and stories is one of the consummate mysteries of the arts—one of the reasons that art for most Asian and tribal peoples is inseparable from religion and philosophy. The magic of art, the skill of creating effigies of revered and mystic animals, for instance, may have been one of the most compelling motives for the creation of the cave paintings at Altamira and Lascaux. This astounding Stone Age art demonstrates the wide diversity of ways we see and describe the world. Though cave painting is admired for its "naturalism," the images are anything but naturalistic. To the contrary, they are highly stylized. For instance, the depictions of cattle at Lascaux use a form of representation that has been described as "twisted perspective." The head of a bull is drawn in profile, and yet both horns are shown as if representing a frontal point of view—as if two cameras had photographed the beast simultaneously, in profile and in full face. The impact of this perspective is startling. Centuries later, Picasso's cubist approach to spatial representation was profoundly influenced by this Stone Age "twisted perspective," which he claimed to have observed in ancient Iberian sculptures and reliefs.

The apparent intent of both Picasso and his Paleolithic forebears was to create an art of essence rather than an art of appearance. It is a sacred art that deals with *revelation* rather than *observation*. Art historian Herbert Read makes an important observation about this kind of animal imagery, which is found in numerous nonindustrial cultures: "In such representations there is no attempt to conform with the exact but casual appearances of animals; and no desire to evolve an ideal type of animal. Rather from an intense awareness of the nature of the animal, its movements and its habits, the artist is able to select just those features which best denote its vitality, and by exaggerating these and distorting them until they cohere to some significant rhythms and shape, [the artist] produces a representation which conveys to us the very *essence* of the animal."

Such a purpose may explain the twisted perspective of Paleolithic cave paintings. What distinguishes twisted perspective is the fact that the painter's approach is not descriptive of a single optical point of view but is concerned with the painter's consummate experience of the animal: the experience that confirms that cattle have two horns is more important to the painter than the optical fact that only one horn is visible when the animal stands in profile. When exploring the arts of ancient Egypt and the Near East, we find the same *essential*, rather than pictorial, attitude toward representation.

This diversity of representation in art has not had much impact on the Emperor, who still insists that the visual arts are supposed to depict the world as *he* sees it. He gazes at the stylized forms of Egyptian reliefs, with their predominant angularity, with eyes and shoulders in frontal view while heads and legs are in profile, and he wonders if that kind of spatial form is the result of

22

artists who were simply unskilled at their craft and could not properly draw what they saw. The Emperor is unaware that the notion of representing a scene as it would appear to a single observer at a single moment was as alien to the Egyptian artist as it had been to Paleolithic painters (Janson). And so the Emperor presupposes that artists have always attempted to match appearances with cameralike exactitude. "This is not the case, nor is it the case that artists of one period 'see' more 'correctly' and render more 'skillfully' than those of another. It seems rather to be the case that artists represent what they *conceive* to be real rather than what they *perceive*" (Gardner).

Even if we insist upon the veracity of the optical world as it seems to exist, still we must recognize that very few forms of art have taken much interest in such "realism." Even a cursory exploration of cultural history makes it clear that verisimilitude has been important only to the artists of a few times and a few places. In fact, such realist art is currently called "illusionist art," insofar as it strives to create the illusion of "optical facts."

On the other hand, one of the startling discoveries of twentieth-century physics has been a vision of reality that is remarkably similar to the nonillusionist visions of the great majority of artists throughout global history. Physicist Werner Heisenberg devised a revolutionary concept that has come to be known as the "uncertainty principle." It suggests that we cannot observe the world without changing it. "What we observe is not nature itself," he wrote, "but nature exposed to our method of questioning." Art is just such a method of questioning, and what it sees and depicts results from what it asks of its subject matter. The kinds of questions that artists ask transform their perceptions into ritualized experiences, into active metaphors that illuminate sacred and personal visions of the world that are called mythologies.

As for naive, empirical reality, it is little more than a perceptual convention of a particular time and place—a useful but banal fiction. French philosopher Michel Foucault found the notion of Western reality discouragingly middle class. And if, as many physicists and philosophers now confirm, reality is malleable and transient, then who can claim to know and see the one and only "reality"?

Still, there are those who defend the universality of artistic realism by claiming that art is an outgrowth of a universal and transcendent attribute of Homo sapiens called "human nature," presumably a ubiquitous and inborn aspect of human consciousness. Anthony Marcel disagrees. He is a psychologist at the Medical Research Council of the Applied Psychology Unit of Cambridge University, and he believes that recent studies suggest that *consciousness* may not be an entirely inherent part of so-called human nature. To Marcel, it seems that consciousness itself may be at least partly learned: "I go along with philosophers who believe that consciousness is to some degree a social construct. Every culture holds certain tacit beliefs about the nature of reality and perceptions that shape experience. In a radically different culture, people's phenomenal experience may be literally quite different from ours."

As Arthur Zajonc has pointed out, "The sober truth remains that vision requires far more than a functioning [optical] organ. Without an inner light, without a formative visual imagination, we are blind." The veracity of this statement is exemplified by Zajonc in his recounting of an event in 1910. Two French surgeons achieved a successful operation on an eight-year-old boy who had been blind since birth because of cataracts.

> When the boy's eyes were healed, they removed the bandages, eager to discover how well the child could see. Waving a hand in front of the boy's physically perfect eyes, they asked him what he saw. He replied weakly, "I don't know." "Don't you see something moving?" they asked. "I don't know" was the boy's only reply. The boy's eyes were clearly not following the slowly moving hand. What he saw was only a varying brightness in front of him. He was then allowed to touch the hand as it was moving; he cried out in a voice of

triumph: "It's moving!" He could feel it move, and even, as he said, "hear it move," but he still needed laboriously to learn to *see* it move. Passing through the now-clear black pupil of the child's eyes, that first light called forth no echoing image from within. The child's sight began as a hollow, silent, dark, and frightening kind of seeing. The light of day beckoned, but no light of mind replies within the boy's anxious, open eyes.

Clearly, then, it takes far more than sight to see. It was American painter Arthur Dove who said: "We cannot express the light in nature because we have not the sun. We can only express the light we have in ourselves." Quantum physicist Arthur Zajonc now makes it clear that Dove's metaphor can also be understood as a medical phenomenon.

Seeing is apparently as much a matter of socialization as is the development of consciousness.

Given this variability in the nature of experience, it is little wonder that myth and metaphor are central aspects of the human encounter with experience.

This wide spectrum of representation in the arts is doubtlessly built on the intrinsic relationship the arts always have with the sacred and secular mythologies of societies. So from the outset it is important that I explain what is meant here by the term "mythology." The noted mythologist David Maclagan explains it best:

Myth, in its deep structure as well as in its superficial content, is about this compound relation between body/mind and word/world. It is metaphoric, not in the sense that it uses what we call "figures of speech," mere rhetorical devices, but in the root sense of the word: "carrying across" the convenient boundaries we establish between sexes, seasons, species and stars. This metaphoric leakage is not consciously contrived, nor is it peculiar to myth; it penetrates, in the act, *everything* we do, all the sense we make—even in the most narrowly specialized branch of science.

Barbara C. Sproul observes that "myths involve attitudes toward facts and reality." As such, the questions they raise are most effectively answered by the metaphoric mentality that is at the heart of mythology. Myths constellate a society's grasp of reality. Whether we adhere to them or not, the myths at the foundation of our societies remain pervasively influential. Myths deal

> with first causes, the essences of what our cultures perceive reality to be. . . . So it is no accident that cultures think their creation myths the most sacred, for these myths are the foundation on which all later myths stand. In them members of the group can perceive meaning. . . . But because of the way in which domestic myths are transmitted, people often never learn that they *are* myths; people become submerged in their viewpoints, prisoners of their own traditions. They readily confuse attitudes toward reality (proclamations of value) with reality itself (statements of fact). (Sproul)

Like the Paleolithic cave painters, the artists of ancient Egypt and medieval Christianity had distinctive worldviews. They had unique mythological responses to the most fundamental questions about their existence and purpose in the cosmos. These ideologies were the unquestioned basis of *reality* and moral value in their works. They didn't have to explain the content or justify the political and moral attitude of their efforts. They didn't have to justify their style and technique of representation. They worked within a socially unified process of thought and consensus that grew out of the worldview of their cultures. Their audiences existed within the same frame of reference and in the same reality, the same mythology. Thus, in their art there was in the truest sense "nothing to understand." "Meaning" in the arts only comes into existence when the mythology of a society dissipates and no longer supports the worldview of artists. Today, when the content of art has lost its ideological function and context, we look at it as a historical document or as a totally independent creation of expressive forms—or ideally, as a combination of both art form and historical tradition. We need not be Christian in order to respond to the creations of Dante, Memling, and Bach. The appeal of their religious works persists not because of, but in spite of, their total grounding in Christian mythology. In a unified society, art exists in the context of communally held paradigms. In a society whose mythology has corroded, art can only exist in the context of "meaning," which is determined by the value judgments of individuals and/or political groups. When art ceases to operate out of a mythological context, it becomes the province of the individual rather than the voice of the group. This individuation and secularization of art fundamentally changes the relationship of the arts to their audiences, bringing into play the necessity of rationally grasping ("understanding") the intention of the artist rather than directly experiencing art in its mythological and communal context. Artists of industrial societies that no longer retain viable myths are, of necessity, the creators of personal mythologies. Such artists often picture themselves as modern alchemists. Choreographer Eliot Feld said that artists who are very lucky and talented are capable, like fabled alchemists, of changing "base metals into gold." In this metaphoric sense, common experience is the base metal, while art is the gold. For this reason, Feld explains, to talk about what you have created is to turn gold back into base metal. "You don't really explain your art by talking about it. What you do, unfortunately, is explain it away."

This mystical and alchemical view of the artistic process was a central conceit in early Christian and Byzantine art, which was deeply influenced by the metaphysical ideology of Asia and the Near East. The medieval vision of art was strongly Asiatic in its other worldliness, which distinguished it from the worldly idealizations of the arts of classical Greece and the naturalistic arts of Rome.

27

Roman mural painters had devised elaborate illusionistic methods that enabled them to suggest a reality beyond the two-dimensional surface of the wall. The creators of early Christian mosaics also disdained the flatness of the wall surface, but, in contrast to the Roman artists, they did so in an effort to achieve an "illusion of unreality—a luminous realm peopled by celestial beings or symbols" (Janson).

This early Christian art expressed an attitude about visual representation that was very different from that of the arts of Greece and Rome. Greece had been devoted to the humanization of Hellenic gods and, at the same time, to the deification of mortal heroes and leaders. The art of Rome was essentially secular in its attitudes and was used almost entirely in the service of the nobility, with an emphasis upon creating portraiture and monumental statuary of powerful rulers. Then, from about A.D. 450, the fashion of creating outward likenesses, typical of Roman and early Christian art, gave way to images built upon a spiritual ideal not unlike the arts of the Paleolithic cave painters, the artists of the Near East, and the artists of tribal communities. From the fifth century onward there would be no more portraits in the Greco-Roman style for almost a thousand years. The creation of a realistic imitation of the appearance of individual persons, and even the realistic depiction of the human body, ceased to be the primary concern of artists in the West. The emphasis now had shifted to the abstract and the spiritual. The famous mosaics of Santa Vitale at Ravenna typify this mystical element of early Christian and Byzantine art. Justinian and his empress, Theodora, accompanied by various officials, are depicted in a manner hitherto unknown in the Romanized West: exaggeratedly tall and slender figures, with tiny feet that float in the air; small, almond-shaped faces dominated by large, gazing eyes; and ethereal bodies that are incapable of any movement other than elegant ceremonial gestures. There is no reference in the figuration to muscular movement or human emotion. The dimensions of secular time and space have given way to what Jacques Le Goff has called "sacred time and space"—an eternal present portrayed as if heaven were a golden limbo. The solemn, exclusively frontal images of Justinian and Theodora give the impression of a celestial rather than a secular court. At Ravenna, art is no longer aimed at a worldly glorification of nobility; it is dedicated to the depiction of lords and ladies in a mood of spiritual otherworldliness, a style that arises from the influences of Asian mysticism and that hearkens back to the mythological mood of the Altamira cave paintings. Gradually even the spiritualized emperors of the Byzantine world are exiled from the arts of the Middle Ages, as the great lords of the secular world are subdued and displaced by biblical characters in whom the ideals and conflicts of Christianity are visually ritualized.

Church windows and frescoes vividly dramatize the tales of saints and prophets. The Annunciation, the Nativity, and the Crucifixion are celebrated in countless works of art. The expulsion of Adam and Eve from the garden, the martyrdom of saints, and the lamentations of prophets are vividly depicted on altar panels and in frescoes and paintings, forming a vast visual archive of biblical teachings that enrapture the preliterate population. Once again art is in the service of religious mythology—and the church becomes the major patron of artists, replacing the Roman state and the Byzantine lords who had controlled the subsidy of art for several centuries.

Then, in the fifteenth century, a subtle revolution began in the subject matter of religious painting. In the foreground of paintings that celebrated biblical events there began to appear tiny secular figures: the images of the princely families whose newfound wealth allowed them to commission works of art in exchange for their modest visual representation as witnesses of great religious events. As these dukes and princes became more powerful their images in sacred paintings became larger and larger, until at last their faces appeared in full-size portraits that rivaled those of the Roman nobility. The religious emphasis of divine painting had been literally moved into the backdrop. The noble personages were portrayed in the luxury of their homes, surrounded by finery, which included a modest religious painting depicted on the wall in the background.

The Tower had fallen. And mythic experience was lost to the West, becoming the questionable legacy of eccentrics and outsiders.

Antonin Artaud warned us that if we insist upon observing our acts critically and lose ourselves in a concern for their imagined form and meaning, instead of being impelled by the experience of their force, then all the magic will leave our lives. Campbell cautioned that we must not be misdirected into a search for the meaning of life instead of seeking an experience of life. If we stray from the hero's path and flee from our mythic journey, then all the magic—the bliss—leaves our lives. At such a point, the Tower falls—and we fall with it. Intuition and imagination die in the mouth of reason. Logic bursts like lightning from the patriarchal sun, striking the Tower and demolishing our ability to be engaged in life, leaving us with form and meaning, but without an experience of ourselves that gives context to the form and meaning we think we find in the world around us.

IV.

The Hierophant

Body as Metaphor

The enigma is that my body simultaneously sees and is seen. That which looks at all things can also look at itself and recognize, in what it sees, the "other side" of its power of looking. It sees itself seeing; it touches itself touching; it is visible and sensitive to itself.

Maurice Merleau-Ponty

The realm of ritual and ceremony is presided over by the Tarot figure known as "The Hierophant": originally a high priest of ancient Greece, who is depicted in the Tarot deck as a man of great stature and wisdom seated upon a throne. His emblematic role as the pontiff of ritualism makes the Hierophant an ideal symbol with which to begin a discussion of the mythic and metaphoric function of the human body in the history of art.

The body is the central actor in the life of ritual. The body is both a witness of the world and an organ of expression that conveys its experiences of the world. The body ritualizes those experiences in the gestures and movements of mime and play and dance. The body transforms experience into ritual actions. It transmutes sensations and beliefs into the physical acts of art and the ceremonies of daily life. And in this way it creates rituals that are quite literally the embodiments of a society's and an individual's mythology. The movements of the body "give visible existence to what profane vision believes to be invisible" (Merleau-Ponty). The movements of the dancer and the actor are not devices borrowed from "the real world in order to signify prosaic things which are absent" (Merleau-Ponty). To the contrary, the dancer and actor give bodily expression to visions that exist only at the threshold of profane experience. Like rainbows, the gestures of dance and theater have only a virtual existence. They are visible surges of energy that are intangible. As spectators it seems to us that these surges of energy occur when the actor or dancer acts upon the world, but for the performers the experience is just the opposite. They are quick to inform us that it is the world that acts upon them. It is not their movements but the space surrounding them that defines their actions and makes their bodies visible.

The body is the place where humanity achieves the ritualization of motion as art. The body is the organism in which motion makes visible the sacred forms of life itself. Our bodies live through motion. And thus motion is the most important and pervasive means by which many tribal and Asian peoples celebrate living.

As Susanne K. Langer (1957) observed, "Strange as it may seem, the evolution of the dance as a high art belongs to prehistory. At the dawn of civilization, dance had already reached a degree of perfection that no other art or science could then match." But the choreographic achievement of primal peoples was largely dismissed by Western societies, for whom dance was a savage "dumb show" lacking refinement, discipline, and intellectual content. Until the founding of a highly mechanized European form of dance, eventually called ballet, dance was rarely given serious attention as an art form, and was, as an activity of the mortified flesh, rejected by Christianity and given no subsidy by the church. Only later, during the extravagant reign of Louis XIV of France, did ballet assume a central role in court life, mainly because Louis himself was an avid performer and often appeared in lavish dance pageants. But official Christianity had no love of dance. It was the only world religion that actively abhorred dancing and refused to include it in its orthodox services (except during a brief period, before the eighth century, when it was used unofficially in miracle plays and other religious theatrics).

After centuries of believing in a mythology concerned with the mortification of the flesh and the celebration of the disembodied soul, it is difficult for most people of the West to grasp the existence of something as seemingly contradictory as the "spiritual body," which implies the unification of spirit and flesh. But among the great majority of the world's peoples, past and present, the spiritual body is not an oxymoron, but an apt description of the mystic and trancelike energy that rises through consciousness during rituals and dance ceremonies. In the tribal fusion of dance, song, and music is an experiential "art" before art existed. Nothing in this richly metaphoric ritual form is the equivalent of the West's self-conscious idealizations of art and beauty. If you agree with those who believe that action came before conjecture in human societies, then you will recognize in bodily gesture and motion humanity's most fundamental and expressive act—evolved to a sublime achievement long before the emergence of the first civilizations of the West. Now and in the past, dance and theater are the inclination of Asian and tribal peoples to idealize action as magical forces. There is substantial physiological basis for this viewpoint. We are born with organs of perception that provide us with our only means of experiencing ourselves and the world. As Maurice Merleau-Ponty observed, the body "touches itself touching; sees itself seeing." Our perceptive organs include not only the senses of touch and sight, smell, hearing, and taste, but also a sense of balance and of rotation, which the semicircular canals in the inner ear reveal to us through successive impulses sent to the brain. In addition, we possess a kinesthetic sense that operates through little understood receptors in our muscle tissues and through our tactile sensitivity to pressure and texture, and which helps us realize when we are moving and on what kind of surface we are moving. From birth we are taught to recognize the ways in which the movements of our bodies work for us practically: swimming, driving, writing, eating. But bodily movement has other functions, and tribal peoples and the populations of Asia are as aware of them as they are of the purely practical ways in which bodily motion serves us. Every sentient state expresses itself in movements that are not necessarily utilitarian or representational, but that nevertheless reflect the specific quality of the ideas and feelings that cause them. The relationship between sentience and movement affects everything from the expression in our eyes to the flow of adrenaline in our bloodstream. In its most fundamental artistic form this spontaneous link between sentience and movement is called mime or dance, a gestural expression that is a direct, nonverbal, unreasoned assertion of ideas and sentience expressed in the form of motion. From this fact it becomes clear that gesture is an extremely powerful force in human experience, especially if we happen to live in one of the countless societies in which less importance is given to words than to actions.

Just as many visual artists and composers of the twentieth century have been strongly influenced by mythic and ritual art forms, so too have many contemporary choreographers and theater directors. Antonin Artaud was virtually obsessed with the trance dancing of Bali, rituals performed by dancers who submerge themselves in a hypnotic state in order to put themselves in touch with the ineffable spirits of their animistic cosmos, who offer their bodies as the expressive instruments of intangible natural forces that can only act out rituals by taking over the bodies of the entranced performers. Artaud insisted that theatrical reality is different in kind from ordinary reality, that it is self-defeating for the stage to attempt to copy everyday life. As with the expressionist painters and choreographers,

> this reaction against naturalism implies a rejection of the philosophical assumptions of Western civilization. Presenting conventional social themes or realist characterization exacerbated the fundamental inauthenticity of stage performance, because it simply reinforced the falsified world of appearances; consequently theatre could only escape from pretence by setting its own standard of what is real. The stage was to present inner rather than outer truth, which would be validated by audience response: a "world touching the real" through its "direct relation to the agonies and preoccupations" of each spectator. (Innes)

For Artaud, as for the surrealists and such abstract expressionist painters as Robert Motherwell, the conjunction of trance and depersonalized images and gestures expressed "the automatism of the liberated unconscious" (Artaud).

Dance has been as influenced by ritual as theater. Photographer Barbara Morgan was closely associated with Martha Graham:

> I had just seen one of Martha's concerts. I can't exactly remember whether it was "Primitive Mysteries" or "Frontier," but I was very excited and it aroused memories of my experiences in the American Southwest. So I asked Martha

36

very directly, "By any chance have you been influenced by the Indian and Spanish dance ceremonies in the Southwest?" She said to me: "Absolutely, that's one of the greatest inspirations in my entire life."

Graham was not the only choreographer to be influenced by ritualism. Before Graham's ground-breaking "Primitive Mysteries," Vaslav Nijinsky had caused a scandal in Paris when he used highly erotic and ritual gestures in his choreography for Igor Stravinsky's 1913 revolutionary score "Le Sacre du printemps" and Claude Debussy's equally avant-garde "Prélude à l'après-midi d'un faune."

It is possible to attribute much of the thrust of the global and, particularly, the French and American rebellions against the strictures of formal ballet, theater, poetry, music, and architecture to the influences of primal arts and rituals.

The avant-garde mentality in the arts of the twentieth century has been highly focused upon myth, ritual, and what might be called spirituality—the expressionism that bursts from the subconscious: intuition, passion, and irrationality.

By itself this might seem atavistic, a retreat from contemporary issues in a way that must isolate avant-garde [artists], condemning their work to irrelevance once their technical innovations have become generally accepted. But seen in a wider philosophical . . . context, it is precisely these qualities that link them to the mainstream of modern thought. Most of those mental attitudes we customarily accept as representing what is specifically contemporary about our intellectual climate—materialism, scientific empiricism, agnosticism, rationalism—are in fact carry-overs from the nineteenth century. The premises and interests of psychology and social anthropology, both founded around the turn of the century, are far more typical of our age. . . . In particular the search for quasi-mystical "roots" reflects a really significant revaluation of so-called "primitive mentality," through which these new sciences have given fresh relevance to myth and myth-opoeic qualities. (Innes)

Perhaps no single group of scholars were more responsible for the twentieth-century interest in mythology and mythopoetics than James Frazer and his fellow members of the Cambridge School of Anthropology. Yet Frazer's 1890 publication of *The Golden Bough* carried with it an inclination to retain much of the bias of nineteenth-century rationalism, suggesting that myths were simply mistaken explanations of the natural world. Mythology was largely regarded by Frazer and his colleagues as false conclusions resulting from ignorance and a lack of exacting, empirical observations. For most pioneer anthropologists, "mythical meant inferior, synonymous with 'false' " (Innes). Then researchers like Carl Jung, Ernst Cassirer, Susanne K. Langer, Mircea Eliade, and Joseph Campbell reversed this negative judgment of mythology and ritual by seeing it in the context of symbolic language, an externalization of the world of dream and the subconscious.

This late-nineteenth- and twentieth-century fascination with mythology and ritual was entirely alien to Europe in the centuries before the Renaissance. Until the middle of the fifteenth century the Christian church was virtually the only patron of art, and this largely anonymous art was required to make statements about Catholic dogma—morality, cosmology, and absolute truths that relied upon the conviction that Christian mythology, unlike other mythologies, represents a factual history. As I have already noted, the Renaissance grandees who later dominated the art market had very little interest in religious philosophies, but they were interested in using art to promote their own reputations and to heighten their social rank and prestige. Each patron endeavored to commission works of art that would outshine those sponsored by rivals. It is clear in the relationship between the art of the Christian church and that of the grandees that the nature and purpose of expression changed drastically. That change is even greater when we consider the transformation of primal rituals into ecclesiastical art. And the most drastic change of all was the transformation of the art created for Renaissance patrons into art produced almost entirely with the motive of self-expression by later artists who created their works without sustained patronage.

The arts and rituals created in the West have often described personal visions, but they have also served nationalistic causes. There have been numerous efforts among various political movements to construct art that glorifies specific political points of view or celebrates various ethnic and gender groups. But whether the intention of an artist is tribal, social, political, or highly personal, the process of ritualizing experience is essentially the same. With a Western historical perspective it is possible, for instance, to grasp how and why the competitive flamboyance of the era of Louis XIII of France was central to the formative character of court dancing and ballet in the seventeenth century, and how it eventually led to the rococo mannerisms in the salon paintings of Watteau, Fragonard, and Boucher. And in more recent times it is equally clear that the stark Freudian emphasis upon the interior world influenced the emergence not only of expressionism in dance, theater, painting, and literature, but also brought about the cult of personality that people such as scenic designer Gordon Craig and dancer Isadora Duncan came to symbolize. These relationships between the driving forces of culture and the forms of art demonstrate the crucial and diverse ways in which human experience is ritualized on every level of consciousness—from era to era and from place to place.

This centrality of ritual is particularly clear in the gestural languages of dance and theater. Beyond the purely expressive powers of movement, there is also the highly contagious nature of bodily activity, which lends a mysterious and provocative aspect to the way in which ideas and feelings are communicated in the theater. Yawning is the most obvious example of this contagion of gesture from body to body. So too is the desire to stretch when we see someone else stretching. Because of the inherent contagion of motion, which makes onlookers feel in their own bodies the exertion they see in others, the actor or dancer is able to convey nonverbally, even nonsymbolically, the most intangible and metaphysical experiences, ideas, and sentience.

The body is capable of communicating in its own bodily manner. But it is only since the beginning of the twentieth century that the power of gesture as a communicative medium has been fully appreciated in the West. Primal peoples all over the world, including Europe and America, as well as Asiatic peoples, had understood and focused on this effective aspect of ritual since long before the rise of the earliest civilizations. This emphasis upon ritualism persists today in primal and in Asian cultures, but, as I have already indicated, it dissipated greatly in the West with the advent of Christianity, except, of course, as it was applied, in a disembodied form, to orthodox ceremonies such as the Mass.

When we consider how powerfully movement and gesture influence all of us, it isn't difficult to understand why most of the world's population regards an action as the embodiment of a mysterious force. Ritualistic societies believe that gesture can shape the circumstances of nature if rituals can focus the contagious power of movement on animals and supernaturals. This premise of "sympathetic magic" is at the root of most ceremonial uses of ritual. The imitation of an animal (essentially in movements, but also in costume) is believed to have an influence upon the animal itself. This practice, called "homeopathic ritual," is the basis of most hunting and fertility rites. It probably resulted from a long history of less complex usages of bodily motion until it was determined that actions of a certain kind were highly effective: Depicting the pursuit and slaying of an animal might influence the animal powers to sacrifice one of their kind so human beings might eat and survive. At such a point, thought and action are fused in a form unknown in the West except, perhaps, in the specialized process that separated from the practical activities of life and became known as "art."

In this effort to move closer to the centers of power in nature, ritualists often imitate and transform themselves into things of the natural world that invest them with vision and strength. They receive power through chants and songs. Through their dances they touch unknown and unseen elements that they sense in the world around them but over which they feel they have little or no control. It is perhaps an error to speak of the "imitation" of animals, because the ritualist's actions are designed not for emulation but for transformation. Today's actors and dancers have consciously rediscovered this same process: They do not simply *perform* movements and gestures. Through intense kinesthetic projection of ideas and sentience as pure bodily expression, they *become* the movements and gestures they enact. They become part of the spiritual body.

Ideas and feelings are merged in the spiritual body. Words—chanted, sung, or spoken—are valued in ritual primarily for the reaction they produce within the singer rather than for any effect they might have on others. The first stage of ritual is almost always the rising of the singer/chanter on his or her own song to a plane of mystical power—a place of contact with the forces that move the cosmos. The words and sounds of a song or chant are only the small, visible aspect of a far greater mystery that lies beneath and beyond syntactical speech. For this reason the nature of ritual music requires the comprehension of a larger idea, a sound or a word or two that convey something far wider and truer than what is actually spoken, sung, or sounded.

No one knows for certain just how ritual originated, but there is in many mammals, including of course humans, a relationship between intense feeling and involuntary bodily movement and vocal utterance. Due to the stresses of movement upon the belly and upon the diaphragm, there is a tendency for vocalization: sighs, grunts, groans, pants, cries, or murmurs. It is the kind of noise people make when they sit down or when they are surprised, dismayed, or experience intense pleasure. The contractive movement of many rituals also results in the forced exhalation or inhalation of breath, causing a variety of vocal sounds. It is possible that some of the songs or chants that accompany rituals are the result of such vocal utterances that involuntarily occur during movement. Whatever the origins of song and its physical relationships to movement, we know from ethnologists that song and dance are intrinsic in most tribal cultures—the dancers accompany themselves with sounds of rhythmic accents produced by clapping or stomping. It is often conjectured that once the energies of the performance accelerate, making self-accompaniment difficult, the beat and the vocal sounds are picked up by a less active dancer or bystander who eventually becomes the "orchestra" of the ritual. In this way, theater and dance emerge as forms distinct from music in the ritual arts.

The seeming rusticity of much primal behavior makes Western people devise a self-serving ideal of themselves as civilized, which sets them widely apart from other peoples. They are inclined to forget that the same impulses that give form to people of other cultures are active in all societies despite wide diversities. The twentieth-century Western mind is a product of its gradual withdrawal from an awareness of the natural world and its place in it. Westerners "think" that nature serves the purposes of the West because divine intention made them the dominant and superior beings of the cosmos. Such a construct is so fundamental to Western mythology that it is believed and acted upon even by the most secular of people. Avid ecologists often demand the protection of the planet for future generations of human beings, rather than for a less anthropocentric vision: the grandeur and sacredness of nature and the realization that human beings are simply a small aspect of the natural world.

The response of all peoples to their environment is largely ritualistic. The Western notion of human beings as the crown of creation is simply a self-serving aspect of the process of mythologizing and ritualizing nature. Such ritualization of experience is a type of cultural idealization. In the case of many Asian and tribal cultures, the aim of the rituals is to bring the human community into a close and cooperative relationship with nature. In the Western world the effort is in the hope of neutralizing (rather than ritualizing) nature. Ritual and mythology deal with ambiguity on the level of ambiguity—in the same way that art deals with reality as metaphor. On the other hand, the "civilized" mentality of the nineteenth century, which greatly influences the West today, is inclined to turn ambiguity into certitude and orthodoxy. The central method for this transposition from a world of essences to a world of objects and appearances, as philosophers Ernst Cassirer and Susanne K. Langer have indicated, is through the use of words as the definitive framework of realism. Langer (1942) informs us:

> Words are certainly our most important instruments of expression, our most characteristic, universal and enviable tools in the conduct of life. Speech is the mark of humanity. It is the normal terminus of thought. We are apt to be so impressed with its symbolistic mission that we regard it as the only important expressive act, and assume that all other activity must be practical in an animalian way, or else irrational—playful, or atavistic (residual) past recognition. But in fact, speech is the natural outcome of only one kind of symbolic process. There are transformations of experience in the human mind that have quite different overt endings. They end in acts that are neither practical nor communicative, though they may be both effective and communal: I mean the actions we call *ritual.*

Ritual is a symbolic transformation of experiences that no other medium of expression can adequately contain. Because it springs from a primary human need, it is an activity that arises without artistic self-consciousness, without any necessary adaptation to a pragmatic or a conscious purpose. Its growth is "undesigned" in the same sense that primal architecture is undesigned. Its patterns, for all their intricacy, merely express the social process of a unique people who are largely unconscious of the social structure in which they live. Ritual is never successfully imposed upon a people. When such missionary efforts are made the imposed ideology is thoroughly assimilated into preexisting ritual forms and thus neutralized. For instance, the Aztecs simply applied the names of the Christian saints imposed upon them by missionaries to their own ancient pantheon of gods.

The province of ritual, including movement, gesture, song, image, and nonsyntactical words, has been continually assaulted in the West as mindless and compulsive because it does not sustain the certitude and orthodoxy of the language-bound mentality of industrial peoples. Freud saw rites as acts that must be performed out of sheer inward compulsion, like emotional regurgitation. It is now apparent that Freud was wrong, and that ritual acts are often creative and expressive on the highest levels of consciousness, the spontaneous transformation of external as well as internal experiences. There are countless rites among the people of Bali, for instance, such as the awesome Barong and Wayang Wong performances, that contradict much of what Freud assumed about ritual acts. These Balinese ceremonies are not necessarily unconscious outpourings of feelings into shouting, prancing, and rolling on the ground, like a baby's tantrum. As soon as an expressive act is performed intentionally, without compulsion, it is no longer simply "self-expressive," in the narrow, psychopathic sense. Instead, it becomes logically expressive, but not necessarily in the kind of logic conveyed by words. Neither is Balinese dance simply a set of emotional signs; rather it is a metaphor for an *entire experience*. Instead of completing the natural history of emotions, the dances denote feelings and ambiguously summon these feelings to mind without actuating them. The dance is expressive, but in a special sense. I use the word "expression" to suggest a deliberate conveyance of values rather than simply an emotional outburst or a public tantrum.

The process of civilization may be contradictory to the process of art and ritual. In civilization as we know it in the West, the power of these activities is gradually displaced and dismissed as people embrace the dogma of cause and effect and pursue the control of nature by methods that alter the casual circumstances of their essential existence as a people and a society. At such a time the power of actions and images ceases to be a prime object of the community. Movement and gesture, chant and song, incantation and imagery persist, but only so far as they express aims and principles that have little to do with their original impulse and purpose. In southern France, for instance, a folk dance called the farandole is still performed. It is a labyrinth-patterned dance common in European folklore derived from an ancient symbol found on Greek coins. The snakelike winding of the farandole of Provence, in ancient times a colony of Greece, closely resembles a journey to the middle of a maze; it is a vision of the passage of a dead person to the land of the afterlife, a passage fraught with danger from evil powers. In performing an ancient funeral dance that slowly winds toward the middle of a man-made labyrinth, the ancients were demonstrating that people possess the power, through sympathetic rites, to direct certain events of nature. This winding farandole was a means of mimicking the spirit of the dead person and helping it on its way. Today, the farmers of Provence still perform the farandole, but without any conscious purpose other than the enjoyment of music and movement. In this case the expressive form of the ritual has been abandoned. What remains is neither art nor ritual but something else: an entertainment, an empty gesture like the ceremonial act of shaking hands or a game not unlike hopscotch, whose once significant ritual meaning has been lost.

Rituals are products of hundreds of generations, a slow selective process by which certain actions, images, and incantations are retained through repetition. These rites possess strong magic to the people who practice them. They do not easily vanish and leave only a game (a seemingly purposeless pattern of exuberant physical movements) except under specific duress and over a great period of time. Sooner or later in the forward push of Western civilizations toward a totally controlled and verbalized construct of nature, a mimetic dance form made its appearance—a dumb show, a substi-

tution for words built on the syntax of words. Out of this pragmatic dance-mime came the separation of drama, dance, and
music. Ultimately, not only power and expressivity, but also dance
motion itself passed from the rituals of civilizations, and a purely
literary drama of ideas and facts came into existence. This is the
basis of much Western banal realism in the arts: images, structures,
sounds, gestures, and figures of speech that attempt to imitate
prosaic words.

The forward plunge of Western civilization, and its influences
on non-Western cultures—which some still look upon as progress—has brought the impulse to express feelings under the too
rigid domination of reason, and this, in turn, has caused the
Western mind to think of itself predominantly as a perpetual spectator of the world, afraid to create its own artistic forms because
they might fall outside the conventional preconception of sanity
and reality. Until very recently, Western people were cut off from
their own bodies and from expressive activities by their own con-
straint and embarrassment. This, of course, is particularly true of
men in certain cultures, who often have a profound fear of all forms
of expressiveness except rage and an occasional outburst of self-
pity. There is some validity in the anecdote about the man who
loved his wife so much he *almost* told her so!

To be out of touch with our physiological selves means that
we lack a body that can function in harmony with our ideas and
feelings. Consequently, we tend to "leave the dancing to women,
queers and savages"—thus reassuring ourselves of the old Judeo-
Christian assessment of the body and its movement as liabilities and
as a humble organism over which we possess little if any control.
Without an articulate body, without facial expressions that genuinely reflect our states of mind, without arms and hands and torsos
that respond to the self and relate to external events, we cannot
participate in our world or, for that matter, in our own emotional
lives.

The Hierophant of the Tarot cards still reigns over a marvelous realm of ritual. We urgently need his influence in our lives. In

the ritual performance there is an idealized transparency, a configuration in which the totality of human experience becomes brilliantly luminous and visible. The feelings intrinsic to ritual are probably no more fundamental or primitive than the loftiest sentience of any of the arts. The ideas inherent in ritual motion, in dance and theater and performance art, may appear simplistic at first because Western people, at least until Isadora Duncan, did not believe that something as inarticulate and fanciful as dancing could possibly convey anything profound or significant. That is perhaps true of much of what used to be called ballroom dancing. It was a dance form that had been in a long decline from its ritual purposes when the youth of the 1960s began efforts to rediscover the ancient heritage that in the United States and Europe had been kept alive only by African-American social and religious dancing. What black dancers had sustained was the potential of relating dance to the most ecstatic rather than the most prudish and uninspired aspects of the human condition. That many people felt so bereft of their bodies in the rebellious era from 1960 to 1970 that they had to undertake courses in "body awareness" attests to the degree of decline of physical sensibility among Anglo-Americans.

It is perhaps significant that in the age of Dante, the Hierophant of the Tarot cards, who had been the ancient Greek master of rituals that celebrate the human body, was renamed "The Pope," who is the master of Christian ceremonies that detest the human body.

As Martha Graham once noted, gesture is stupendously human, and that is why modern people of the West find it so difficult to comprehend. They are eager to escape their bodies and live through what they envision as their souls. But this dichotomy need not exist. The concept of the spiritual body is pervasively human and exists among all people, including pre-Christian Europeans. If there were better words to describe the merging of body and soul, perhaps it would be easier to articulate this idea that is so alien to many of us; but in that case it would be doubtful that there would be any reason to talk about ritual or ceremony or the arts in the first place. There is nothing really "spiritual" in the concept of the spiritual body, but there isn't another word that suggests all the qualities of nobility, loftiness of thought, and intensity of ideals and feelings that we normally exclude from our connotation of the word "body." The intent behind the term "spiritual body" envisions not just the anatomical body but all the still-mysterious physiology by which the body experiences itself and the world, the amplification of the senses into vision and the puzzling process of perception and thought by which the purely physical "brain" re-creates itself as something called the "mind."

Many people have little concern or faith in the Cartesian materialism that imposes the Western dichotomies of mind/brain and soul/body. We live in our bodies. A body is all there is of us. That thought terrifies and even agonizes us, but there is nothing we can do to change it. We are a perishable and fragile animal among countless other life-forms. Yet we can live fully within our bodies, for the primal unity of body and spirit is the one and only aspect of our humble existence that is ultimately life affirming. It frees us from ourselves. It liberates us from that unthinkable Copernican cosmos, with its infernal gears that move some pathetic, calculated clock by which only Western civilization is supposed to be able to tell the correct time.

Artists, like ritualists, stand somewhere outside and beyond the value systems of the now dominant culture. They are aliens in their own nations, and yet they have seen drastic revisions in attitudes since the turn of the century that have made room for them at the very center of society. There have been revolutionary changes in our ideas about our bodies and our world: about gender and sexual orientation, about race and ethnicity. We have come to understand the difference between equality and conformity, between unlimited industry and ecology, between nature and progress. And we have arrived at a vital new vision of that extraordinary organism of expression called the human body.

The Hierophant remains the supreme priest of rituals of the human heart. He vanishes for a time and then he is mysteriously reborn. He is as perishable as everything that exists in nature, because nothing is definitive and nothing is ultimate. Only the basic principle of ritual is enduring. "And out of it, like the cycles of nature itself, rises an endless succession of new springs out of old winters" (Martin).

V.

The Magician

Originality and Illusion

Why should we honor those that die upon the field of battle, when a man may show as reckless a courage by entering into the abyss of himself.

W. B. Yeats

The Magician is a delightful character, part enchanter and part con man. In the Tarot deck he is depicted as a gentleman standing at a table, wearing a hat with a double nimbus in the form of the eternal number eight. In his left hand he holds a rod pointing to the heavens, while his other hand points downward toward the earth. Metaphorically, he exists somewhere between heaven and earth, and, accordingly, he is believed to represent a number of fascinating attributes: originality and free will, trickery and guile, creativity and imagination, sleight of hand and deception. What symbol could better serve for contemporary artists, who tirelessly strive to speak their own minds in their own ways, but also want to be heard and appreciated by their communities; who live in alienation but strive for acceptance; who are immersed in a reality of their own, but want to relate to the larger social reality of their world?

Artists are magicians. Though once they were vital practitioners who stood at the very center of primal societies, now they have been so mystified that they no longer seem to be part of the everyday world of the West. Ironically, artists were less alien when they were part of a society that survived on mythology than they are today in demystified Western society. Thus the West is bereft of myth, and God has been demystified; while its artists, who were once a vital and coherent part of society, have been mystified as aberrations and outsiders. They lack acceptance not only because their efforts are regarded as highly rarified and impractical, but also because their reputations are stained by distrust in a society that associates art with falsity and deceit.

British physicist and philosopher L. L. Whyte deplores this view of art and artists: "The genius of man lies in his growing faculty for enchantment without illusion."

Such enchantment is the impetus of the arts. It emerges from an experience compounded of a stream of recollections that vacillates between all the material events of one's life and imaginary and invented events. It is a fabrication without illusion because we recognize that identity itself is a fabrication. When philosopher John Locke was attempting to understand the epistomological basis of self, he made the famous statement: *I am what I remember my self being.* Thus he explains identity as an aspect of memory. But it is a type of memory that is not responsible to commonsense realism. Instead, memory includes not only what is consciously recalled but also those events that are lost to consciousness as well as those memories that are invented through acts of the imagination. Freud himself recognized the phenomenon of false but identity-constitutive memories. Psychoanalytic experts continue to question why well-adjusted people put together remembrances that are material realities with remembrances that are clearly invented; while in the arts it is abundantly clear that this peculiar human inclination to invent one's memories exists at the very core of what we mean when we speak of imagination and creativity.

Novelist Isabel Allende has remarked:

> I've been a foreigner for the past twenty years. I don't have
> roots anymore. My roots are in my memory and my writing.
> That's why memory is so important. Who are you but what
> you can remember? I have a very bad memory, so I invent my
> memories all the time, and I remember things that never
> happened. I'm a great liar. Now I'm called a narrator because
> I make a living with my lies, but before I was just a liar.

Nobel laureate in literature Isaac Singer has said that when he was a child, people called him a liar, whereas now they call him a novelist. Apparently his motives did not change, only the perception of his motives was reevaluated.

Science reportedly deals with fact. Art deals with expression and meaning. That distinction connotes a world of differences.

Kurt Vonnegut, Jr., once said that we must take great care about who we pretend we are, because that is who we will become.

It is a comment that shakes the basis of the empirical notion of identity and reality, but that has never been of great concern to Vonnegut. He also said,

> I do not furnish transportation for my characters; I do not move them from one room to another; I do not send them up the stairs; they do not get dressed in the mornings; they do not put the ignition key in the lock, and turn on the engine, and let it warm up and look at all the gauges, and put the car in reverse, and back out, and drive to the filling station, and ask the guy there about the weather. You can fill up a good-size book with this connective tissue. People would be satisfied, too.

That kind of truth is not what Kurt Vonnegut, Jr., is after. Nor are many other artists.

John Irving, writing an autobiographical essay for the *New York Times Book Review,* said that although he was writing a memoir, his readers should be forewarned that as a novelist he was very apt to talk more about what could have and should have happened than about what actually happened, because what actually happened is less significant and interesting than what could have happened.

So it seems that we must now ask a question that would be unthinkable in any but a materialistic society such as the one in which we live: Does art have any relationship to empirical truth?

The answer is an unqualified no. The arts, even in their most naturalistic mood, do not denote truth; they connote something beyond empirical truth. Wallace Stevens agrees. He said, "The final belief is to believe in a fiction, which you know to be a fiction, there being nothing else; the exquisite truth is to know that it is a fiction and that you believe in it willingly." He also insisted, in way of an explanation for his statement about fiction, that "reality is not what it is. It consists of the many realities which it can be made into."

All of these statements by renowned and supposedly trustworthy writers create a great uneasiness among prosaic people such as the Emperor, who staunchly believe that words are designed as vehicles of facts and truth. For the Emperor, the opposite of a truth is a lie. And it is virtually impossible to convince the Emperor that there can be truth in deception. To him the Magician is simply a charlatan. The Emperor grasps only the negative aspects of magic: its deception, trickery, and guile. He cannot grasp its marvelous creativity and imagination, because he cannot find such qualities in himself. As far as the Emperor is concerned, the Magician is an incorrigible liar. This becomes a case of the "Magician's new clothes."

The Emperor is convinced that when it comes to truth and reality there are no substitutions or alternatives. Something is either truthful and real or it is untruthful and unreal. For this reason he regards mythology as falsity, metaphor as double-talk, and the arts as pretty little fallacies at best, or, at worst, abominable extravagances.

The nineteenth-century Swiss historian Johann Jakob Bachofen would have problems with such a stolid point of view about truth. He postulated what became an influential theory about the importance of women early in human history. His point of view had a strong impact on several major scholars and artists of his day, including such celebrated German writers as Friedrich Nietzsche, Rainer Maria Rilke, Hugo von Hofmannsthal, and the American anthropologist Lewis Henry Morgan. Today Bachofen's famous matriarchy theory is almost universally discredited. His critics point out that there is no historical evidence that a matriarchy ever existed. For them that "factual error" is the end of the debate. But such a dismissal is a bit facile. Bachofen himself made a strong distinction between what he called "ideas" and what he called "facts." "What cannot have happened was nonetheless thought," he insisted. And what is thought and felt and imagined by the people of a society (factual or not) is essential to our understanding of the nature of that society. If our notion of "history" ignores the inner life of artists and people in general, we end up with all the "facts," but we are likely to miss the point.

Why is this? Because there is far more to truth than just a succession of facts. That is why, in Bill Moyers's anecdote about Joseph Campbell, he made the humorous distinction between Campbell's getting the "story" while all he got were the "facts."

> Any culture is a series of related structures which comprise social forms, values, cosmology, the whole of knowledge and through which all experience is mediated. Rituals [like art] enact the form of social relations and in giving these relations visible expression they enable people to know their own society. Rituals work upon the body politic through the symbolic medium of the physical body. (Douglas, M.)

The Emperor is not aware of how works of art are made. Nor does he understand the impact that the ritual life of the arts has on the societies in which they are produced. He is confused because he believes that anything that is not truthful cannot be meaningful. For instance, he is apt to insist that if a religious event is a myth rather than a historical fact, then it cannot possess religious meaning. The Emperor: "Either Jesus Christ walked on the water or he did not walk on the water." And if he did not walk on the water, then there was no miracle and the story has no meaning. For the Emperor, there is no other possible conclusion to reach about such mythical events. And so, in the case of the arts, he readily reaches the conclusion that artists, like all mythmakers, are simply high-class counterfeiters.

Yet in other societies art is such a pervasive form of expression that there is no need to have a word for it in hundreds of tribal languages. But in the West there is so great an emphasis upon the artist as a disreputable outsider and a speaker of incomprehensible languages that making art is generally looked upon as some kind of con game.* The common assumption is that modern art is

---

*Witness an October 1993 program of *60 Minutes* during which an entire segment dismissed late twentieth-century art as a sham.

baffling because the artist wants it to be baffling. Many people believe that the modern arts have no place in our society because artists do not want an audience of everyday people. Those who are unfamiliar with the arts assume that modern art has no tradition or history because it recklessly pulled anchor from the beautiful, sentimental, and accessible arts of the past in order to demonstrate its unquestionable originality. The notion of the quest for unlimited originality has become the predominant consensus of the purpose and meaning of twentieth-century arts.

Many people have the impression that novels, sonatas, paintings, poems, films, sculptures, pots, textiles, and dramas are the products of complete originality. Two popular clichés often used to respond to art are the expressions "That's interesting" and "That's different," which essentially mean that the speaker has not grasped the nature of his or her artistic encounter.

The history of art makes it very clear that originality has played a very small part in the lives and works of most important artists and artisans. So it is difficult to imagine why so many sophisticated people still insist that innovation and novelty are prime requirements of masterful arts.

We need to make a distinction between originality and individuality. And that distinction necessarily invokes a contrast between the way art is conceptualized by the West and by many other societies. "Originality" betrays an ego that identifies itself as the ultimate source of inspiration and craft, whereas "individuality" in art identifies with a group and its historical and communal tradition.

Of course, the public is not alone in seeing artists as supreme egoists. Many renowned artists, as well as many fledgling ones, are devoted to self-aggrandizement, thrusting upon the public a curiously contradictory view of the creative personality as both egocentric and mystical. But the fact remains that the creation of art is an activity necessitating a personal craft that is refined and secure but is nonetheless a process carried on largely in an unconscious state—almost to the point of being subliminal and anonymous.

The West is disinclined to accept this impersonal view of artistic inspiration. It continues to envision art as the final proof of free will and creative self-determinacy in its long devotion to the self-image of the "Faustian man," the essentially male product of a tradition that developed ideals for "organizing deliberate behavior which had no direct relation to humanity's instinctive and spontaneous activities" (Whyte).

In contrast, many Asian and tribal peoples have rejected the entire premise of originality—or they are innocent of it. They tend to see the creative person as an individual with more facility than others for drawing inspiration and vision, not from the "self," but from the communal soul, variously known as *mana,* from the Melanesian, and *orendas,* from the Iroquois—both terms roughly meaning "life forces" (Highwater 1981).

Since the West persists in the endemic notion that originality and only originality is the very essence of the creative process, it is not surprising that people gasp in indignation when an artist is accused of plagiarism. To the contemporary Western mind, infringing upon another person's art is the ultimate sign of a failure of originality. Contrarily, in the arts of other peoples, "plagiarism"—leaning heavily upon preexisting art—is something of a virtue.

This contrasting way in which the West and other societies view originality is more significant as an expression of attitude rather than a description of the actual working practices of Western artists, for on close examination it will be discovered that "quotation" is a commonplace among many of the greatest artists of Europe and America.

So we must not summarize the entire mentality of the West in the example of just one moment of history, for the Western mind possesses its own genesis and its own period of tribalism and so-called paganism. For instance, until very recently there did not exist in the West an awareness of or an interest in the kind of idiosyncratic personality who believes in originality as the ultimate source of art. Even the conception of authorship, as a demarcation of a specific person, was nonexistent until the age of Pericles (300 B.C.). And as Herbert Read has pointed out,

> Even when in later historical times the artist was differenti-
> ated from other craftsmen, . . . even then there was the
> strongest impulse to achieve an ideal uniformity, and al-
> though distinct personalities (individualities) do emerge
> among the sculptors of classical Greece, it is very difficult to
> ascribe any personal accents to the work of a Myron or a
> Praxiteles.

They may differ considerably in skill, in their fulfillment of the ideals of Greek aesthetic perfection, but they do not express, and were not expected to express, uniqueness or originality. Their artistic style was, in Read's word, "impersonal" to the point of bearing more resemblance to the creations of tribal artisans than to the fabled egocentric producers of Renaissance art.

The contrast between individuality and originality is the most complex distinction between the ways twentieth-century peoples look upon themselves and their artists.

The iconography and forms of art grew very gradually out of the profound experiences of communal histories. This process was universal—in Europe, Africa, Asia, Australia, and in the Americas. The modes of art have such spontaneous relationships to a people's reality that art is capable of speaking to them in silence, without deliberate interpretation or "instruction." The experience of art is virtually automatic, like the experience of dreams. The metaphors of such communal art are so pervasive within certain cultures that they are not defined or understood as metaphors but, rather, are experienced spontaneously, almost as if they were aspects of the "self." In many of these same societies the West's strict demarca-tion between a waking state and a dream state does not exist. Even in the grammar and syntax of many languages, the dream is not isolated from the waking state but is discussed as an aspect of a person's entire consciousness. Therefore, art is easily grasped as an endowment of the community rather than the property of an individual. In Bali, the instruments of the gamelan orchestra are usually "owned" by a community and made available to accomplished performers. The cave paintings of the Australian "People of the Dreamtime" (the Aborigines) belong mutually to the tribe and the very rock face upon which they are painted. In contrast, the assumption of the West is that people with creative imagination not only produce original things, but also hold legal ownership to whatever it is they originate . . . like a patented product.

There is nothing inherently evil about the stress upon originality in the West, but as soon as we begin to believe in art as predominately the result of originality, then the relationship of the artist to people and the relationship of his or her art to tradition is "materialized" and highly confused, both by copyright laws and by public consensus.

Originality is a conception that promotes elitism in art and denies the profound relationship of artists to societies. Nonartists have become so alienated from their own artistic capacities that they often express amazement at the activity of creation: "How do you think of the stories you write?" they ask in humble bewilderment. "How do you imagine the things you paint?" "Where do you find the music you compose?" Art seems to be utterly beyond them, while, in fact, it is the very essence of who and what they are!

And because they cannot grasp the ubiquitous capacity of mammalian animals for creative acts, they come to the conclusion that creation can only be the result of a rare and mysterious originality that they do not possess.

This reckless adoration of originality in the West is contradictory to all its history, and especially to twentieth-century history, when, early on, our most original artists were greatly influenced by their ideas about the function of tribal arts, and when, at the close of our century, postmodern artists explicitly favor the reimagining of classic images and myths and forms and the abundant infusion into their new work of elements freely drawn from works of the past. One of the most brilliant practices of T. S. Eliot in his masterful poem "The Waste Land," written in the 1920s, was a form of literary collage or montage using extensive paraphrases and quotations from a vast variety of literary works that served as "objective correlatives": doorways between Eliot's poem and the elaborate verbal images and ideas of earlier authors. In fact, Eliot provided a five-page appendix to the thirteen-page poem, in which he provided source notes for his fifty-one references and quotes from the works of other authors.

Many creators of great art have not even been aware of the public obsession with originality. Or, if they have been aware of it, they clearly ignored the mandate. "The characteristic of medieval storytelling is that you don't invent the story, you develop it. You take a traditional story and interpret it—give it new depth and meaning in terms of the conditions of your particular day." (Campbell 1990). Borrowing melodies from existing music was also a commonplace throughout the Middle Ages. Of the 2,542 surviving works of the troubadours, at least 514, and perhaps another 70, have melodies that have been reckoned to be imitations or borrowings. A fifth or more of this entire genre of music was clearly "unoriginal." Later, Vivaldi borrowed from his predecessors, and then the elder Bach borrowed whole compositions from Vivaldi. It was not a game or a deceit. Making music in the baroque period had very little to do with originating melodies. It was a process intent upon individualizing something out of a tradition—making it "new" through an *expression* that was individual.

Charles Ives is among the most interesting composers of North American musical history, but he is one of the least "original" at the same time that he is the most individual. He not only quoted Brahms and anybody else whose tunes interested him, but he also used a vast amount of folk materials with a passion. He played no favorites when it came to his borrowings. He even quoted himself in at least half of his own compositions.

The stupendous individuality of late-nineteenth-century French painters such as Manet—with his burnished light and color values—was deeply indebted to the works of the seventeenth- and eighteenth-century Spaniards Velásquez and Goya, who were equally indebted to the late-sixteenth-century Italian Caravaggio. Nor was the twentieth-century British composer William Alwyn fearful of occasional quotation. In the slow movement of his elegant and moving 1970 "Sinfonietta for Strings," he subtly quotes the love theme of Countess Geschwitz from Alban Berg's opera *Lulu*. In Dmitri Shostakovich's "Symphony No. 15" op. 141, one of the late and highly personal works by the modernist Russian composer, there are elaborate quotes from Rossini's opera *William Tell* and a quotation of the "fate motif" from Wagner's *Götterdämmerung*. The employment of paraphrase is highly visible in the works of surrealist painters who created vivid parodies of subjects borrowed from classical and Renaissance art. There recently has been something of a legal furor about postmodern painters who freely use other people's photographs, ingeniously incorporating them into their graphics and paintings. And there has also been a good deal of controversy about the recycling of popular tunes by rap artists, who transform bits of music by other songwriters by physically manipulating turntables backward and forward as music is reproduced mechanically.

Clearly, originality cannot be the basis of our appreciation of any of these artists who openly employ the influences and innovations of other artists. We admire them because they have a special and personal way of interweaving all that they borrow, a sense of form and style—and a startling, liberal imagination—which result in things that did not exist in any of the materials they appropriated.

In a more mechanical way, appropriation also has been encouraged in the technical education of artists in academies of the past. Copying the masters was supposed to be an excellent learning tool. Even critics encouraged artists to look to their nationalistic "roots" for inspiration. Most early Americans in the arts were so inclined to lean on European models that in the 1930s critics like George L. K. Morris urged them to borrow from Native American art rather than the arts of Europe. "American Indian art is the only true American art," he said. And American artists "should study Indian art in order to develop independent of European aesthetic values."

It was advice that sounded rather quaint until art historians began to notice the relationship of African art to the works of Derain, Picasso, Matisse, and Giacometti. John Ashbery, as well as many other critics, has noted again and again that Picasso's art was rather conservative and realist until *Les Demoiselles d'Avignon* (1907), when the influences of African and early Iberian iconography made an appearance in his painting.

As for the American Indian connection recommended by George L. K. Morris, it is easily found in the art of Rothko, Newman, Motherwell, Hartley, Pollock, Gottlieb, and many other leaders of the first internationally acclaimed arts movements of the United States. This quasi-Indian influence is not only visible in the works of these painters, it is also documented by their own statements. And despite a current testiness among certain political arbitrators about cultural appropriateness, which I will discuss elsewhere in this book, there is little question that the idea, if not the facts, of a romanticized Native American cultural identity has had a highly pervasive impact on Anglo-American sensibility in general, and in the American arts in particular.

The visuals arts are only part of the story of this cross-cultural exchange. In dance, Indian rituals had a clear bearing on the choreography of Martha Graham, and the influence of the artifacts of the Toltec-Maya culture of Central America (specifically the *chacmool* sculptures) on the works of England's Henry Moore is apparent. Native American melodies make an appearance in countless American and European musical compositions, from Henry Cowell and Aaron Copland to Antonin Dvořák. Working conversely is the strong influence of the art of the British painter Francis Bacon on the paintings of American Indian painters T. C. Cannon and Fritz Scholder, and the effect of the cubist style of Picasso on the images painted by Hopi painter Michael Kabotie.

Originality is an illusion. Artists work within a tradition—frequently with materials that "belong" to someone even though they clearly do not belong to anyone except the heritage itself. This is not to diminish the exceptional invention of artists or to denigrate the vividness of individuality in the arts. I am not talking about petty theft. I am not talking about kids with empty heads and nothing to say who steal their term papers from textbooks. I'm talking about artists who have a great deal to say, who have a distinctive point of view, and a style and an individual talent that nonetheless spring from a *communal otherness*, from a mythology, and from the ritual life of a people.

The indignation that always surrounds accusations of plagiarism—the lack of originality—sounds a good deal like the Victorian animus toward adultery. Originality in the arts is the same kind of illusion as fidelity in human relations. It may exist, but it is hardly commonplace, given recent survey statistics. To insist upon something that is illusory or—at best—rare is not a matter merely of being unreasonable. What it finally comes down to is being immoral by insisting upon a morality that is both impossible and meaningless.

It seems to me that the "plagiarist" is not the immoralist. It is those whose ignorance of the artistic process places the artist in a position of indignity who are finally immoral. A great *created* work of art cannot be plagiaristic any more than it can be original. Its connection to the world ultimately depends upon its capacity to celebrate what already exists in ways that invent what does not yet exist. Edgar Allan Poe summed it up years ago in his famous observation "All literary history demonstrates that for the most frequent and palpable plagiarisms we must search the works of the most eminent poets."

VI.

The High Priestess

Myth as Discovery

Whereas the simile of Dante is merely to make you see how the people looked, and is explanatory, the figure [of speech] of Shakespeare is expansive rather than intensive; its purpose is to add to what you see.

T. S. Eliot

She sits on a throne between two pillars and beneath a high canopy. She has an open book in her hands, and she is impressively robed. Her name is "The High Priestess," and she is the figure of the Tarot deck who represents wisdom and serene knowledge; intuition and penetrating understanding. In her Egyptian image she is shown to be veiled, her face only half visible. She is a delicate contradiction: obscured clarity, earthy empress, and guardian of secrets who, inevitably, illuminates what exists only in the shadows.

No Tarot symbol better represents that fragile place in our minds where mystery becomes discovery and discovery remains mysterious. The French symbolist poet Stéphane Mallarmé was keenly aware of the domain of the High Priestess, for he was alluding to her when he said that realists take things just as they are and put them before us,

> and consequently they are deficient in mystery: they deprive the mind of the delicious joy of believing that it is creating its own impressions. To name an object is to do away with three-quarters of the enjoyment of the poem which is derived from the satisfaction of guessing little by little: to suggest it, to evoke it—that is what charms the imagination.

The High Priestess, like myth itself, exists as a contradiction without the need for resolution or mediation. In reflecting on her own "status as a fiction that speaks truth, like a mask that conceals the surface in order to reveal hidden depths," she spans the world of polemics and tells us everything at the same time that she tells us nothing (Segal). As a result, those who live with mythologies are provided with the opportunity of testing themselves against a delirious recognition: the discovery of a reality that seems unreal but which is ultimately a reality beyond reality. In this way, the achievement of myth is not unlike the achievement of the artist. "It is the function of creative individuals not only to represent the highest transpersonal values of their culture, thereby becoming the honored [spokespersons] of their age, but also to give shape to the compensatory values and contents of which it is unconscious" (Neumann). Underscoring Neumann's observation is the work of Arthur Rimbaud, who is probably the quintessential model of twentieth-century sensibility: "I had to give up my life in order to be."

Rimbaud was the explosion that blew a gigantic rupture in nineteenth-century sensibility. Though he died almost a decade before the beginning of the twentieth century, he attended the cesarean birth of modernism. He was not the first nor the last of such cultural guerrillas, but he was certainly the most ferocious and resonant. Like his contemporary Friedrich Nietzsche, Rimbaud obliterated the prudent boundary between good and evil. He passionately believed that the final truth could only be discovered in the deepest abyss of the human psyche. Rimbaud stumbled out of reality. He stepped beyond that frame of mind that we designate as sanity. As Wallace Fowlie has indicated, Rimbaud's rebellion against French middle-class rationalism was so perilous that it blew him out of history into a fictive and unthinkable time-before-history. As we read Rimbaud's poems in the hard-glazed brittleness of his unique language, we see more and more clearly the contours of the strange myth from which his experiences sprang. It was the myth of a time before time, beyond good and evil. "The myth of the void is as true as the myth of the creation, and for the creative artist, the first myth, that of formlessness and nothingness, is the most terrifying story of mankind" (Fowlie).

Rimbaud dedicated himself to the myth of nothingness, both as a personal lamentation and also as one of the most remarkable expressions of the religious and social crises of the West at the close of the nineteenth century. *Je est un autre* . . . I is another, Rimbaud proclaimed with a grammatical inconsistency that emphasized the unraveling of the self.

The crisis that is implicit in the words of Rimbaud is the result

of a world that has lost its mythic moorings. Jungian philosopher
Edward F. Edinger has written:

> History and anthropology teach us that a human society
> cannot long survive unless its members are psychologically
> contained within a central living myth. Such a myth provides
> individuals with their reason for being. To the ultimate ques-
> tions of human existence it provides answers which satisfy the
> most developed and discriminating members of the society.
> And if the creative, intellectual minority is in harmony with
> the prevailing myth, the other layers of society will follow its
> lead and may even be spared a direct encounter with the
> fateful question of the meaning of life.

He continues by saying that it is evident to thoughtful people that
Western society no longer has a viable, functioning myth. It therefore has no basis on which to affirm life or to determine the nature
of absolute good and evil.

Rimbaud vividly depicted the plunge from certitude as well as
the frantic efforts of people to stay afloat in the resulting quagmire
of cultural and religious anarchy. As such, Rimbaud was Neumann's archetype of the honored spokesman of his age, but he also
gave shape to a vision of the world of which his contemporaries
were still largely unconscious. The researches of Freud, Jung,
Darwin, Frazer, Einstein, Marx, and many other pioneers of a new
mentality largely rejected the neat patterns of mechanized nature
as conceived by Descartes. Such highly diverse philosophers as
Henri Bergson and Martin Heidegger became determined for the
first time in the history of the West (or at least since the time of
Plato's agnosticism) to take the great leap beyond reason in order
to see how reason itself might look from the outside—that is, from
the point of view of some other potential of comprehension
granted the human animal. What such philosophers were facing in
the early nineteen hundreds was the crisis of symbols, of myth and
metaphor and language.

This bewildering situation at the close of the nineteenth century was not unique in human history. Rimbaud's works make visible that crisis of belief and of language, indeed a crisis of all symbolic expression in our time, much as the tragedies of Euripides vivified the tumult of belief and symbols in Greek civilization during the fifth century B.C. Despite the radical differences in their eras, both Rimbaud and Euripides faced "the juncture when the validity accorded to poetry and myth passes over to philosophy and conceptual thought" (Segal). In Rimbaud's visionary sojourn in hell and Euripides's myth of Dionysus at Thebes we are confronted by parallel themes: "the irreducible, enigmatic quality of the great, powerful symbols of myth" and the threatened, precarious status of those same symbols in societies that have lost the prevailing power of their mythologies (Segal). Not coincidentally, the tone of both Rimbaud's *Une Saison en Enfer* and Euripides's *Bacchae* is excessive, irrational, and bizarre. In the *Bacchae,* rationality and irrationality collide. This apotheosis reflects the conflict between two implacable but irreconcilable aspects of Greek culture: mythos and logos—"the metaphoric and conceptual modes of thought, written deep into the intellectual history of the late fifth century" (Segal). It is a conflict that is reenforced by the ascendancy of literacy as the facility for the organization, presentation, and transmission of knowledge. Oral tradition gave way to writing and the literate dedication to the sifting and analysis of facts.

> Plato's banishment of mythic poetry from his ideal state rests on a similar attempt to replace symbolic with analytical means of reach and communicating truth about the human condition. With the growth of analytical thought comes the increasing importance of prose, already well developed in the last quarter of the fifth century and soon virtually to supplant poetry as the primary medium of artistic expression and the main vehicle of cultural values. In this situation the poet no longer regards himself as the transmitter of stable cultural values, a master of truth, but rather as a creator of his own fictions. (Segal)

In this way, the predicament of Euripides is very similar to the situation in which Rimbaud found himself at the close of nineteenth-century France. The focus of both Rimbaud and Euripides is the effort to know what must not be known. "The unconscious is knowledge," says Jacques Lacan, "but it is a knowledge one cannot know that one knows, a knowledge which cannot tolerate knowing it knows." Though this dedication to "forbidden knowledge" is far clearer to us in Rimbaud, because of his proximity to our era and our sensibility, both he and Euripides created their works on the brink of frenzy, balancing on the very edge of our indecision about what can and cannot be acknowledged by consciousness. Through a myth of his own Rimbaud dared to break down the barrier between ignorance and discovery. Through a moribund myth of the Greek past, Euripides dared to retrace the irrational path that leads to Dionysian chaos and bliss and, in so doing, discovered the fallacy of literalism and the vitality of metaphor.

The works of Euripides and Rimbaud are but two examples of the ways in which myth becomes discovery. There has been a persistent recapitulation of this enduring conflict between similes that describe things as they are and metaphoric myths that describe things as they could be or should be. Between prose that informs us and poetry that changes us. Between data that lead to cognizance and myths that lead to discovery.

Dante Alighieri, the Italian poet born in Florence in 1265, is often regarded as the greatest poetical power of the West. He is said to have given "voice to ten silent centuries" (Carlyle) when he composed his epic poem *The Divine Comedy*. The work consists of one hundred cantos in terza rima, an Italian verse form in tercets: the second line rhymes with the first and third of the succeeding triplet. This elaborate form of versification was invented in Italy and eventually made its entry into England in the sixteenth century, where it was later used by both Shelley and Byron.

Dante had an astounding control of both language and poetic form. In a manner that seems almost nonchalant, he addressed himself in *The Divine Comedy* to the description of nothing less than the universe: a comprehensive moral, religious, and political scheme, a journey through Hell, Purgatory, and Paradise. The result is a staggeringly complex and opulent display of literary prowess. The immense encyclopedia of Catholic dogma had been transformed into poetry, achieving an extraordinary description of the fullest bloom of medieval culture, which had taken place during the century that ended just as Dante began work on his *Divine Comedy* in 1300. Influenced by the social climate of his time, the rise of towns, and the growing importance of the middle class, Dante was the primary writer of a new phase of European literature, one aimed at a secular audience and involving novel elements of humor, satire, allegory, beast fables, and bourgeois realism. Accordingly, Dante composed his epic not in Latin but in the everyday language of Tuscany, and the influence of his writings was so great that the Tuscan vernacular became the standard language of Italy.

Dante's language is concrete and vivid, making use of familiar words and comparisons, with few excursions into literary invention. As Eliot has suggested, Dante was not a visionary, but a cataloger of his age, using explicit similes with clear and easy references, rather than metaphors that evoke ambiguity. For the readers of his age there was nothing to comprehend or to fathom in Dante's depiction of the cosmos. However removed and naive to us may seem his view of things, no one of his own time would have questioned his philosophy and religion, which was that of Aquinas; his science and cosmology, which was that of Aristotle; or his depiction of the universe, which was that of Ptolemy. Nor would Dante's contemporaries have blinked at his literal belief in absolute sin and divine retribution and punishment. Heaven and Hell were real to the people of Dante's Christendom, and sin and its consequences were also real. The Christian's struggle for salvation was therefore no figure of speech, but a genuine struggle against sin emanating from within each person as well as evil coming from the outer world. Realism and simile served Dante well, for they transmitted the pragmatic mentality of his age, which was dominated by Pope Gregory the Great's legacy of blind faith. For Dante there was no such thing as the "natural" as opposed to the "supernatural." There were no spiritual ambiguities; no unanswered questions. Aristotle, Aquinas, Ptolemy, and Gregory had laid out the scheme of things, and from that scheme there was no possible deviation, except for heretics like Peter Abelard, who dared to proclaim that he could believe only what he understood. But understanding had nothing to do with Dante's immense literary gift; for him there were no options when it came to faith. And so he dedicated himself to the art of designation, depicting with utmost realism the Christian concept of all things human and divine.

Thus Dante himself was a Campbellian hero, whose journey of discovery, paradoxically, did not take him into the unknown, but rather into a territory meticulously mapped by Christianity: Hell, Purgatory, and Paradise. The framework of that journey assumed a cosmology that is totally removed from the Western twentieth-century picture of the cosmos. In the Ptolemaic conception of Dante's time the Earth is the cosmic center about which all other things move: a ball suspended in space around which revolve, one arranged within the other in concentric circles, nine spheres or heavens, the speeds of which increase in proportion to their distance from the Earth. The sphere nearest the Earth is the moon; then in order come Mercury, Venus, the sun, Mars, Jupiter, Saturn, and the fixed stars. The ninth circle is the crystalline sphere, or premium mobile, from which all the rest take time, space, and movement. Encircling all is the empyrean: motionless, timeless, and spaceless—the seat of the Judeo-Christian god.

Eternally separated from God is Lucifer, whose fall caused the earth to gape with fear; so a cavity, roughly cone-shaped, was created, with its apex at the center of the Earth. In this dismal place—which is also the center of the cosmos—is Lucifer, "emperor of the dolorous realm," fixed in ice. From its rim to the center, where Lucifer abides, Hell has nine circles, each receiving certain categories of sinners, who are nearer to Satan in proportion to the gravity of their sins.

Keeping to the strict geographical realism of his era, Dante tells us that Purgatory is located on top of a mountain, created by the upheaval of soil when Hell was formed. On top of this mountain originally was the garden called Eden, the earthly paradise, inhabited until their fall by Adam and Eve. But the garden had been transformed into Purgatory, with its seven circles where penitent souls are cleansed of their sins.

Nothing better exemplifies Joseph Campbell's notion of "the concretization of mythology" and its transformation from metaphoric allusion to historical and geographical fact than the utterly contradictory realistic/mystic world that Dante described in *The Divine Comedy*. When we are startled or dismayed by the literalism of religious fundamentalists at the close of the twentieth century, we should realize that such literalism has had a long history. In fact, as historian Herbert J. Muller has pointed out, the whole of medieval history in the West is the story of a fictive obsession that converted marvelous myths into incredulous truths:

> No other age has created such splendid, preposterous fictions; none has been at once so artful and so artless in its make-believe, and so blind to its solid, original achievements. For the fictions were not simply lies. They were spontaneous growths, rooted in an innocent, impassioned piety. They flowered luxuriantly in the imaginative ignorance of the holy past and a lofty indifference to vulgar fact. All that mattered was the pure, Catholic ideal. Enthralled by magnificent theories, [the people of the Middle Ages] were not troubled if no one tried to carry the theories out. At no time in the world's history has theory, professing all the while to control practice, been so utterly divorced from it.

Dante's task as a poet was to express what he believed to be known and believed by all Christians. Nothing else existed; and, if something else did exist, it didn't matter. What drove Dante was the fictive "unity of the Middle Ages." But that famed unity was not just a religious fiction.

> There was a practically universal agreement on the basic ideas by which people professed to live. Catholicism was not only the one Church but the primary inspiration of art, the main source of education, the accepted basis of all philosophy, science, political theory, and economic theory. (Muller)

People of the Middle Ages all knew the same absolute truths about the human drama. It was pictured in every cathedral's stained glass windows, sprawled magnificently across the walls of every church and chapel. It was praised in orations and sermons, in oratorios, masses, and motets. From the creation to the last judgment, every moment of the Judeo-Christian mythology was a vivid and real aspect of the life of the medieval people. It was not just "religion" to them, it was *drama*—the epic story of their own lives. As such, Catholicism was the basis of a rare sense of unity in Europe. "There were no strict nationalities, no fixed boundaries, no armed frontiers, no passports" (Muller).

Yet contradiction abounded within this Catholic unity. It was possible to hold ceremonies in which vanity was renounced—with great pomp. Those who celebrated austerity and celibacy were also renowned for the abundance of their bastards. Christian compassion lived side by side with the public torture and the execution of heretics. "Their high sense of honor was a blend of fine conscience and rude egotism that enabled them to set up an ideal of selfless fidelity, seek personal glory, gratify their love of fighting, maintain standards of justice, and wreak a barbarous vengeance on their enemies" (Muller).

The Divine Comedy is a synthesis of medieval thought and feeling. Dante was not the herald of things to come but the chronicler of an age of faith that, unbeknownst to the faithful, was eroding and collapsing all around them. His epic is a synthesis of medieval sensibility exalting the Roman world that Dante's generation believed had not declined but had somehow been renewed in the so-called Holy Roman Empire of Charlemagne—which was not holy, not Roman, and not an empire. Charlemagne's unique domain was the beginning of Europe and not the continuation of Rome, and the idea of the Holy Roman Empire was an essential Christian fiction that transformed the Vatican from a center of spirituality into a Christianized autocracy.

The Divine Comedy derives its power and its weakness from these contradictions: the collisions of the sacred and the secular. It fused "sensual, moral, intellectual, and spiritual values in the elaborate symbolism and allegory beloved by medieval people" (Muller). It abounds in the matter-of-fact language of reality, picturing the ineffable in terms of the concrete. It is, as Eliot suggested, explanatory rather than evocative, depictive rather than reflective; it uses similes that heighten reality rather than metaphors that change reality. Though *The Divine Comedy* aspires toward an evocation of the soul in bliss and in torment, it is remarkably full of the business of the world: "vulgar, mean details; the sublime message is introduced by fierce invective, which becomes simply nasty when Dante gloats over the infernal torments of his political enemies" (Muller). In short, a work typical of the contradictory mentality of the Middle Ages: steeped in the loftiest ideals and permeated by a foreboding of spiritual bankruptcy.

Beyond the specific elements of *The Divine Comedy* that help to define the Middle Ages, there is a more fundamental key to the understanding of Dante and medieval mentality, and it is discovered in the personality of Dante himself: an elaborate symbol of the Faustian spirit, "that insatiable, inextinguishable willfulness that distinguished Western civilization from all others" (Muller).

That same Faustian nature impelled the sixteenth-century achievements of William Shakespeare, but it manifested itself in an entirely different manner from the way it influenced the works of Dante. While Shakespeare's contemporary Ben Jonson was, as Dante, an apostle of conscious art, Shakespeare himself was a person who lived in the world of make-believe: a playwright, actor, and theatrical manager who was so much in touch with the Elizabethan public that he epitomized the spirit of his age without conscious effort. Friedrich Hebbel, one of the great writers of nineteenth-century theater, noted that the tragic impulse of Shakespeare's art was not always to be found within the complexity of individual characters, though it is a commonplace to ascribe to Shakespeare a profound grasp of psychological characterization. Hebbel, however, suggests that behind Shakespeare's tragic sense was a distinctive Elizabethan dilemma: the clash of the medieval and the modern sensibilities. Thus, though virtually all of Shakespeare's plots were derived from traditional medieval legend, contemporary chronicles, classic literature, and existent dramas of his own day, he brought to these familiar subjects an entirely unprecedented depth of experience and interpretation. Living, as he was, on the threshold of modernism, he managed to infuse new depth into the allegorical characters of his medieval prototypes and the archetypal vision of Greek dramatic tradition. And he achieved this not as Ben Jonson might have attempted, through carefully examined facts and observations, but through an exceptional poetic gift—the ability to use an entirely invented and unrealistic language that no Elizabethan spoke in daily life—to insinuate and to imply states of mind that might otherwise escape description. Ultimately the entire framework of Shakespeare's theatrical manner grew out of his exceptional inventions of language and metaphor. Even the broad outlines of his borrowed plots were interpreted in terms of poetic and symbolic meaning, rather than in the calculated and staid realism of his contemporaries.

Shakespeare's metaphorical approach was just one important aspect of his art. He also invented a literary approach that made it possible for him to build theatrical characters with a psychological depth that was to be found nowhere else among the writings of his contemporaries (with the possible exception of John Webster). It is precisely this combining of metaphoric ambiguity with specific psychological characterization that gives the works of Shakespeare their unique theatrical and literary personality.

Three hundred years before Shakespeare, Dante had embraced the allegorical mentality of the Middle Ages, fashioning his *Divine Comedy* in a literary manner born of parable, with an eagerness for realistic detail. Several centuries before Dante, Euripides concerned himself with the struggle of humankind against destiny. His keenly chiseled figures, like sculptures of the archaic period, are not merely human. They are archetypical characters that, to this day, still resonate with a verity that has nothing to do with verisimilitude. Shakespeare achieved a different, but equally sublime, effect. Since he lived in an era that was still touched by the supernaturalism of the Middle Ages, magical and enchanted characters and events flow through his most solemn tragedies: ghosts, witches, apparitions, and demons. (It is not by coincidence that Japanese filmmaker Akira Kurosawa could impressively interpret the plays of Shakespeare in the fantastic manner of Kabuki theater, a theatrical genre that has more than a bit in common with the stylization of medieval miracle plays.)

The witches in *Macbeth* are pivotal characters in the tragedy, not simply colorful ornamentation. They are depicted in the most robust medieval manner, as if they stepped from a painting by Hieronymus Bosch. They typify the mood of the fifteenth century, an epoch that had began

on a note of humanistic optimism and ended with a waning strength of spirit, and an erosion of confidence in the moral and religious authority of the Church. Contemporary poetry is filled with dreary pessimism and foreboding, anticipating another Fall of man and seeming to see ahead the disasters of Christendom in the time of the Reformation. (Gardner)

When Macbeth and Banquo first approach the witches and hear their quizzical prophecies, it is as if three irreconcilable worlds have collided: one still rooted in the medieval dread of the supernatural; another impelled by the skeptical attitudes of an emerging modernism; and the third recalling the archetypical heroes of ancient Greece. To this improbable blend of classical and medieval models, Shakespeare adds an unheard of innovation: the psychologically dimensional personality that would become the centerpiece of modern literature. Edith Hamilton notes that Lady Macbeth is at first very much like the Clytemnestra of Aeschylus in her emotional monumentality and archetypal presence: a prototype rather than a flesh and blood person with a psychological history. But gradually Lady Macbeth changes, assuming a depth of individuality inconsistent with the scheme of Greek tragedy. While waiting for Macbeth to kill the king, she says to herself, "Had he not resembled my father as he slept, I had done't." This phrase, as Hamilton points out, infuses the kind of idiosyncratic *identity* into Lady Macbeth that Aeschylus would never have given his Clytemnestra. Aeschylus was concerned with Clytemnestra as a form, a type, a symbol, not as a personage with an inner life and a unique and complex history.

The Clytemnestra of Aeschylus, like the Pentheus of Euripides, alludes to an aspect of the transcendent spirit of the Greek ideal. Greek tragic characters are similar to Platonic forms—imprecise shadows of an absolute reality we cannot perceive or comprehend. In sharp contrast, Lady Macbeth alludes to that aspect of the human psyche that is both individual and transcendent. Not an idea and not an allegorical personage, but a literary character wrought of flesh and mind—both perception and conception.

By and large, the impact on today's audiences of both Greek and Shakespearean drama is similar, but the components of language and symbolism in these two theatrical forms are distinctive, as surely as the communicative manner of Dante and Shakespeare are both highly effective but widely different from each other.

Interpretation only comes into existence when the prevailing mythology of a culture begins to erode. L. L. Whyte tells us that "thought is born of failure." While there exists an unquestioned dogma, there is no need for interpretation. And without interpretation, there is no possibility of discovery.

81

Dante was a descriptive, not an interpretative, poet; he applied an unquestioned set of criteria without the impulse or the need to reimagine or reevaluate what he described. He simply applied those values that he found in the reigning worldview. That worldview was implicit in the religious paradigm of his society; though, in fact, that paradigm was on the brink of dissolution.

Euripides and Shakespeare lived in vastly different times from Dante and from each other, but they shared a central social experience: a mood of profound skepticism caused, at least in part, by the disintegration of the supportive mythologies of their distinctive cultures.

In the *Bacchae* Euripides looked back into the moribund cult of Dionysus, with its emphasis upon gender ambiguity, abandon, intuition, imagination, and the vision of uncontrolled "nature" of which women have always been the ambivalent symbol in the West (Highwater 1990). He had to reimagine the Dionysian vision in terms of the demystified social order of his own secular era, by which time the gods had been so humanized as to be rendered metaphysically insignificant. He had to interpret the abiding dilemma of the Periclean age, when logos replaced mythos as the driving force of life, and when the ancient goddess and her kinship with unbridled nature was submerged in a new social order revolving around the patriarchal repudiation of nature (Highwater 1990). This he achieved with brilliance through the theatrical manipulation of archetypal characters whose animation arises out of mythic spirit rather than out of distinctive human personality; characters who are monumental concepts in the pagan masks of persons dramatically pitted one against the other. Euripides presented his audience with architectural personae, not with dimensional personalities.

In *Macbeth* Shakespeare borrowed from the highly theatrical folklore that lingered into the sixteenth century, tales of witches and ghosts. He drew upon the morality plays of the Middle Ages, dramas focused upon the conflicts inherent in authority, retribution, destiny, and ambition. But in dealing with such familiar subject matter, he could not rest upon the interpretations of the past nor rely upon the philosophical consensus of the audience of his time. In Elizabethan England the age of skepticism was already shattering the informing mythologies of Western Christendom. The Reformation was contesting the religious authority of Rome. Now there were no easy and accessible standards that playwrights could depend upon as the philosophical foundation of their works. The grand allegorical design of the cosmos imagined variously by Athens and Rome was being dismantled. Shakespeare's contemporary, the poet Edmund Spenser (author of *The Faerie Queene*), relied upon a reactionary devotion to a vanishing creed and its archaic language, which was loaded with preconceptions. Shakespeare, on the other hand, felt compelled to invent a new language of vision that might enable him to *explain* evil and retribution and not simply to *describe* them—however vividly—as Dante had. Shakespeare had to reinvent the world and describe it in terms of his own mythology, his own paradigm. And since Elizabethan language was built upon an obsolescent mythology and not the visions that were the bases of Shakespeare's own vision, he had to construct a metaphoric language capable of making poetic sense out of revolutionary subjects that defied the traditional approach of poets who confirmed the realities of their unified and systematic societies.

To achieve this purpose, Shakespeare could not rely upon descriptions of an external and fixed reality to determine the evolution of his plots and the moral behavior of his characters. He could not design his tales so all the dialogue and all the action led gracefully to the one and only socially acceptable conclusion and the inevitable moral lessons. Instead, he had to illuminate something as subjective and insubstantial as the psychology of his characters, the ruminations of his interior self that Dante and Euripides would have found irrelevant and unaesthetic. As Camille Paglia has pointed out,

> Shakespeare uses language to darken. He mesmerizes by disorienting us. . . . Shakespeare's language hovers at the very threshold of dreaming. It is shaped by the irrational. . . . The

83

essence of Shakespeare is not the objet d'art but the metaphor. Metaphors are the key to character, the imaginative center of every speech. They spill from line to line, abundant, florid, illogical. They are Shakespeare's dream-vehicle of Dionysian metamorphosis. The teeming metaphors are the objects of the medieval great chain of being suddenly unstacked and released into vitalistic free movement.

Macbeth is not the traditional medieval hero of the tragedy bearing his name; he is far more reminiscent of the antiheroes of the twentieth century. He is not driven by a religious code of behavior, nor by a monumental sense of Christian destiny. He is not an allegorical figure, set in dramatic motion in order to illustrate a moral battle. He does not speak in maxims. Instead, he is motivated by the trace of a complex impulse that arises, invisibly and mysteriously, from consciousness. The exterior world merges with an ambiguous interior mentality. Shakespeare could take nothing for granted. He could not compose with the comfortable security of writers who lived in states of faith. His most brilliant characters are his most enigmatic creations: Hamlet, Lear, Othello, and Macbeth. Even Iago, who seems to represent an unmotivated but indisputable evil, is, finally, intriguingly complex rather than simply villainous.

In each scene he wrote, Shakespeare faced the unknown, and to deal with such a calamitous, expressive dilemma, he created a rich metaphoric language capable of expressing passions rarely discovered in literature before his time: metaphors of cynicism, desire, longing, ambition, defeat, love, and hate; words that captured a reality that was not yet fully real.

Tomorrow, and tomorrow, and tomorrow,
Creeps in this petty pace from day to day,
To the last syllable of recorded time;
And all our yesterdays have lighted fools
The way to dusty death. Out, out brief candle!

84

Life's but a walking shadow, a poor player
that struts and frets his hour upon the stage,
And then is heard no more; it is a tale
Told by an idiot, full of sound and fury,
Signifying nothing.

Dante lived in the twilight of a world that still believed in its central mythology, and he could therefore attend to the business of making poetry without great concern for meaning. His poetry is descriptive rather than interpretative. Shakespeare, in contrast, lived in an era of disunity, torn between the past and the future, when the central beliefs of his world were in decline. He therefore could not rely upon the communal faith of his audience but had to use a metaphoric mentality that allowed him to reimagine and vivify the familiar characters and plots he borrowed from others.

In short, like many postmodern playwrights and authors, he had to reinvent the past in order to create the present. It was a predicament not unlike the one in which the Greek playwrights of the age of Pericles found themselves. But whereas the Greeks dedicated themselves to a monumentalism that gazed philosophically and dramatically upon characters as microcosms of the human condition, Shakespeare devised a radical approach: He began with monumental and archetypical characters that allude to vast, transindividual conditions, but then he awakened the oblique psyches within these symbolic characters and transformed them into personalities capable of reflecting both the general and the specific. The device with which he achieved this effect was multifaceted, but one of its major components was the use of metaphoric language, which not only tells us what people look like and what they are saying, but also tells us what they are thinking and feeling—and why they think and feel as they do. By no means do all adventurous twentieth-century writers ascribe to Shakespeare's psychological realism, but his influence on the tradition of the dominant Western literary style is enormous.

One of Shakespeare's most remarkable achievements remains

an abiding and central concern of major writers, bringing to mind the mythic nature of works by James Joyce, Franz Kafka, Virginia Woolf, William Butler Yeats, Federico García Lorca, Tennessee Williams, T. S. Eliot, Ezra Pound, William Gaddis, William Faulkner, Thomas Mann, and practically all the other nonrealist authors of the twentieth century. Shakespeare resolved the conflict between similes that describe things as they are and the metaphoric and mythic language that describes things as they exist in the imagination. He abandoned the kind of prose that merely informs us and created a poetry that changes us. He distinguished once and for all between data that lead to cognizance and visions and myths that lead to discovery.

VII.

The Empress

Rituals of the Land

The whole of nature is a metaphor of the human mind.

Ralph Waldo Emerson

The female figure of the crowned Empress of the Tarot deck sits on a throne and holds the symbol of power in her hand: a scepter with a globe at the end. Some interpret the globe as a symbol of the earth. She is said to represent feminine power, natural energy, fertility, and the powers of terrestrial creation. Her realm includes every aspect of the human response to the environment: agricultural mythologies, rituals of the changing seasons, and beliefs about how buildings and gardens should be created. The Empress is the guardian of the natural world and an ideal symbol of the earth rituals enacted by human beings throughout history.

The marks we make upon the earth tell us who we are.

The world is modeled upon paradigms. The land is constantly changing because our vision of it changes. What Emerson said bears repeating: "The whole of nature is a metaphor of the human mind."

At the core of such metaphoric vision, as Mircea Eliade points out, is that universal "mythical behavior" that is our only means of understanding the fundamental reality of our world.

> The marks people make on the ground reflect the philosophy of the time. . . . The groves and temples of Arcadia, the radiating avenues of the imperial center, the neatly ordered municipal garden, and the spoils and effluent of industrial rapacity, are each the product of a certain cosmology, a certain view of the nature of the universe and its relationship to human beings. (Mitchell)

The pyramids, the slums, the gardens of Versailles, the dammed rivers, the New York skyscrapers, the landfills, even the cottage gardens of English peasants—each of these earthworks tells us something about ourselves at a particular time and in a particular place.

89

Once the earth was the realm of the wizard and the alchemist, the ritualist and the magician. But since the eighteenth century the earth has been the domain of science. Frances Yates has tried to understand that drastic transition in the custodianship of nature:

> The basic difference between the attitude of the magician toward the world and the attitude of the scientist toward the world is that the former wants to draw the world into himself, whilst the scientist does just the opposite; he externalizes and impersonalizes the world by a movement of will in an entirely opposite direction.

Positivist science claims something called "objectivity," which is simply *subjectivity* trying to disguise and to supplant itself with a delusion of detachment. The "impersonalized world" is the source of the fable of objectivity that physicist Werner Heisenberg deflated when he suggested that the mere presence of an observer, scientific or otherwise, insinuates meaning upon reality, all of which reconfirms Emerson's view that nature is a metaphor of the human mind.

The earth, the land, the buildings we build, the gardens we make can be regarded, not just as the terra firma so dear to scientific materialism, but as a succession of ritualized conceits— the stage upon which we enact our imaginal lives as cultures and as persons. Whether we call these central conceits scientific or mythological is irrelevant. As David Maclagan suggests, we literally create the land on which we live:

> In many American Indian myths [human beings] are only one part in the whole of creation; in our own Book of *Genesis* "Man" is the apex, the focal point of creation. . . . But in some cosmogonies creation almost frowns on man: for the Aztecs, the cosmos was highly vulnerable and insecure and people were bound to offer their blood, or even their lives, in order to sustain it. In other cultures the natural world is

considered of little real importance; for many Hindus the whole drama of creation is indeed merely theatrical; a performance which, once its message has been understood, is no longer necessary.

Our sense of place—of cosmic space—is largely determined by the manner in which we see ourselves in relation to nature. That perception varies drastically from culture to culture. Among many tribal peoples, for instance, there is an extraordinarily sharp awareness of spatial relationship. But it is a sense of space quite distinctive from the one we find in the history of painting in the West. Tribal people usually have a keen eye for the details of their environments. They are extremely sensitive to every change in the position of the common objects in their surroundings, creating what is some sort of exacting experiential interior "map" of the environs. The tribal person is rarely lost, even under the most difficult circumstances. When rowing or sailing, the tribal person

> follows with the greatest accuracy all the turns of the river.
> . . . But upon closer examination we discover to our surprise
> that in spite of this facility there seems to be a strange lack
> of [a tribal sense] of space. If you ask [a boatman] to give you
> a general description, a delineation of the course of the river
> he is not able to do so. If you wish him to draw a map of the
> river and its various turns he seems not even to understand
> your request. (Cassirer 1944a)

The comprehension and apprehension of space in Western society is of a quite different order, representing a distinctive way of ritualizing nature. For instance, in the West "perspective" is the art of delineating solid objects upon a plane surface so as to produce the same conception of relative positions and magnitudes, or of distance, as we conceptualize out of our cultural experience of space in nature. In this way, perspective is the result of how we interpret and therefore how we see space.

Though we might be inclined to believe that the optical activity involved in spatial perception is universal and, therefore, the same for all human beings in all times and places, quite the opposite is true. Space perception is a highly ethnocentric interpretation existing in numerous forms, but the most characteristic ones are these:

Tiered Perspective: It suggests space by placing levels of activity one above another; all figures are about the same size, with the lowest level in the composition reading as the closest to the viewer. This type of drawing is found in early Christian art, such as the Isenheim Altar by Matthias Grünewald; it is also found among many non-Western cultures, such as the Javanese and Balinese societies.

Reverse Perspective: Parallel lines do not converge as they move away from the viewer, and objects do not get smaller as they recede, but depth is suggested by providing two points of view and showing more sides and parts of an object than could possibly be seen from a single viewpoint, thereby using the flatness of the painted surface as an aesthetic entity that is often entirely filled. It is a technique similar to the twisted perspective of the Paleolithic cave paintings, which, as noted earlier, deals less with illusionist "appearances" and more with the artist's essential awareness and knowledge of the painted subject matter. Reverse perspective is seen in many Byzantine paintings, as for instance the fourteenth-century *Birth of the Virgin* from a fresco in the King's Chapel of the Church of Sts. Joachim and Ann, in Studenica of the former Yugoslavia. It is also seen in the drawings of tribal peoples and in the paintings of children.

Aerial Perspective: Since air is not entirely transparent, an ever-increasing layer of obscuring atmosphere gradually interpolates itself between the seen objects and the viewer; therefore as objects get smaller with distance, the eye fails to see detail and contrasts diminish as they turn to a middle gray. In his *Landscape with St. Jerome* of about 1520, Joachim de Patinir makes use of aerial perspective, with generally warm foreground colors that shift to cool blue in the background.

Linear Perspective: This is the form of perspective that is most familiar to us in illusionist paintings, which commenced roughly with the Renaissance. In this spatial technique, space is suggested by the use of the mathematical conception of the oblique line: parallel lines (edges of planes) appear to converge as they become more distant from the observer, and if uninterrupted they converge at a point on the horizon line (actual curvature of the Earth and the viewer's eye level), and the objects close to the observer overlay and obscure more distant objects when they are in the same trajectory of vision. Distant objects become proportionally smaller as they are placed farther and farther back from the foreground. Linear perspective is essentially a mathematical scheme invented by artists of the Renaissance, who were often also mathematicians.

> The position of the observer of a picture, looking "through" it into the painted "world," is precisely that of any scientific observer fixing his gaze upon the carefully placed or located datum of his research. There is little doubt that linear perspective, with its new mathematical authority and certitude, conferred a kind of aesthetic legitimacy on painting by making the picture measurable and exact. (Gardner)

Thus, with the Renaissance, the metaphor changes from an experiential paradigm to a scientific point of reference. The art of painting becomes something very similar to cartography, a science that would be incomprehensible to the tribal boatman who knows the river experientially but would see no relationship between that experience and the kind of aerial view of the river that is depicted on maps.

We see nature in drastically different ways depending on our point of view. We see what we expect to see. And, therefore, we ritualize nature in ways that are constantly changing. Our point of view not only influences the art of visual representation; it also sways our conception of how gardens and buildings should be made.

The manipulation of earthly space recapitulates our visions of the workings of cosmic space. Therefore, in the great ceremonial camp circle of the Sun Dance of the American Plains Indians, in the architecture of the Sun Lodge itself, there is a carefully prescribed master plan that is not a matter of simply accommodating rank and bestowing places of honor, but is also a reflection of a cosmic design and rhythm that reverberates through every aspect of the Native American relationship to the earth, to nature, and, ultimately, to the conception of nature.

Astronomer Ray Williamson reports that "much of the art and the architecture of American Indians of a millennium ago can be better understood in relation to celestial events."

Thus, the sacredness of space is not limited in the tribal mentality to the relation of place to earthly directions and mythic history, but is also closely and accurately related to heavenly movement. It is a use of "scientific observation" distinct from the application of the mathematical linear perspective to the art of illusionist painting. In a monumental structure at Hovenweep in New Mexico, dating from the thirteenth century, the ancient native people incorporated two special sighting holes in the walls, one aligned to the summer solstice sunset on June 21, the other to the winter solstice sunset on December 21. In this way, though the tribal conception of astronomical motion is accurate, it is built on a spatial paradigm also, and not on a worldview that is essentially abstract and mathematical. The same must be said of the great stone circles of England and Brittany, as well as early architectural structures such as the Nuraghi of Sardinia and the great temples of Malta.

British archaeologist Colin Renfrew makes some decisive points along these lines:

> Most of us have been brought up to believe that the Pyramids of Egypt are the oldest stone-built monuments in the world, and that the first temples were situated in the Near West, in the fertile land of Mesopotamia. There, it was commonly thought, in the homeland of the first great civilizations, metallurgy was invented. The knowledge of working in copper and bronze, like that of monumental architecture and many other important skills, would then have been acquired by the "less advanced" inhabitants of surrounding areas, and gradually have been diffused over much of Europe and the rest of the Old World. The early prehistoric monuments of western Europe, the megalithic tombs with their colossal stones, would document one very striking instance of this diffusion of ideas. In Britain, we have similarly been led to believe that the riches of our early bronze age and the sophistication of Stonehenge itself reflect, in comparable ways, the inspiration of the more sophisticated world of Myceanaean Greece.
>
> It comes, then, as a shock to learn that all of this is dead wrong! The megalithic chamber tombs of western Europe are now dated earlier than the Pyramids—indeed, they rank as the earliest stone monuments of the world—so an origin for them in the east Mediterranean seems altogether implausible. . . . The traditional view of prehistory is now contradicted at every point.

We now plainly see that the theories about the supremacy of certain traditionally admired centers of Western "civilization" are rather pathetic bits of nationalist self-aggrandizement and historical fraud.

Implicit in the self-serving refocusing of admiration on patri-

archal Near Eastern and Greek societies at the expense of the
so-called pagan and matrofocal cultures of the Mediterranean, is
the story of the Empress—better known today as the Goddess:

> The earth used to have, as it were, a goddess to call her own,
> because the earth and all creation were of the same substance
> as the Goddess. Earth was her epiphany: the divine was
> immanent as creation. Our mythic image of earth has lost this
> dimension. So we must set out to discover what has hap-
> pened to the goddess image, how and when it disappeared,
> and what were the implications of this loss. Since mythic
> images implicitly govern a culture, what did this tell us about
> a particular culture—as our own—that either did not have or
> did not acknowledge a mythic image of the feminine princi-
> ple? It begins to seem no coincidence that ours is the age
> above all other that has desacralized nature: generally speak-
> ing, the earth is no longer instinctively experienced as a living
> being as in earlier times, or so it would seem from the
> evidence of pollution (itself a term that originally meant the
> profaning of what was sacred). . . . From Babylonian mythol-
> ogy onwards (c. 2000 B.C.), the Goddess became almost
> exclusively associated with "Nature" as the chaotic force to
> be mastered, and the God took the role of conquering or
> ordering nature from his counterpole of "Spirit." (Baring/
> Cashford)

One of the first and most vivid mythic accounts of the decimation of the power of the Goddess is found in both the epic of
Gilgamesh that dates from the Akkadian civilization, centered in
Babylon circa 1200 B.C., as well as the earlier Sumerian fragments
from 2500 B.C.: *Gilgamesh and the Huluppu Tree.*

As William Irwin Thompson recounts this central tale, Gilgamesh, the king of the city, the man who most exemplifies Faustian personality and progressive civilization, takes it as his project
to go forth from the city to slay the spirit of the forest.

Here are the roots of the ecological crisis of our civilization. The furniture of civilization comes from the death of forests, not merely of trees. Men no longer ask permission of the guardian spirit to take the minimum for their needs; they march in pomp and glory and level the entire forest. Gilgamesh does not realize, though, that when he slays the spirit of the forest and cuts off the city from nature, he gives a new life to death. Before, all the processes of culture were connected with the cycles of nature; in death, tribal man simply returned to the Great Mother. But when civilized man sets up walls between himself and the forest, and when he sets up his personal name against the stars, he ensures that the now-isolated ego will cry out in painful recognition of its complete alienation in the fear of death. ⌣

There is an unmistakable association between the notion of the "conquest of the forest" and the various conceptions that have determined the forms of cities, buildings, and gardens since earliest times.

American archaeologist George Kubler has noted that our conception of architecture has been dominated for so long by the pragmatic need for shelter that "we lack the sense of buildings as sacred and monumental form apart from shelter." In sacred and monumental architecture, it is not necessary to enclose and cover chambers and rooms; it suffices, as in ancient America and contemporary Java and Bali, to mark out a space by solid masses or groves or gardens—or simply to inscribe the space with a system of lines and shapes. The grand design of the ninth-century Buddhist structure called Borobudur, located in central Java, attests to this scheme of a sacred structure entirely without an interior design, for this, the largest stupa in the southern hemisphere, is built as a colossal series of ascending terraces without enclosures. Similarly, the *pura* (temple) of Bali is a bright outdoor place entered through the highly ornamental *candi bentar* (split gate) that leads into enclosures surrounded by freestanding walls marking, but not enclosing, numerous courtyards that are open to the sky. The sprawling Nazca Lines that mark the Peruvian desert of South America, as well as the numerous earthworks of the pre-Columbian mound buildings of the Mississippi and Missouri rivers, are examples of inscribed lines and freestanding mounds that have an architectural basis.

Such architecture is an expression in honor of a sacred place, revered not because of an event that took place on the site, but because there is a belief in something powerful and transcendent emanating from it—a spring, a geyser, a mountain, a valley, a rock, a center of the earth's spirituality which native peoples often call the "earth's navel."

The architectural concepts of other times and other places give less emphasis to "earth centers" and tend to focus on orientations in relationship to the sky. At Teotihuacán, in the valley of Mexico (the most ancient true city of the ancient Americas), architectural planning was focused on geometric positions that related to the sun, particularly the annual zenith setting occurring every year on June 21. The distribution of hundreds of small structures was determined by a cosmic order, and "the spatial arrangement reflects the rhythm of the universe" (Kubler). The shift from earth to sky orientation usually accompanies the shift from matrofocal to patrofocal social orders. With a sky orientation not only are structures planned in terms of mathematical schemes related to celestial movement, but they also tend to be associated with a revolution in attitude about the ownership of the land itself; it passes from being a communal or tribal possession to being a matter of individual or familial ownership, a shift associated with the emergence of various hierarchies of rank and power.

The buildings of primal peoples tend to uphold the convictions of the romantic movement in architecture espoused by such luminaries as Frank Lloyd Wright: namely, the use of materials immediately available at the building site (so the structure reflects its environment, rather than imposing itself upon the land and standing remote from its surroundings); and a celebration of "the nature of materials," rather than encouraging the typically Western effort to disguise brick and wood and stone so they look like something other than what they are.

Of all the ways in which the ritualization of land is made visible, perhaps the ways in which gardens are made is the most revealing, betraying the precise attitudes of various societies toward the natural world. Gardens reflect a wide variety of attitudes about nature: Each garden is a metaphor that makes a statement about the outdoors. For some cultures the notion of a "garden" does not exist because the entire world is envisioned as that primordial landscape, or "paradise garden," implied in most myths of the creation. But in drastically different cultures, the garden is a wall of defense against the chaos and invasiveness of "wilderness" and "nature."

As such, gardens are a reflection of the age in which they are created. From historical evidence it seems that the gardens of ancient Egypt, Greece, and Rome were rather formal affairs: walled and secluded oases, often porticos, atriums, or rotundas open to the sky in the houses of the wealthy. An inscription in an Egyptian tomb reads: "May my soul sit on the branches of the grave garden I have prepared for myself; may I refresh each day under my sycamore." When describing the garden of Alconous in *The Odyssey*, Homer recounted: "Their fruit never fails nor runs short, winter and summer alike, it comes at all seasons of the year, and there is never a time when the West Wind's breath is not assisting."

Islamic gardens preceded medieval European ones and were highly sophisticated in ways that do not make their impact felt in Europe until much later. The gardens of the Persian and Islamic empires "share a religious heritage, intellectual philosophy, and environmental attitude that remain influential today. A direct line of influence runs from Persia and Islam, to Spain's Alhambra and Generalife, to the modern gardens of major designers of America and Europe" (W. L. Douglas). In the Near East, water was a precious commodity, and it was used sparingly, usually as a single jet or in a small linear channel faced with brightly colored titles. Shade was equally precious in the arid environment of the Islamic Empire, so trees and covered passageways were used to great advantage. The Islamic influence gave the medieval European garden its fundamental scheme: an enclosed, secluded place of meditation—a microcosm of paradise.

In contrast, the oriental garden has a quite different plan and reflects a unique attitude toward nature. There is a famous anecdote claiming that the people of Japan love nature so much that they can't leave it alone.

> In China and Japan, one is told, man blends with nature; there is no dichotomy, such as exists in the West, where man is inclined to oppose the forces of nature. . . . In art and daily life Japanese like to use natural images to express human emotions. Japanese novelists are masters at weaving natural metaphors and images into the fabric of their stories. (Buruma)

In the central Japanese religion, Shintoism, everything in nature is potentially sacred. The Buddhists view human beings as only one element in the natural cycle of life and death. Man is an inseparable part of nature. "The Japanese attitude to nature is not therefore simply a matter of love, for it is tinged with a deep fear of the unpredictable forces it can unleash. It is worshipped, yes, but only after it has been methodically reshaped by human hands, for the Japanese love of nature does not extend to nature in the raw, for which they seem to feel an abhorrence" (Buruma).

Likewise, in medieval European monasteries the gardens turned their backs on the hostile, barbaric world and were inwardly oriented around a central, walled garden, which were crucial elements for the development of gardening in the West. "The monastery's cloister . . . shows a relationship to Roman and Persian antecedents. Divided by two intersecting paths, the resulting quadrants held plants with both ornamental and religious significance.

In the center would be a water feature: a well to drink from, a cistern for watering and bathing, or a tub holding fish for lenten meals" (W. L. Douglas). The painters of the fifteenth century often depicted Paradise as such a walled medieval garden with fruit trees and flowers, birds and animals.

In contrast, the garden of the Italian Renaissance was a strictly geometric and symmetrical arrangement, giving rise to our notion of the "formal garden," with its overwrought elements of Roman antiquity and aristocratic splendor. Nature so entirely disappears into the grid system and architectural control of the Renaissance garden that even the hedges and trees are trimmed into rigid geometric shapes and forms. The French carried this mechanistic scheme to its ultimate Cartesian extreme in the fifteenth century with the so-called parterres, elaborate mazes and geometric patterns created with clipped box hedges or woody low-growing herbs entwined by labryinthian pathways covered by colored gravels.

In complete contrast was the invention in England of a type of landscaping that attempted to imitate the freedom of nature, eventually becoming the renowned British herbaceous garden, which imitated the charm of the cottage gardens of peasants. Such gardens, with their earthy simplicity and rambling disarray, were part of the British reaction against formality and bloated sophistication, becoming, in the nineteenth century, a major social and artistic trend called the Arts and Crafts movement, a celebration of many elements of folk art and country living. Thus, in the eighteenth and nineteenth centuries, England gave rise to a virtual revolution in garden design.

Ever since this radical redirection of attitudes about nature in England, the gardens of the world have been an eclectic affair, combining many different elements borrowed from every possible tradition of gardening, producing the romantic gardens of the nineteenth century and the mixture of every possible gardening fashion in the twentieth century.

With the persistent revision of the ways that gardens and

buildings are made, we have come a great distance from the ancient myth of the spirit of the forest. And yet that potent mythology remains at the center of much of our thinking, either as the goal of our aspirations or as the abhorrent chaos of the natural world that we hope to control with clippers and lawn mowers or escape entirely by closing it out of our lives with sturdy walls. Whatever our point of view, each method is an expression of rituals of the land.

Whatever our attitude about the control of nature, the forest remains a place of magic. And the magic forest is always full of adventure.

No one can enter it without losing his way. But the chosen one, the elect, who survives its deadly perils, is reborn and leaves it a changed person. The forest has always been a place of initiation; for there the demonic presences, the ancestral spirits, and the forces of nature reveal themselves. There human beings meet their greater selves, their totem animals. And thither the medicine man conducts the youths of the tribe in order that they may be born again through gruesome initiation rites. The forest is the antithesis of house and hearth, village and field boundary, where the household gods hold sway and where human laws and customs prevail. It holds the dark forbidden things—secrets, terror—which threaten the protected life of the ordered world of common day. In its terrifying abyss, full of strange forms and whispering voices, it contains the secret of the soul's adventure. Somewhere in this monstrous region, this seat of darkness, the castle of Merlin still stands. Its countless windows look out upon the secrets that lurk around it, the doors are open to travelers from every quarter of the globe, and paths lead from the castle into the farthest reaches of the world. The castle is the heart of darkness, its countless eyes see and know all, and it offers to each of the elect a different approach to the mystery. (Zimmer)

The ritualization of land is a form of "art" only for those who have found it necessary to invent the notion of art. For all other people, rituals of the land are an unconscious but pervasive aspect of the planetary life cycle. Among people with a concept of "art" as a nonutilitarian expressive form there is a long-standing exclusive attitude that does not recognize so-called crafts as legitimate art forms. But *anything* becomes art as a result of the "impregnation of ordinary reality with the significance of created form" (Langer 1957). This is what Susanne Langer has called the "subjectification of nature."

Unquestionably, many casual activities are distinct from art, for instance, whenever significant form is not the intent of the maker of an object or activity. But, if the maker is intent upon recapitulating or originating a form built on sentient significance, then the results are not simply a matter of craft or artifact. Such an activity is *art* in the most inclusive sense of the word, whether it be a brilliantly prepared meal, a beautifully plowed field, a handsomely made pot or textile, a splendidly built temple, an imaginatively conceived garden, or the ritual planting of a sanctified grove of trees.

> Wherever art takes a motif from actuality—a flowering branch, a bit of landscape, a historic event or a personal memory, any model or theme from life—it transforms it into a piece of imagination, and imbues its image with artistic vitality. The result is an impregnation of ordinary reality with the significance of created form. This is the *subjectification of nature* that makes reality itself a symbol of life and of feeling. (Langer 1957)

Robert Hughes has said that, until about fifty years ago, images of nature were the most fundamental key to feeling in art.

> Nature—its cycles of growth and decay, its responses to wind, weather, light, and the passage of the seasons, its ceaseless renewal, its infinite complexity of form and behavior

103

on every level, from the molecule to the galaxy—provided the governing metaphors within which almost every relationship of the Self to the Other could be described and examined. The sense of a natural order, always in some way correcting the pretensions of the Self, gave mode and measure to pre-modern art. (Hughes 1981)

But today we live in a world that we ourselves have made entirely—and in which nature has little visibility. We are so out of touch with nature that there are chickens on display at the zoo in Central Park in New York City, lest urban children believe that chickens are simply those dismembered and plastic-wrapped pieces found in the supermarkets.

> The problem for art, then, was how to survive here, how to adapt to this habitat. . . . The idea that we would live immersed in a haze of almost undifferentiated images, that the social function of this image-haze would be to erode distinction rather than multiply the possible discriminations about reality, would have been unthinkable to our great-grandparents—let alone to our remote ancestors. (Hughes 1993)

It is, therefore, not unexpected that some late-twentieth-century artists decided to try to find a way back into nature, to invent a method of ritualizing landscapes into dreamscapes capable of bringing the power of the natural world back into their art. Their achievements are usually called Earth Art or Earthworks and constitute an artistic movement that made a major impact during the late 1960s and early 1970s.

Earth Art, along with conceptual art and performance art, deemphasized the final work and placed emphasis upon how the work came into existence; process became more important than effect. "The idea was to open the gallery doors, to let in nature and daily life" (Lippard 1990). The hope was that art would escape to the freedom of the streets and fields, where it would presumably be welcomed by a populace hitherto intimidated by so-called high art. "This enterprise was not entirely successful, but the whole tendency toward the 'dematerialization of the object' did introduce a healthy number of new subjects and concerns into experimental art" (Lippard 1990).

Among these new subjects was a focus upon the landscape as a significant aspect of the geosphere—something very different from the romantic terrain celebrated in eighteenth-century French and English landscape paintings or even in the luminous revisionist worlds painted by impressionists like Monet or postimpressionists like Cézanne and Van Gogh. Earth Art transformed the act of depicting the world into a process combining aspects of architectural designing, ritual theater, sculpting, and pottery making. Lucy Lippard notes that the intent of these artists was not very different from the goal of geologist Paul Leveson, who wrote that his task was "to interpret the earth to society, to bridge the gap between pattern and process." Another major influence on the makers of Earth Art were the megalithic monuments of England and the Mediterranean—the structures at Stonehenge and the ancient temples of Malta. "The hermetic quality of the awesome stones and mounds was compatible with Minimalism's obdurate silence. The combination of nature and monumental scale also characterized New York modernist sculpture at the time" (Lippard 1990).

Perhaps the key figure at the outset of the Earth Art movement was Robert Smithson, an artist and amateur geologist with an interest in crystallography, mining, and the formative processes of the earth's surface. His attitude about nature had no relationship to the idealizations that, until then, had been typical of artists working with landscapes. He deplored pretty views and grand vistas. A self-declared antiromantic, Smithson nonetheless admitted his attraction to that quintessential romantic focus upon myths and prehistory. As he put it, he had "a tendency toward a primordial consciousness. . . . Our future," he declared, "tends to be prehistoric." His most celebrated earthwork was the 1970 project

105

entitled *Spiral Jetty*. It is a curl of bulldozed rocks, built at the edge of Great Salt Lake in Utah, projecting a quarter of a mile into the then-shallow brine. At times Smithson's earthwork is not visible, because the lake rises and covers it, and recently, it may have covered it permanently. As Robert Hughes has observed, visiting *Spiral Jetty* when it was visible was something of a pilgrimage, something it had in common with many remotely located earthworks. Such Earth Art clearly was defying the museum orientation of prior art forms; remaining aloof from public and critic alike; and finding its celebrity in the rumors and reports of those willing to undertake the pilgrimage of discovery.

> Smithson created the suggestion that his gigantic pe-
> troglyph, imposed on the surface of the lake, had been there
> almost forever. Seemingly located outside the stream of mod-
> ernist time. . . . Its spiral form was full of archaic implications.
> (Hughes 1993)

Smithson was killed in a plane crash in 1973 while surveying a new earthwork. But his influence prevailed and impelled an entire generation of artists intent upon creating Earth Art in far-flung and often remote parts of the world.

American sculptor David Barr is such an artist, who incorporates elements of sacred architecture in his work. One of his pieces is a model of the earth that encases a huge geometric form called a tetrahedron. Its four equally spaced points pierce the globe's surface at East Island, in South Africa, on Greenland, and in Papua New Guinea. The project might have ended with the model, but Barr believes art should be "manifest," and so he applied his model to the actual earth as if an invisible tetrahedron spanned the inside of the earth with its four outer corners just barely protruding from the ground. He and his colleagues traveled to the four selected points, and in those remote but mathematically exact points of the tetrahedron, they implanted small marble pinnacles marking the protrusions of each of the four imaginary lines that span the inside of the earth.

Says Barr,

> When I visit a cathedral, for all its architectural beauty, I don't feel the presence of the sacred. It seems so detached from the earth. But when I look at the ancient world, at all the stone alignments and sites like Stonehenge, I see the works of people who had such intimacy with nature that they believed the earth and cosmos are sacred. They were plugging into that with everything they made. And that's what I'm trying to achieve in my work.

The marks we make upon the earth tell us who we are.

The meaning we see in the world is probably more a reflection of ourselves than of some fixed and final truth. As Loren Eiseley puts it, "Man's quest for certainty is, in the last analysis, a quest for meaning. But the meaning lies buried within himself rather than in the void he has vainly searched for portents since antiquity."

All of the structures built by humankind are expressions of who we are, for all reflect the mentality of the people who produced them. Architecture, gardens, earthworks are ritualizations of the land. They are model paradises that embody our visions of ourselves and of the cosmos. Those visions change from time to time and from place to place. And if our visions are not god given and eternal, they are nonetheless significant as a metaphor of our minds.

VIII.

The Lovers

Revelation as Pleasure

He has stepped out of the glowing darkness of chaos into the cool light of creation. But he does not possess it yet; he must first draw it truly out, he must make it into a reality for himself, he must find his own world by seeing and hearing and touching and shaping it.

Martin Buber

A flaming cherub appears in the sky above three figures. The Lovers: a man in the center and two women who hold him and gaze at him with passion. The Lovers of the Tarot deck are often associated with Adam and Eve, but they have little relationship to the biblical narration of the impending Fall or the moral struggle of good and evil. Instead, the Lovers are said to represent qualities greatly valued by human society: the consciousness of beauty, the capacity for deep feeling, and, above all, the experience of pleasure.

Though we take such attributes for granted as quintessentially human, their biological existence, from a Darwinian perspective, is rather mysterious. Our inclination to see objects in terms of feeling and significance rather than simply in terms of their use is a biological oddity. As Roger Fry put it, "Biologically speaking art is a blasphemy. We were given our eyes to see things, not to look at them."

John Maynard Smith, the British biologist, has attempted to comprehend the evolutionary basis for our looking at things "subjectively," which seems to serve no substantial role in our survival as a species. From the point of view of evolutionary logic, there is no explaining impractical human facilities such as that complex collection of responses we call "love" or the rather mystifying attribute of love called aesthetic "pleasure." Though Maynard Smith made fundamental contributions to evolutionary theory, and is considered a rather strict Darwinian thinker, he has recently conceded that he does not understand why organisms have feelings. As *Time* magazine put it, in a discussion of Maynard Smith's research:

> After all, orthodox biologists believe that behavior, however complex, is governed entirely by biochemistry and that the attendant sensations—fear, pain, wonder, love—are just shadows cast by that biochemistry, not themselves vital to the

111

organism's behavior; they are affected by the material world but don't affect it. Well, if that is the case and feelings do not *do* anything, then why do they exist at all?

This is hardly a trifling question. The fact that we experience the world and also have the capacity to *respond* to it is of central significance to our lives. Without the capacity for *sentience* (a term I use to indicate a response that combines both thought and feeling), there would be no basis for either a moral or an aesthetic dimension in life. So we must ask, if, from an evolutionary point of view, subjective experience is an optional and nonpragmatic feature of the human organism, how can it be explained in terms of Darwinian theory?

When pressed for an answer, John Maynard Smith says that although the existence of subjective experience may have no strictly scientific explanation, it could still have what he chose to call a "metaphysical" interpretation. It is striking that a major figure in theoretical science has reached the point at the end of the twentieth century where he can consider an ineffable explanation for issues that, earlier on, members of his discipline would have refused even to consider, insofar as such a consideration admits a possible explanation of reality that is beyond an inductive solution. Admittedly, there are also evolutionary biologists, like the renowned William D. Hamilton of Oxford, who fundamentally disagree with Maynard Smith. But still, we may speculate with some authority that sentience is a by-product of biology that is unessential to evolutionary survival yet serves some opaque and unknowable "purpose." It is perhaps this mysteriousness of human sentience that has allowed us to transform it into a central metaphor of our curious and unique humanness.

When we feel like we are fully human our lives seem to be driven by passion. We assume that art reflects that perfect intensity of living. And so, within every great work of art we sense the driving force of a passionate and life-affirming energy. It is a passion compounded equally of mind and body, of feeling and thought. But Susanne Langer cautioned us not to think of such art as "emotional," but, rather, as symbolic form that conveys sentience.

> Why should common sense find the concept of art as a direct expression of actual emotions easier to accept than the concept of the art symbol? It is because the latter idea requires a distinction which is not always easy to make and maintain. It takes some analytic effort to distinguish between an emotion directly felt and one that is contemplated and imaginatively grasped." (Langer 1967)

Emotions are felt as experiences that originate within us. An emotion itself is different from the contemplation of an emotional experience. Contemplating an emotional state of mind is, therefore, distinct from the actual occurrence called "having" that emotion. "No wonder, then," Langer continues, "that when artists are said (by themselves or someone else) to be engaged in expressing an emotion they are *ipso facto* supposed to be having [that emotion] and to be giving vent to it, as they might by shouting or gesticulating," and by such an emotional display to be "causing the same emotion in each person who sees or hears their self-expressive display."

Langer insists that the artistic excitement felt by the onlooker is best called "intellectual excitement" and not simply an instantaneous and presently occurring emotional state. It is, according to Langer, "the feeling of heightened sensibility and the mental capacity which goes with acts of insight and intuitive judgment." This is what artists feel as they work and, afterward, what they evoke in those people who appreciate their creations.

I call this "intellectual excitement" *passion*, but in a sense far wider than that term's use in popular psychology. I prefer a definition of passion that is taken from the ancient Greek conception of the passions and that extended into later times in the philosophy of Spinoza.

113

Self-preservation is the fundamental motive of the passions, according to Spinoza, but self-preservation alters its character when we realize that what is real and positive in us is what unites us to the whole, and not what preserves the appearance of separateness. (Russell)

For me, "passion" is best defined by the Latin *perturbationes animi,* a term that includes all states of feeling and thought for which human beings are dependent upon the outer world.

Joseph Campbell called this "intellectual excitement" *bliss*— the awareness of being wholly alive—though, unfortunately, some naive critics confuse Campbell's "bliss" with mere sensual indulgence and creature comfort. The Taoist philosopher Al Huang called the Campbellian bliss by a different name: "fire." Unfortunately, as Huang has often noted in his lectures, in most of us the fire has gone out. French-American composer Edgard Varèse was observing this same tragic circumstance when he said that all of us are born with genius but most of us keep it for only a few moments. After those precious moments the fire is extinguished by the pragmatic demands of the world. "Even the pilot light goes out," Al Huang has quipped. "People walk around smelling gas, and they don't know what it is!"

Kierkegaard said that he could easily foresee his fate in an age when passion has been obliterated in favor of learning, in an age when an author who wants to have readers must take care to write in such a way that the book can easily be perused during the afternoon nap. The abstract expressionist painter and art theorist Hans Hofmann remarked that art students of his day seemed to have a great deal of talent but a severe lack of passion.

The incapacity to experience and to act out passion is currently endemic, particularly in masculine American culture. In fact, the control and obliteration of passion is seen, by many Western societies, as a unique, male virtue. And, therefore, the spiritual aspects of passion are no longer associated with pleasure. Pleasure has become a biological response deprived of humanness. As a result, many of us can no longer experience Campbellian "bliss."

Joseph Campbell was keenly aware of this tragic loss of the capacity for bliss in our lives. He saw this paralysis of spiritual passion not merely in terms of the individual but in a sweeping historic frame of reference, which charted the transformation of the engaged and life-affirming mythos of primal peoples into a disengaged and life-negating mentality. He called this basic shift of paradigm the "Great Reversal" (1968).

From what we know of the temper of early cultures, it is safe to assume that the myths, rites, and philosophies first associated with these [wheel-shaped] symbols were rather positive than negative in their address to the pains and pleasures of existence. However, in the period of Pythagoras in Greece (c. 582–500? B.C.) and the Buddha in India (563–483 B.C.), there occurred what I have called the Great Reversal. Life became known as a fiery vortex of delusion, desire, violence, and death—a burning waste. "All things are on fire," taught the Buddha in his sermon at Goya, and in Greece the Orphic saying *"Soma sema:* The body is a tomb" gained currency at this time, while in both domains the doctrine of reincarnation, the binding of the soul forever to this meaningless round of pain, only added urgency to the quest for some means of release. In the Buddha's teaching, the image of the turning spoked wheel, which in the earlier period had been symbolic of the world's glory, thus became a sign, on one hand, of the wheeling round of sorrow, and, on the other, release in the sun-like doctrine of illumination. And in the classical world the turning spoked wheel appeared also at this time as an emblem rather of life's defeat and pain than of victory and exhilaration in the image and myth of Ixion, bound by Zeus to a blazing wheel of eight spokes, to be sent whirling for all time through the air.

It seems to me that since the sixth century B.C., with few exceptions, the impetus of the Great Reversal has affected every aspect of the mythic mentality of both the East and the West. For instance, this life-negating mythos has been willfully used by Christianity as a moral basis for deploring corporeal satisfaction and sensual pleasures and, in general, for the stigmatization of the body and its functions. Art—like sex and all things carnal—is viewed as degenerate because it demands and requires the sentient activity of our denigrated bodies. Without our bodies there can be no art, for the body is an indispensable organ of expression.

Why are so many people of the industrial world threatened by art? Why do they become so angry about works of art? Why is the artist viewed as a person of questionable morality? Why do so many people dismiss art as a self-indulgent and willfully obscure pastime?

Undoubtedly, there are many answers to these questions, but I am particularly interested in those that deal with passion and pleasure in the arts.

Art enables us to glimpse a reality that lies outside the realm of what we are normally aware of, and so the reaction that art arouses in us is not quite of this material world. We spend most of our lives "seeing" objects without looking at them, because we conceptualize objects in terms of their purpose or use. We rarely look at objects as entities unto themselves, as pure sentient experience. In art, passion is felt not for this world of objects of use, but for a symbolic reality somehow beyond the world of useful objects. It is for this reason that we often speak of the remoteness of art—not in the sense of its being obscure or distant, but in the sense that it is less than concrete. The impression made upon us by art is tantalizingly brief. Hardly are we aware that the veil has been lifted before it is suddenly lowered; hardly is the vision glimpsed before it passes. It is an experience that invokes Plato's cave, on whose walls are cast the shadows we mistake for reality. We are Plato's creatures, forever bound in a cave so that even our heads cannot move. Behind us is a fire, and the shadows of a world we cannot see are cast upon the wall before us. We cannot escape our bonds. We can never look back at the reality that we imagine exists somewhere behind and beyond our view. We must believe in the shadows, for we have no access to the reality they reflect. We can neither imagine nor speak of that reality because it is beyond our experience and outside our communicative capacities. The poet William Blake believed that the body is Plato's cave and therefore, he insisted rather sadly, "The body is the grave of the soul." But the arts change biology into metaphors that imagine the fire we cannot see. They transform the ordinary into the extraordinary. Through the sensual and metaphoric transformation of a reality composed of shadows the arts are able, at least momentarily, to allude to the fire.

When the words *passion* or *pleasure* are applied to the arts, these terms assume the possibility of a great variety of meanings. Many discussions of pleasure in the arts are evocations of a romantic nineteenth-century notion of beatitude, an aesthetic sensibility that is far behind us and entirely out of touch with twentieth-century convictions of artistic experience. By now we have come to understand that standards of beauty are as evasive as the aesthetic philosophies that attempt, unsuccessfully, to define them. We have come to the existential conclusion that we may be able to describe what art does, but we cannot truly define what it is, let alone determine what "good" art is versus when it is, presumably, "bad" art. Every judgment is tenuous. Every definition is transitory.

Henry Moore may have defined the central artistic doctrine of the late twentieth century when he asserted that he was not interested in the expression of beauty but in the power of expression. It is a good articulation of a stance that radically altered our perception of art from what it had been in the midnineteenth century. It obliterated the niceties of "artistic beauty" and ushered in an era of concentration upon expression.

Though we presume that bewilderment and consternation are unique responses to aspects of art in the twentieth century, in fact, such reactions have prevailed in response to every artistic effort that has defied the prevailing precept of beauty, whether that be the hallucinatory imagery of Goya's black paintings and Bosch's

dreamscapes or the luminous abstractions of Turner, the disso-
nances of Gesualdo's madrigals or the dramatic percussiveness of
Beethoven's middle and late symphonies. The power of expression
has always superseded the urge to express "beauty" in the works
of seminal artists, because beauty is only a social convention,
whereas the power of expression is the result of idiosyncratic
revelation and vision.

So there are often times in our artistic experience when we are
deeply distressed by what we are experiencing at the same time that
we are intensely moved. The curious result of this transaction is a
peculiar kind of pleasure. It is an experience of pleasure that has no
singular form or quality. After all, a García Lorca tragedy doesn't
give us pleasure in the same way as a meditative and solemn Rothko
chapel in Houston. Pleasure has as many facets in the arts as it has
in sexual experience. Today the encounter of "beauty" is no longer
the sole basis of artistic pleasure any more than the experience of
romance is the necessary basis of pleasure in sex.

One of the most fascinating aspects of art at the close of the
twentieth century is the inclination of artists to intermix the conventions of beauty and pleasure. I recall the intense satisfaction of
watching the devastating war film *Platoon* and realizing that the
director had made the brilliant decision to use Samuel Barber's
hauntingly lyrical and elegiac *Essay for Orchestra* as the accompani-
ment to the film's most horrific and brutal moment. Two dozen
years earlier, I had been equally intrigued by Jean Cocteau's decision to set his highly narrative and surrealistic ballet *La Jeune
Homme et La Mort* to an abstract and nondramatic composition by
J. S. Bach.

Neither of these artistic efforts resulted in what is conventionally called the expression of beauty, but both provided an intense
kind of artistic pleasure.

The problem with conventions of beauty is that they are
circumvented by cultural biases. The Western audience is alienated
by Kabuki theater because of its expectations of beauty. That
audience is equally alienated by the music of Alban Berg because

Berg did not provide a familiar encounter with the nineteenth-century convention of beauty. These artists were not concerned with our precepts of beauty. They had something quite different on their minds, and it is this difference that I think we should celebrate. Artistic experiences—from the experience of the works of the Marquis de Sade and Jean Genet to the works of Richard Wagner and William Wordsworth—provide us with radically different kinds of pleasure. An essential aspect of art in our century has been the redefinition of what we mean by pleasure. What I think we have learned is that we come away from art with a unique sense of pleasure because artistic pleasure is the result of revelation.

It is a revelation that exists, as Thomas Mann suggested, where thought and feeling merge. It seems to me that the experience of that precarious junction of human emotion and contemplation is what artistic pleasure is all about.

But if art provides pleasure, why are people afraid of the experience of art?

I don't think people are afraid of artistic pleasure. I think people are either afraid to have or are unable to have the revelation that provides such pleasure. When the music of Debussy was first performed it shocked his cultivated audience. To our ears it is music that is so atmospheric that it seems almost insipid, but in 1895 *Prélude à l'après-midi d'un faune* outraged music lovers. They experienced no pleasure because they could not avail themselves of the revelation of the music. And when an experience cannot become revelation it cannot become pleasure.

Rollo May has theorized that "creativity occurs in an act of encounter and is to be understood with this encounter at its center. . . . Out of the encounter is born the work of art." And out of the encounter/experience is born the response of the audience to the work of art. "Is there some place where reality speaks our language, where it answers us if we but understand the hieroglyphics?" (May) These mysterious signs—the hieroglyphics—are ruminations of the unconscious that rise into consciousness as our experience becomes intensified.

This heightened consciousness, which we have identified as characteristic of the encounter, the state in which the dichotomy between subjective experience and objective reality is overcome and symbols which reveal new meaning are born, is historically termed *ecstasy*. Like passion, ecstacy . . . is a temporary transcending of the subject-object dichotomy. (May)

It is epitomized by Cézanne's assertion that he had to give his body to his painting in order to supersede himself; that when he painted trees he was not interested in mere trees but in something called "tree-ness."

People cannot get out of their own way; they often put a barrier between themselves and experience. This can be done by ideologues; it can be done by bureaucrats; it can be done by people who simply expect of art what they have already gotten from art—rather than expecting the unexpected. And people who approach art with all kinds of preconceptions, whether political—from the right or from the left—or moral or artistic, deprive themselves of the experience of art. Art cannot speak to those who are waiting to hear what they have already heard. That is the difference between the idea of art and the idea of repertory. One is concerned with idiosyncratic expression while the other is devoted to cultural ventriloquism.

Too many of us ignore what is before us in anticipation of what we expect to be before us. And therefore we don't experience the sentient world; we experience only our preconceptions of the world. This situation always reminds me of the design concept of the international Holiday Inns. The lamp is always in the same place. The bed is always in the same place. No matter where you are—Bangkok or Lima—at a Holiday Inn you can get a hamburger or bacon and eggs. People tell me that they feel comfortable at a Holiday Inn because their surroundings are always familiar. But art doesn't want to be familiar. Art wants to astonish us. Or enrage us. And, above all, it wants to move us. It does not want to accommodate us. It doesn't want to make us comfortable. Art is not a soda pop machine; you don't press a button and get your choice of beverage. What you get from art is an experience, but you have to allow yourself to be part of that experience or it simply will not happen.

Most of our spectator experience is devoid of revelation. It is prefabricated to such an extent that it precludes our participation. People sit passively watching sitcoms on television in which all the familiar middle-class clichés are endlessly repeated. Tired jokes get laughs year after year because people accept the cues that tell them to laugh. But they are not responding to humor; they are responding to cues. A great deal of popular entertainment is built on such audience manipulation, and that is fine and well, except that it is a formula that has a potentially negative impact on audiences: It diminishes our capacity to experience the unexpected. It dims our imaginations. It substitutes icons for experiences. It gives us platitudes while what we need are revelations. Raise the flag and get instantaneous and mindless patriotism. Show pictures of a little girl trapped in a well and get instant sentimentality, while the larger reality and real tragedy of thousands upon thousands of children dying of privation entirely escapes our notice.

The result of the manipulation of the public consensus is a society that believes it has the right to an opinion but does not realize it has a responsibility to open itself to the revelations that are the basis of opinion. There are dozens of television and radio programs each day that encourage us to express our opinions about everything from brain surgery to atomic fusion, regardless of whether we know anything about such complex matters. What this kind of populist pandering achieves is an attitude that effectively protects us from both thinking about things we claim to think about and experiencing things we claim to experience.

As noted earlier, L. L. Whyte, the British physicist, insisted that "thought is born of failure." Unless we are jarred out of our complacency we are not going to indulge in thought and we are also not going to have an experience of our own lives. Most people don't like being jarred. They don't like to admit to failures, and they don't like to think. What they like is for things to be *nice*.

As a result, there is very little rapture left in the world today. Very little passion. These Dionysian virtues have been relegated almost entirely to women and gay men. Apparently, American machismo is incompatible with rapture and passion. But, somehow, for women and gay men such experiences are vaguely tolerated. Women and gay men are a bit like the poor. They are considered of so little consequence that they are left out of mainstream existence almost entirely. The obvious negative aspect of this exclusion is social disempowerment, but there is also a positive side to alienation, and that is a freedom from confining and inhibiting conventions that permits choices of action if not the social freedom to undertake such action. Every step of an adventurous life is a trespass; for each step of our lives we must, therefore, summon enormous courage in order to dare the undertaking of an act or the expression of an idea capable of rousing the hostility of a disapproving society.

The victors of the Western world have won everything, but in the process they seem to have lost themselves. Men have cast themselves in the horrendous role of arbitrators of norms and standards. They have condoned cerebration while they have condemned the celebration of the senses. As the bromides go: They do not dance; they do not cry; they do not indulge in emotional extravagance. In sports and in pornography, they have made a fetish of our bodies at the same time that they have disavowed erotic ecstasy—which is simply another form of rapture and passion. The male body no longer functions as an organ of expression, but as the tool of willful assertion.

Such a worldview is numbing. And so we find ourselves once again slouching toward Bethlehem to be born. And as Martin Buber said, we step out of the glowing darkness of the chaos we have made into the cool light of yet another creation. But we do not yet possess ourselves. We must make the chaos into a passionate reality. We must find our own world through the revelations of seeing and hearing and touching and shaping it even as we shape ourselves.

Perhaps in this paraphrase of Martin Buber's words, we can understand what biologist John Maynard Smith meant when he was asked to explain the existence of subjective experience that seems to have no strictly scientific explanation. Such experience of passion and rapture and revelation might possess what Maynard Smith chose to call a "metaphysical" interpretation. No one is certain exactly what the word "metaphysical" means to us or will mean to the world of the twenty-first century, but at least that enigmatic and inexacting word gives us cause to dream.

IX.

The Chariot

Escape from Reality

Welcome, O life! I go to encounter for the millionth time the reality of experience and to forge in the smithy of my soul the uncreated conscience of my race.

James Joyce

A warrior stands in a chariot drawn by two horses, one black and one white. The horses usually have no bridles and appear to be running headlong. Significantly, this card of the Tarot deck is associated with perplexity and escape, an ideal symbol of the flights of imagination that have been the basis of the decline of artistic naturalism in the twentieth century.

One of the greatest physicists, Albert Einstein, contemplated the dilemma of his field, and in 1938 he produced this revealing simile:

> Physical concepts are free creations of the human mind, and are not, however it may seem, uniquely determined by the external world. In our endeavor to understand reality we must escape from it. We are somewhat like a man trying to understand the mechanism of a closed watch. He sees the face and the moving hands, even hears its ticking, but he has no way of opening the case. If he is ingenious he may form some picture of a mechanism which could be responsible for all the things he observes, but he may never be quite sure his picture is the only one which could explain his observations. He will never be able to compare his picture with the real mechanism, and he cannot even imagine the possibility of the meaning of such a comparison. (Zukav)

Despite Einstein's encouragement for us to escape reality if we are to understand it, literary critic Lionel Trilling was unconvinced by the recommendation of a major physicist (though advocates of naturalism always hurry to call upon the authority of science to vindicate their embrace of the so-called objective world). In his classic book *The Liberal Imagination,* Trilling suggested that the direction of twentieth-century nonrealist literature is disastrous. According to Trilling, the "poetic methods being employed by some contemporary novelists mark the end of an ending." What we really need to do, according to Trilling, is to rediscover the style of writing he chose mistakenly to call "story telling," for primordial story-telling is the opposite of what he was describing. According to Trilling's misconception of the art of the "legender," we must get back to "natural prose" and "good common speech." We are told that "a prose which approaches poetry has no doubt its own value, but it cannot serve to repair the loss of a straightforward prose, rapid, masculine, and committed to events, making its effects not by the single word or by the phrase but by words properly and naturally massed."

Clearly Lionel Trilling was one of many advocates of the revival of a naturalism that was faltering in the early decades of the twentieth century. Fortunately, most of the major writers of our time have ignored his mandate.

"Quite a few protests have been aired in recent years against the sway of the naturalist method in fiction," Philip Rahv wrote in his landmark essay "Notes on the Decline of Naturalism." "It is charged that this method treats material in a manner so flat and external as to inhibit the search for value and meaning, and that in any case it is now exhausted."

The kind of writing that Trilling favored and Rahv disdained is an endless bookkeeping of existence. Such ledgered "objectivity" is not possible in a society in which there is no central and sustaining mythic system, with accessible and universally significant symbols and forms. Such realistic books can only be written for readers who have not yet emerged into the contemporary predicament and are continuing, somehow, to live in an ideological past. They do not realize that life is nowhere seen steadily and whole, but under a number of perspectives relative to nothing central. Never before has the interpretation of cultures been so worldwide—or disintegration so universal.

Behind all literature is a common expressive impulse. But expressiveness is not a single, uniform power in any art form. It constantly changes, at least on a certain level, as public values change. What is amusing to one era is not necessarily so to another. The playwrights of the English Restoration presumed that rape was a comic twist of plot, while the poets of the English Romantic period depicted rape as the tragic circumstance of a helpless female, and the writers of the late twentieth century regard rape as a political outrage. As Michel Foucault has noted, the politics of truth are constantly changing.

The quality of sentience changes from one era to the next, and in ways often so subtle that even the most undefinable qualities of life—those with no direct relation to emotion—also change.

The kind of straightforward story-telling demanded by Lionel Trilling is wishful thinking in our era. It cannot exist without faith, and faith in the West is obsolescent. Western literature, with its concrete clock time and explicit geography of place, faces the same problems of credibility faced by organized religion. Much as faltering religious faith deals with its obsolescence by assuming an unconditionally prosaic, literal, and fundamentalist stance, so literature, in facing the demise of certitude, has evolved a number of naive forms of realism that attempt to deny the fact that today's writers cannot describe the present or the future in the moribund language of the past.

The alternative to the bankruptcy of literary naturalism has preoccupied many of the most celebrated critics and writers of the West. "The literature of vision," as David Daiches calls this alternative form, "tends to come into prose as part of the reaction against what is regarded as an over-formulated, and therefore not sufficiently objective, type of fable literature." The personal sense of truth replaces the formulas of a civilization. Since physics asserts that there can be no such thing as "objectivity" without the paradigms of a stable civilization, the paradox of the twentieth century world of literature is discovered in its futile search for an objectivity that only leads to greater subjectivity.

This "literature of vision" is very different from prior literary forms dominant in the West. First of all, the subject matter is not easily fitted into a linear structure and organized on the basis of character motivation and the chronological succession of events. Kenneth Burke distinguishes two kinds of literary composition: "syllogistic progression," in which the reader is led from one part of the composition to another by means of naturalistic relationships; and "qualitative progression," in which the reader is led, according to a "logic of feeling," by means of association and contrast. What Burke has called qualitative progression is the core of visionary literature—the expressive mode of the dreamtime so familiar to tribal storytellers.

Ernst Cassirer points out that "like all the other symbolic forms, art is not the mere reproduction of a ready-made and given reality. . . . It is not an imitation but a *discovery* of reality." And as Einstein affirmed, we must escape reality in order to discover it. "But we do not discover nature through art in the same sense in which the [empirical] scientist uses the term 'nature.' . . . When the scientist describes an object he characterizes it by a set of numbers, by its physical and chemical constants. Art has not only a different aim but a different object" (Cassirer 1944a).

In the early decades of the twentieth century the writers supporting these refutations of naturalism were mostly those who looked to symbolism, fantasy, and myth. "The younger writers," Rahv wrote in 1949, "are stirred by the ambition to create a new type of imaginative prose into which the recognizably real enters as one component rather than as the total substance." Today such literary efforts are highly diversified, though one of the most conspicuous examples of the process described by Rahv is the Latin American approach called magic realism.

"They want to break the novel of its objective habits," Rahv continues. "Some want to introduce into it philosophical ideas; others are not so much drawn to expressing ideas as to expressing the motley strivings of the inner self—dreams, visions, and fantasies."

These writers have steadily produced a new "popular" fiction since about 1945, attracting the massive population of the college-trained and radically changed baby boomers while having minimal impact on both the mass market of literature and the generations of the 1980s and '90s, which have had virtually no interest in writing except as it exists in book-length prolongations of the forms and techniques of magazine prose and the attitudes and styles of exposé journalism.

But many young and attentive readers of literature have made fundamental alterations in the way Western people "perform a book," to use Vonnegut's metaphor, and the books they read tend to verge on the cinematic, which, in part, explains the widening use of literary techniques that reflect the new "visual literacy" of the 1980s. "Events," Harry Levin noted as early as 1941, while discussing the novels of James Joyce, "are reported when and as they occur; the tense is a continuous present." That description is close to the abstract imagery of music videos and visionary films, like those of Meredith Monk and Godfrey Reggio. "In its intimacy and in its continuity," Levin continues, *"Ulysses* has more in common with the cinema than with other fiction. The movement of Joyce's style, the thoughts of his characters, is like unreeling film; his method of construction, the arrangement of this raw material, involves the crucial operation of *montage."*

This montage, as well as the animation and crosscutting epitomized in the works of pioneer filmmakers such as Georges Méliès, Sergei Eisentein, and D. W. Griffith, has been so entirely absorbed into global mentality that we no longer balk at their "unnaturalness," but grasp these once avant-garde filmic techniques as authentic and cogent representations of the ways we see and think. Writing about the cinema in 1916, Harvard psychologist Hugo Munsterberg affirmed this amazing impact of filmmaking on perceptive sensibility when he said, "It is as if the outer world were woven into our mind and were shaped not through its own laws but by the acts of our attention."

This kind of vision of time and space in modern fiction bears the same relationship to naturalistic writing that the film does to the stage. The time and space of the cinema are essentially abstract. In the early days of filmmaking it was traditional to hire great actors of the theater, such as Sarah Bernhardt, and to film silent sequences of classic melodramas with the stationary camera focused on the entire stage from the vantage of a spectator in the third row center. There were virtually no close-ups, none of the exceptional intimacy of the later cinema, no movement of the camera, no flashbacks, crosscutting, iris shots, or any of the other manipulations of time and space that we take for granted in today's cinema and video. Event followed event in strict clock time, producing an internal rhythm that, as we view most of these old films today, seems painfully naive, tedious, and slow. Nothing better illustrates the naturalistic bookkeeping of existence than a film like *Queen Elizabeth* (1912), featuring Sarah Bernhardt and directed by Henri Desfontaines and Louis Mercanton.

It was only gradually that the temporal and spatial attitudes of cinema (and literature and the visual arts) fundamentally altered Western traditions of perception. "It is no more true to say of Joyce, than any other artist," Levin concludes, "that his work enlarges the domain of consciousness. . . . Bergson himself, the philosopher who held the fullest realization of the fluid nature of time and experience, also held that the intellect 'spatializes.' Consequently our imitations of life, no matter how complete and complicated we try to make them, are bound to be one-sided and over-simple." The intellect spatializes, and only in the dreamtime of mystics, primal peoples, poets, and visionaries can we fully grasp the ineffable that lingers just beyond the reach of intelligence.

"Depth and movement alike come to us in the motion picture world not as hard facts but as a mixture of fact and symbol" (Munsterberg).

There have been wide-ranging factors that contributed to the decline of naturalism. Through the influence of psychology, Western literature, dance, painting, and cinema recovered a primordial inwardness, which combines the naturalistic description of the mental process with the antinaturalistic depiction of the subjective and irrational. Another factor has been the tendency of naturalism, as Thomas Mann observed in his remarks on Zola, to turn into the mythic through sheer immersion in the typical. It seems apparent that naturalism cannot hope to survive the world of nineteenth-century technology and industry of which it was a product. For what is the crisis of reality in contemporary art and society if not at bottom the crisis of the dissolution of this familiar and obsolete world? Naturalism, which exhausted itself in taking an inventory of this world while it was still relatively stable, cannot possibly do justice to the phenomena of its own decline. Its sole basis of survival is its ability to depict the melancholy tenacity and perfidy of those countless people who insist upon lingering in a world that no longer exists.

A new visionary attitude has gradually come into existence. This alternative Western viewpoint has not simply affected the subject matter of the arts but has, more essentially, produced new techniques for dealing with time, space, and character. As we have suspected since the time of Shelley, and as we have known decisively since Walt Whitman, poetry has largely abandoned the expository mood of Dante, Pope, and Dryden. It has assumed in the West so metaphoric an attitude that we commonly use the term "poetic" as an opposite of the word "realistic." But visionary mentality is not limited in the West to poetry and so-called poetic license. From Tolstoy's fearsome image of "a peasant muttering something . . . working at the iron" that haunts Anna Karenina both when she first encounters her lover, Count Vronsky, and later at the moment of her suicide, to the famous apparition of wild horses that appears to Gerald in D. H. Lawrence's *Women in Love,* an alternative, "cinematic" abstraction of time and space has come to dominate the most reality-bound art forms: literature and the visual arts.

Meanwhile, those who are reactionary or faithful or both continue to require discursive explanations from the arts. In painting, this demand for "realistic clarity" produced a long line of mass-market modernists, especially during the art boom of the 1980s. In dance it gave us choreographers who artfully mixed a bit of modernism with populist mindlessness. And in literature the demand for "realism" elevated the commonplace efforts of authors of great craft but little vision to positions of literary prominence, while many of the major authors of our day remain virtually unknown by the reading public: Jorge Luis Borges, William Gaddis, Walter Abish, Jakov Lind, Miguel Angel Asturias, William Gass, Ronald Sukenick, and Alejo Carpentier, to name but a few.

In the escape from reality, artists are seeking a visionary facility that imparts a separate experience of the world—a form of communication with an alternative objective. This alternative is not a beautified phrase or an illusive verbal dodge; it is not a substitution for "straightforward prose, rapid, masculine, and committed to events." It is an effort, contrarily, to get the meaning-bound "language" and "objects" and "feelings" out of the arts by refusing to accept the traditional responsibility of artists to depict "realistically" what is before them and what is happening to them and, instead, to begin again the arduous effort to reinvent reality.

In *The Magic Mountain* (1960), Thomas Mann saw this visionary quest as a projection into Jungian consciousness:

> Now I know that it is not out of our single souls we dream. We dream anonymously and communally, if each after his fashion. The great soul of which we are a part may dream through us, in our manner of dreaming, its own secret dreams, of its youth, its hope, its joy and peace—and its blood-sacrifice.

X.

Strength

Mind and Matter

A language of mythos, a language which alludes to experience but does not attempt to replace it or to mold our perception of it is the true language of physics.

David Finkelstein

A woman or a man with a wide-brimmed hat is seen opening or closing the jaws of a lion. The figure is called Strength. Although there is a great deal of debate about the specific significance of this illusive Tarot card, the effortless vigor of the figure suggests that much can be accomplished by the combination of mental and physical effort. Among the many meanings given to this card, the one with great relevance to my purposes is concerned with the exploration of matter over mind and, alternatively, mind over matter. Such symbolism is an ideal frame of reference for the flights of imagination that have been the basis of postquantum physics. The Tarot figure of Strength is then also an ideal emblem of the immense influences of contemporary physical science and psychology on the evolution of twentieth-century art forms.

Physicists conceptualize a revolutionary way of looking at the world. Artists make that revolution visible and experiential.

Physicists and the creators of modern art movements share a reputation for bringing about radical and irrational change as an act of willfulness and insolence. Many people see twentieth-century art as an "experiment" rather than as an achievement. The public attitude about postquantum physics is similar: It is suspected of being illogical theoretical nonsense without any practical application. It seems to many people that the twentieth century has been dominated intellectually by a bunch of rebels who devoted themselves to the pointless destruction of classical Newtonian physics on the one hand, and, on the other, to the destruction of the classical values of Renaissance art. It is believed that the aim of both physicists and artists is to be original at all costs, including the cost of a comprehending and wide public.

But art and physics change only because reality changes. Art and physics are not amusement parks of the mind. Nor are they complex con games. They are not sleight of hand or parlor pranks one watches meticulously in order to deflate their integrity by detecting their "tricks"; the tricks are found in reality itself. Physics is the observer of those profound tricks, while art is the perfect mirror of the unrelenting transformations of the world that take place as a tricky and chameleonic reality changes moment by moment, reshaping our lives and our cosmos with each of its changes from one paradigm to another.

Again, physicists conceptualize these changes. Artists make them visible.

What physics and art make clear is that there are many different ways of conceptualizing, visualizing, and dramatizing the events, objects, and beings of the world. As art theorist Hans Hess notes, "There are many ways of understanding an event; the very way of understanding it, however, changes the event which has been understood. This is a simple form of stating that an event is one thing as it has happened and another thing as it is comprehended, and of the comprehension there are many forms" (Hess).

Not surprisingly, Hess has paraphrased the seminal concept of one of the most influential thinkers of modern physics: Werner Heisenberg, whose "uncertainty principle" suggests that we cannot observe something without changing it. Though Heisenberg's hypothesis was intended to evaluate observation only at the subatomic level, it has found its way into every aspect of social and artistic thinking, causing endless debate about the differences between a paradigm based upon relevance and a paradigm based upon relativity.

In art and in physics, the relationship of observer to the object of observation has become highly ambiguous and suggestive, creating a great deal of discomfort for the champions of both social relevance and scientific certitude. This predicament raises vital questions. What, finally, is relevant? What, ultimately, is certain? So there are good reasons for this discomfort. Legions of liberal and conservative politicos insist upon the validity of social values that require all action, creative and political, to be relevant— to have a functional and concerned relationship to the community at large. These politicos hope to promulgate attitudes about society that they believe to be built upon the transcultural and universal principles of equity and truth. In short, for them there is nothing relative about the relationship of our actions to our society. We have a social obligation to be relevant and not relative. For them, social responsibility is both definable and fundamental. What is not advantageous to society must be abandoned. It is an attitude with little flexibility and many quandaries, especially in relation to the arts, because it is based upon a presumed absolute: Justice runs its course according to laws, such as the concepts of causality, that are implicit in the cosmos.

Likewise, the defenders of classical physics build their arguments on the assumption that our reality, independent of us, runs its course in space and time according to strict causal laws. We can observe reality, unnoticed, as it unfolds, and we can predict its future by applying causal laws to the events we observe. It too is an absolute.

Keeping in mind these absolutist positions of various politicos and old-guard physicists, it becomes clear why Heisenberg's uncertainty principle is exceptionally unsettling to them. It virtually demolishes their central notions of causality and moral certitude. It levels an essential basis of their scheme of things: the Absolute, which asserts that "the further the bounds of our knowledge extend, the more will it be seen that only one system [of thought] is really coherent, and that only one system is, therefore, ultimately true. . . . In the end, therefore, as thought approaches the Absolute, truth and reality merge" (Joad).

What postquantum mechanics and postmodern art suggest is quite the opposite: Reality constantly changes and, therefore, so do "truth" and "moral principles." The idea of a causal universe and a social order built on universal moral laws is toppled by the uncertainty principle. The absolute is replaced by the relative. And the classical search for universality and uniformity in science and society has come to a dead end. Reality becomes a matter of highly variable conventions, rather than a set of fixed and eternal facts.

We know that thought is expressed by scientists not in words but in a language of symbols which becomes the current equivalent for the reality it attempts to describe. In the same way painters use a language, not of words, but of forms or symbols, to depict a form of reality. This reality is neither objective nor subjective; it is collective; the forms are pictorial equivalents for conventions of social and spiritual life. (Hess)

In the autumn of 1927, scientists working in new fields of physics met in Brussels. This meeting had an enormous impact upon all of the basic assumptions of nineteenth-century science not unlike the explosion of ideas that burst into artistic consciousness at the famous Armory Show in New York in 1913, where pre–World War I America became aware of the most radical elements of the modern movements in the visual arts, revising all of the basic assumptions of nineteenth-century aesthetics.

"The Armory Show proved that a fundamental revolution was taking place in the arts, nothing less than a basic redefinition of aims, forms, and purposes" (McLanathan).

When the show opened in the Sixty-ninth Regiment Armory on Lexington Avenue, it became the largest and most influential art exhibit ever held in America, unveiling to an astounded public the whole visual history of the evolution of modern art from such ancestors as Daumier, Corot, and Goya, through the impressionists, postimpressionists, fauvists, expressionists, cubists, and countless artists representing all the other major movements of modernist art. Some sixteen hundred seminal works were exhibited and seventy thousand people paid to see the show. In every way it was an event of unprecedented importance in terms of the American perception of art. The public was amused by the peculiarities of art forms it had never seen before, while the critics were thoroughly outraged. "The Armory Show had accomplished what its backers intended: it had opened the doors to modern art in America and led the way for the internationalization of art later to take place, and prepared for the eventual sharing of leadership in world art by American painters and sculptors" (McLanathan).

In a similar way, at the congress in Brussels, physicists created a scientific bombshell by formulating a radically new perspective of reality called the Copenhagen Interpretation of Quantum Mechanics. The 1927 meeting, the Fifth Solvay Congress, was where Niels Bohr and Albert Einstein conducted their famous debates; the elder Einstein clung tenaciously to a moribund mentality when he exclaimed: God does not play dice with the universe! Bohr set the new agenda when he responded with the admonishment: Don't tell God what to do!

Bohr was triumphant. In fact, the term "Copenhagen Interpretation" was adapted to describe the results of the congress because it reflects Bohr's new, immense influence. He was a native of Copenhagen.

> The Copenhagen Interpretation began a monumental reunion which was all but unnoticed at the time. The rational part of our psyche, typified by science, began to merge again with that other part of us which we had ignored since the 1700s, our irrational side. The scientific idea of truth traditionally had been anchored to an absolute truth somewhere "out there"—that is, an absolute truth with an existence independent of us. The closer that we came in our approximation to the absolute truth, the truer our theories were said to be. Although we might never be able to perceive the absolute truth directly—or to open the watch, as Einstein put it—still we tried to construct theories that corresponded to that absolute truth. (Zukav)

Another major shift in scientific paradigm that had a crucial impact on social and artistic attitudes was caused by the Everett-Wheeler-Graham theory. According to this theory, called the Many Worlds Interpretation of Quantum Mechanics, there are an endless number of different branches of reality rather than a fixed and singular one. The Many Worlds theory suggests that when something happens, all other possible happenings in the cosmos that *could* have occurred, also occurred, but in different realities. The premise of the theory is based on the notion that when a conscious observer is in the presence of one action of one reality, it splits that reality off from all other realities. The consciousness of the observer also splits. One part of it continues to observe one reality, while the other parts observe all the other realities. A complex, even irrational concept! It is as if physics had become the domain of the multiple spatial mentality of cubism and the multiple temporal mentality of futurism—or of the intoxicating ambiguities of Joyce's *Finnegans Wake.*

The Many Worlds theory is surprisingly similar to the stance of modernist and postmodernist art. It argues that all branches of reality are equally real, though the observer may be aware of only one at a time.

Classical physics had insisted upon the notion of a fixed exterior reality that matches the perceptual reality we believe we experience. But the Copenhagen Interpretation did away with all of that; it did away with the idea of a one-to-one correspondence between reality and theory. It suggested that nature is fundamentally irrational and that the cosmos is governed by chance—and is in a bewildering state analogous to chaos. That such a seemingly irrational point of view could arise from science was a powerful blow to the aggrandized and highly cerebral self-image of Western Faustian sensibility.

Rather than lament the rise of the irrational in science, physicist Paul Davies sees this crucial shift in paradigm as a reflection of the whole history of human myths about cosmology. "In the past," he points out, "humans invoked gods to cause the unpredictable, and to protect themselves from the unpredictable. They viewed the world as a temperamental place, full of caprice and random occurrences. Then, with the growth of science, nature came to be regarded as lawful and the universe to be organized according to strict mathematical principles." Now, all of the grand designs of the scientism of the eighteenth and nineteenth centuries have been squeezed out of existence by the intense influence of quantum mechanics, a mode of thought not unlike the "naked singularity" of black holes, where all of the laws of physics break down completely, and even space and time vanish into an unthinkable point called "the singularity," where "reality" itself is literally squeezed out of existence, resulting in what physicists call "zero volume."

With the threat of a naked singularity at the heart of our cosmos, Davies proclaims, we are brought back once more to the chaotic universe of primordial history—to the fearsome heavens of our most ancient forebears, who rightly understood that absolutely anything can and does happen in the cosmos.

As such, it seems that the advanced thinkers of the twentieth century have reclaimed the most viable and fundamental myths of our ancestors. Despite the brilliance of these myths, most of us reject them in favor of the obsolete mythology of an antiquated positivist science in which modern scientists themselves no longer believe. Why do we appear to reject the discoveries of our most accomplished thinkers? Because the old reality is less troubling than the new reality. A curiosity of the twentieth century is the fact that the great majority of people in the industrial nations that produced these radical revisions of reality are almost totally ignorant of—or completely alienated by—them, if they are at all familiar with them. What is more, most of us are as uncomfortable with the Freudian and Jungian concepts of the unconscious and with recent theories on right-left brain specialization as we are with the Uncertainty Principle and the Many Worlds theory. It is little wonder, then, that the arts of the twentieth century alienate us, since the new realities of science and psychology, with their overtones of universal chaos and pervasive irrationality, were first grasped by artists—dramatists, musicians, painters, dancers, poets, and those visionaries we call mystics and saints. These artists are the perpetual subversives of our world, a "dew" line, to use McLuhan's famous phrase, that sounds the alarm the rest of us cannot hear—a "distant early warning" of revolutions taking place at the very core of our culture.

We live in a world that has no tolerance for ambiguity and

uncertainty. We fervently believe that God does not play dice with our lives. According to the January 1992 "Barna Report," 73 percent of people ages 27 to 45 and 80 percent of people ages 46 to 64 "agree the Bible is the 'totally accurate' word of God" (*Time* 1993).

Intuitive, irrational, or unconscious phenomena, such as radically new visions of the "mechanism" of the cosmos or enigmatic shifts in the conception of our consciousness, threaten us with apprehension and a profound anxiety. The old mythologies provided us with uniformity, predictability, and a comforting orderliness. God was not a gambler. But the new myths of science and psychology, like the new visions of the arts, are fraught with inconsistency, unpredictability, and the inevitable threat of chaos.

Until we change our myths, we cannot change our minds.

Thus we can realistically ask of art the same questions Thomas S. Kuhn has asked of astronomy:

> Can it conceivably be an accident that Western astronomers first saw change in the previously immutable heavens during the half-century after Copernicus' new paradigm was first proposed? The Chinese, whose cosmological beliefs did not preclude celestial change, had recorded the appearance of many new stars in the heavens at a much earlier date. Also, even without the aid of a telescope, the Chinese had systematically recorded the appearance of sunspots centuries before these were seen by Galileo and his contemporaries. . . . Can we say that after Copernicus astronomers lived in a different world? . . . Did these men really *see* different things when they looked at the same sort of objects? Is there any legitimate sense in which we can really say that they pursued their research in different worlds? . . . Today research in parts of philosophy, psychology, linguistics, and even art history, all converge to suggest that the traditional paradigm is somehow askew. . . . Though the world does not [actually] change with a change of paradigm, the scientist afterward works in a quite different world.

What Kuhn has said of today's scientist is unquestionably true of today's artist.

Our adventure takes us into the many worlds and the improbability of modern science. It is the world in which we exist, yet it is a world still alien to many of us. In trying to fathom the vital new mentality of science and psychology, in order to find our way into the world in which we truly live our tenuous lives, we may be able, at last, to recognize the images of our own faces in those "incomprehensible" twentieth-century arts toward which the vast majority of us still feel deep anger and complete alienation. What we disdain, ultimately, is the candor of the portraits that have been painted of us and of our dissolute society by the most discerning and astute portrait painters of our day. The problem is that, like pre-Copernican astronomers, we cannot see what we are looking at because we do not expect to see it. We cannot change our minds until we change our myths.

XI.

Justice

Imagination as Political Power

The victim who is able to articulate the situation of the victim has ceased to be a victim—he or she has become a threat.

James Baldwin

The figure of Justice in the Tarot deck is a magnificently robed man who holds in his right hand the traditional double-edged sword of justice. He symbolizes harmony, fairness, and impartiality. So much for symbolism. In reality, such idealized expectations of justice have been illusive at best, especially for those who stand at a remove from mainstream society. For them, justice is often a dole, given reluctantly by the many who have little concern for the few. Today, as in the past, countless social myths permit an unthinkable act called ethnic, gender, religious, or political cleansing. Nothing could be less just than such conduct. Behind this abhorrent behavior, which has marked the history of almost every nation on earth, there is the familiar mythology of a "chosen people" who envision themselves as the voices and instruments of a manifest destiny, a conviction that presumably provides the divine right to dominate all other peoples.

Political concerns and a preoccupation with the meaning of justice are not usually associated with those who labor at art, and yet hardly an era of human history has passed in which there have not been artists who have either championed a devastating patriotism, like Leni Riefenstahl and her brilliant and abhorrent pro-Nazi films, or produced laments for those lost in political and religious conflicts, like Alain Resnais and his agonizingly vivid film about the victims of Nazism, *Night and Fog*.

Robert Hughes (1990) has written with great force about this subject. After describing the Butte de Warlencourt in the Somme Valley on the French-Belgium border, where World War I German and Allied troops fought a terrible series of battles, he exclaims:

> Thousands of people had died for it, and every yard of earth on and around it has been dug over by high explosive and mixed with their outraged flesh, down to a depth of six feet.

At Warlencourt and all along the Somme, our fathers and grandfathers tasted the first terrors of the twentieth century. There, that joyful sense of the promise of modernity, the optimism born of the machine and of the millennial turning point of a new century, was cut down by other machines. In the Somme Valley the back of language broke. It could no longer carry its former meaning. World War I changed the life of words and images in art, radically and forever. It brought our culture into the age of mass-produced, industrialized death.

The expressive capacity of the arts had always been tested by injustices and human calamities. The ravages of the Middle Ages found a terrifyingly apt expression in the macabre works of Hieronymus Bosch and in the depiction of the Apocalypse in the woodcuts of Albrecht Dürer. In the fifteenth century there was Uccello's poignant but heroic *The Battle of San Romano*. In the sixteenth century Jacques Callot's etching *Execution of Evildoers in a Camp in the Field* expressed a pitiless horror of mindless retribution. In the nineteenth century Francisco Goya created his series of nightmare images, *Disasters of War*, and his outraged sequence of studies and paintings called *The Third of May 1808;* Eugène Delacroix painted his *The Massacre of Chios*, and Honoré Daumier devoted himself to the depiction of the inequities suffered by the poor.

These were strongly political paintings, though their creators, with the likely exception of Daumier and Goya, may have had slight awareness of the social impact of their works. Despite such social innocence, all art forms are essentially political; they reflect the primary workings of societies as well as make visible their governing mythologies. Some art, however, was once clearly devoted to an iconoclastic purpose, impelled by social indignity and an effort to render a picture of society strong enough to effect changes in the world, although, according to Robert Hughes (1981), "The idea that an artist, by making painting and sculpture, could insert images into the stream of public speech and thus change political discourse has gone, probably for good."

But before the demise of our delusions about art's social potency and the capacity of individuals for patriotic heroism, there persisted in works of art, until the twentieth century, an insistent glorification of partisanism: the perennial hero on a horse in the public square, an image, dating from Roman times, that has become an anachronism, an impossible and ironic icon, even something of a terrible joke in the nuclear age.

Withstanding our disillusionment, art can still be the source of tremendous political tension. The 1920–21 posters created by Vladimir Kozlinsky extolled his Bolshevik ardor; the contemporaneous paintings of George Grosz, Otto Dix, and Max Beckmann satirized and shamed the dreadful rise of Nazism. There were also the brilliant leftist murals of Diego Rivera and the proletariat frescoes and mosaics of José Clemente Orozco and David Alfaro Siqueiros in Mexico City. And, of course, there is the most renowned of all political paintings of our era, the fiercely antiwar *Guernica* of Pablo Picasso.

The much publicized antagonism between artist Picasso and Spanish dictator Francisco Franco vividly enforces the political potential of art. Franco had good reason to fear Picasso more than the rebels who openly opposed him. The massive painting by Picasso called *Guernica* was a powerful incrimination of the bombing of the helpless Spanish village of Guernica in 1937, during the Spanish Civil War. But the power of the painting is not militaristic but artistic. Its force arises from the imagination and not from an arsenal of weapons. Its emotional barrage is powerfully impassioned and universal, striking our most responsive sensibility, like the terrifying but incongruous images of a nightmare. It rouses intense indignation and outrage. Art such as *Guernica* is an invincible fortress because its impact resonates long after the blare of warfare is silent. Its impact would persist even if the painting itself were destroyed. Our memory of it is everlasting. An enemy can be intimidated and destroyed. Picasso's painting, however, possesses an imperishable voice, because its force survives long after we cease to stand before it. Its imagery enters our lives and our psyches, lingering like a dream whose grip holds onto us well into the daylight hours.

Picasso was able to transform the victimization of a village into an expressive act so powerful that it was deeply threatening to Franco. As James Baldwin said, "The victim who is able to articulate the situation of the victim has ceased to be a victim—he or she has become a threat." Picasso was just such a threat to Franco. *Guernica* was held in "protective custody" by the Museum of Modern Art in New York and could not be returned to Spain until after Franco's death.

The names and faces of the generals and compatriots who fought on each side of the Spanish Civil War have faded and vanished from global memory, while *Guernica* persists—as art and also as a demonstration of moral indignation. Its indictment draws immense power from the imagery of nightmares: the weeping women, the skewered horse, the enraged bull. As art historian John Berger has remarked, Picasso could imagine more suffering in a horse's head than Rubens normally put into a whole crucifixion. "The spike tongues, the rolling eyes, the frantic splayed toes and fingers, the neck arched in spasm, . . . the Mithraic eye of the electric light, and the suggestion that the horse's body is made of parallel lines of newsprint, . . . the black, white, and grey that retains something of the grainy, ephemeral look one associates with the front page of a newspaper" (Hughes, 1981).

Guernica is haunting. Once seen, no one can easily forget it. Its psychological weaponry was a tremendous threat to a dictator who understood the use of bombs but was mystified, like most politicos, by the uses of art. Although the famous standoff between Franco and Picasso is an obvious example of the political impact of art, the power of *Guernica* is not to be found solely in its vivid depiction of brutality. The painting is not propaganda. It is not designed to be illustrative or didactic. Its visual rhetoric is not the studied sign language of protest posters and political cartoons. To the contrary, the power of *Guernica* is found in the way the artist universalized political reality into a painterly experience that is more terrifying than reality itself, because it creates its own reality, which strikes the viewer as more vivid and real than the historic event the painting presumably depicts. Picasso's political outrage was entirely transformed by the imaginative process, an inexplicable artistic transformation that made the creation of the painting possible.

That same imaginative process, however, is also essential in viewers of the painting if they are to be able to respond to the implications of Picasso's images. In other words, the painting alone cannot illicit response. It is merely a catalyst. Its ultimate political power is found in the complex interaction between artist and audience. That is why *Guernica* is art rather than illustration. It is metaphoric—not factual. It does not teach or inform; it elicits our response through allusions. It illuminates an interaction between artist and audience that is built upon apparition and imagination. That which was the source of vision for the creator must also become the source of comprehension for the audience. It is this kind of *shared* comprehension that gives art its communal significance among tribal peoples—and that once provided great religious painting and music with immense impact upon the devout and the faithful.

Today, when we think about expression and comprehension, we tend to focus almost entirely upon the predicament of young American students who are pronounced to be poorly educated. Many educators point to surveys that suggest that the average high school graduate is technically illiterate, incapable of reading and writing. There are, however, far worse problems than illiteracy. While attending a number of writing institutes in the United States, I have learned from specialists (who are concerned with the techniques teachers use to teach young people to read and write) that their problem is not just the loss of the mechanical ability to read. What concerns many educators even more than illiteracy is the dissipation among young Americans of the capacity for active imagination that allows people to *comprehend* what they read. The result of this dilemma is a widespread *cultural* illiteracy—a mentality not only incapable of comprehending the meaning of a book but also incapable of responding with imagination to painting, dance, architecture, theater, poetry, and all other forms of cultural experience.

For such culturally illiterate people, the *Guernica* is incomprehensible. It contains none of the obvious cues typical of the mass media—cues that illicit easy responses. There is no rag doll in the rubble of battle, no idealized hero on a horse, no holy war with God on our side, and no chosen people whose cause is always righteous and just.

This reliance upon ideological and emotional clichés and the lack of a penetrating comprehension of our experiences is the cause of alienation from our own lives and our cultures. It is a politically devastating condition. It isolates us, not only in terms of what we understand about ourselves and our social values, but also in terms of how well we communicate with one another. An "emotionally illiterate" person can be highly educated and professionally skilled, motivated by serious political aspirations and moral purpose. Yet such people are disenfranchised from all but the most superficial aspects of their societies. Lost to such unimaginative and flat-footed people is not just the capacity to grasp the motives and motifs of their own emotional lives, but also the ability to perform the acts of inventiveness that allow them to make creative judgments and decisions that are more than the ramifications of their religious and political dogmas.

There are no more dangerous people on earth than those who do not understand the mythic and imaginal bases of their strongly held beliefs. Champions, rebels, saviors, and saints who act out of ignorance of their motives are despots to be feared, not heroes to be venerated. Inevitably, we discover that among our most dedicated and highly motivated politicos, reactionary or progressive, there is almost no grasp of the role of imagination in the political arena. They inevitably believe that the arts are a luxury ill-afforded by the disempowered. There is something about the political mind, from Plato and Karl Marx to Adam Smith, that assumes that art is extraneous, that it is a limp rifle in the battle against our common enemies. Nothing could be farther from the truth. Imagination is a political force, because without it we cannot participate fully in our own societies, except as media autotypes for whom opinion becomes a matter of public consensus, for whom information becomes idle gossip, political cause becomes catechism, and profound feeling becomes emotional artifice.

The everlasting outcry of Picasso's *Guernica* is lost on people who are artistically and emotionally illiterate because the results of the artist's imagination cannot exist without the artistic collaboration of the audience. "The secret of the world," wrote Ralph Waldo Emerson, "is the tie between person and event." Theater critic John Lahr said much the same thing in another way: "History is fable agreed upon. So too is identity, which is a story not only arrived at by the individual but conferred by the group. There has to be both a public and private coherence to the story of our self."

Cultural illiteracy breaks the essential continuity between fable and history, between the story of the individual and the story of the group. It demolishes the coherence of a public and private vision of the reality of the self and the group. Cultural illiteracy is the tragic motif behind Yeats's often quoted vision of the modern world:

> *Things fall apart; the center cannot hold;*
> *Mere anarchy is loosed upon the world,*
> *The blood-dimmed tide is loosed, and everywhere*
> *The ceremony of innocence is drowned;*
> *The best lack all conviction, while the worst*
> *Are full of passionate intensity.*

When Emerson speaks of the tie between person and event, he is referring to the bond that is built upon the immersion of all the people of a society into the culture of that society: its language, its context, its mythologies and active metaphors, its emotional experience, and its sense of destiny. Our tragic condition is at least partly based on the fact that we have entered a time in which young people are alienated from the artistic forms, the social history, the mythic imagination, and the sentient visions that make culture possible.

In most non-Western societies, philosophy, faith, and art are inseparable. Since the Renaissance in the West, however, that essential symbiosis has gradually eroded. By the mideighteenth century the arts had gradually slipped into social oblivion, resulting in a tragic and curious situation. We are the only society in history in which artists and their efforts are almost entirely alien to the public.

In contrast, most tribal peoples unanimously grasp their arts as an implicit and unnamed element of their inclusive community mentality. "When art is a necessity there are no art critics" (Hess). But in the West, when art ceased to be the prime "illustrator" of Christian faith, it became a tool of the aristocracy, designating social position and refinement rather than being the Emersonian "tie between person and event." The aristocrats became so refined that they failed to be civilized. And with the decline of the aristocratic art-amateur and the rise of the merchant class, both folk art and "high" art were largely abandoned even as social functions, and they became the concern of a narrow artistic elite.

Now, presumably, one is supposed to be an educated specialist in order to "understand" the arts. The imaginal ability to comprehend anything but the simplest social reality has dissipated radically. The primordial and mysterious relationship of art and faith has been replaced by the mystification of the artist as the practitioner of secret languages inaccessible to all but the few. It is a situation ideally suited to the schism between technology and imagination introduced by the democratization of education and culture, which promoted a pride in cultural illiteracy as an expression of egalitarianism.

This Western decline of cultural comprehension—the terrible rift between art and people—became something of a political dilemma for social reformers who dreamed of a populist culture for the masses. But generations of government-sponsored public art and hours of courses in "art appreciation" failed to create a truly "democratic" joy in art. Reading, writing, and arithmetic were not the answer. Mechanical literacy is a craft; it is not the act of imagination that is essential to comprehension.

Stalin had demanded that artists create works that people could easily understand. Limits were placed upon the imagination of artists and restrictions were placed on the content of their works. Doctrine attempted to control the creative process. Works of art were banned. Artists were publicly humiliated for their failure to resist the influence of Western decadence. Art was required to be politically relevant, to address party lines, ultimately to repudiate itself—even if such demands deprived art of the integral sensibility that makes art possible. The results were horrendous both artistically and socially. Politicizing art ironically deprived art of its political power. Whether we look at the monumental art commissioned by Hitler or the bureaucratic art commissioned by Stalin, all of it was an artistic imitation—artistic transvestism, if you will—but it was not art. And such political control of art is as nefarious in the Senate of the United States and at the National Endowment for the Arts as it was in Stalin's USSR and Hitler's Germany.

In the wake of government control, art has suffered great losses, and the people made few gains. British playwright Tom Stoppard pointed to the irony of such bureaucratic situations when he wrote, "The further left you go politically, the more bourgeois they like their art." One might add that the further right you go politically, the more totalitarian the control of the arts.

Since the ancient days when the first "artists" painted the caves at Altamira with marvelous imagery filled with power, the arts have lost much of their vigor and all of their communality. Sculptor David Barr puts it this way:

> In our culture, "knowing"—for all its practical good—has alienated us from feeling. So we have to build sanctified structures, like churches. And we believe that God lives in

those churches, but doesn't live in the rest of the world. For people like me, who are uncomfortable in the cathedral, we begin to suspect that sacredness doesn't exist anywhere. And so, for many artists, the only remaining place of mystery is inside one's self. Admittedly, this egocentric point of view has become the source of a lot of creative arrogance. And much of the nonsensical and self-indulgent "art" that such egotism has produced has become the justification for many people to reject art entirely.

As far as David Barr is concerned, once art is reintegrated into society, there will be no need to bring the people to art or to bring art to the people. But to get art back into the social community, we have to regain that imaginative capacity that makes us an intrinsic part of our culture. To recover the ability to *read* a painting or a sonata, a play, a dance, or novel is an immensely difficult task, not unlike the efforts today of the people of the former Soviet Union to discover a capitalist socioeconomic system they have never known. Such reforms are not simply matters of political determination, social policy, and education. They are processes of psychological transformation that are far more profound and far more illusive than civic reform. It will take time.

Meanwhile, we continue to be so remote from the capacity to experience (and to be touched by) art that we have devoted ourselves to the hopeless effort of *understanding* it. When we discover that we cannot enjoy art simply by understanding it, we accuse it of falsity and we tend to reject it entirely, while, at the same time, we insist that the things we *can* understand are *real art*—which brings us right back to the aesthetics of Stalin and Hitler.

The problem with the popular success of intrusively political art of dubious form and style is that it reinforces and justifies our artistic illiteracy. It is propaganda that makes us feel socially justified no matter our ignorance. It doesn't challenge our imaginations. It doesn't enhance our comprehension. And it also tends to institutionalize the neglect of so-called decadent art—which is often excellent art that doesn't fit into our particular political agenda.

Despite its reputation as an impractical and nonpolitical activity, art is nonetheless an implicit element of human nature. Imagination is also a vigorous political power, because without art we are alone. Our societal relationships dissipate into a suffocating solipsism. For art is that Emersonian "secret of the world that is the tie between person and event." And between person and person. There is nothing alien or elitist about art unless we feel left out of it. In that case, we should probably reexamine ourselves. Artists cannot create art for "the people" until people renew their capability for artistic experience. It takes as much talent to respond to art as it takes to create it.

Again, art is a staple of humankind—never a by-product of leisure or elitism—and so urgent, so utterly linked with the pulse of feeling that it becomes the singular sign of life when every other aspect of civilization fails.

The failure of communication between artists and people is caused by an artistic illiteracy that makes it impossible for us to "read" a significant painting or to "experience" a profound piece of music or a meaningful novel. As much as we believe in the power of data, cultural illiteracy is an impairment that mere information cannot alleviate.

"The sober truth remains that vision requires far more than a functioning physical organism. Without an inner light, without a formative visual imagination, we are blind" (Zajonc).

The attainment of a capacity for aesthetic response is infinitely more subtle than learning the mechanics of reading and writing a language. Despite such difficulties, until we rediscover methods to awaken a capacity for vision in all our communities, we will continue to be in danger of losing ourselves, even if we win the entire world. Technological knowledge is essential to the betterment of our societies, but the "ecology of the human imagination" may turn out to be a far more urgent issue of our times.

XII.

The Hermit

Invisible Art

By making art a specially precious part of life, we have demoted it from being all of life.

Margaret Mead

The bearded Hermit is dressed in long robes and carries a lamp in one hand and a staff in the other. His attire is a monk's habit and cowl. His lamp is lighted by a star. And he leans heavily upon his staff, bent with age. The "Old Man," as the Hermit is often called, represents self-illumination, solitude, and seclusion. He is a silent and mysterious figure, unwilling to give up his secrets. And as such he is an ideal analogy for the type of "art" that is so massive in scale or so remote in location that it is clearly intended to be hidden from the sight of human beings.

Maurice Merleau-Ponty has said that "the entire essence of time, as of light, is to make visible." In some cases, that is not necessarily the essence of art. For whatever we call "art" in our world is, in the worlds of others, often at its highest realization when it is invisible.

Some of the most famous examples of invisible art are the massive earthworks of the Peruvian desert plain in South America called the Nazca Lines. The designs are astonishingly varied: There are at least eighteen kinds of birds alone and about twelve other animal forms—monkey, spider, whale, dog, and others. There are, however, no human or humanoid forms on the plain itself; the only human figures appear on the slopes of the distant hills, where archeologists have found burial mounds. In addition, there are more than one hundred complex and abstract geometric designs consisting of straight lines, parallels, triangles, trapezoids—all executed with the utmost precision. The dimensions of these designs vary widely—the straight lines, for instance, measure from about a mile to as much as three miles in length. The monkey figure is about twenty-five feet long, while the spider is about ten feet long. There is one bird, a hummingbird, with extended wings measuring about forty feet across! The desert plain of Nazca is not sandy; instead, the surface is composed of iron oxide of a light brown color. If this topsoil is removed, one finds a yellowish subsoil. It is this contrast between the color of the surface and that of the subsoil that enables the designs to be seen. The Nazca Lines are not the result of a laborious accumulation of earth shaped into various designs; it is, instead, the calculated scraping away of the topsoil in complex lines and shapes that outline geometric designs and effigies because of the contrasting color of the subsoil.

The survival of the lines some thousand years after they were made is possible not only because of the seclusion of their location, but also because of the fact that rain is exceptionally rare in the vicinity. The designs were apparently made by the Paracas/Nazca peoples who inhabited the valley between 300 B.C. and A.D. 900. The purpose of the lines is unknown, although their massiveness in a remote area suggests that they were intended to be "invisible" art—not made to be seen—since there are no local heights that afford a good view, which is necessary because they are so extended in space that they cannot be readily grasped when an observer stands in their midst. The most vivid experience of the Nazca Lines is relatively recent, afforded by an airplane and aerial photography, though, of course, the lines long predate the invention of aircraft.

Because we are inclined to insist upon a pragmatic motive for the enormous effort required to create the many forms of invisible art that exist in various parts of the world, there has been wild speculation about the purpose of the Nazca Lines, which have long baffled theorists. The hypotheses about the lines are spectacularly bizarre. They have been explained as ancient landing strips for extraterrestrials and as graphic flattery offered up to the heavenly gods of the Nazca, though we have little knowledge of the religion of the Nazca people. They have also been explained as terrestrial maps guiding departed souls back to their living relatives; as ancient highways of a people who, it so happens, had no wheeled vehicles; as primordial racetracks of a people who did not have horses or any other animal capable of racing; and, more probably, as ritual dance grounds or processional "avenues." One particularly curious speculation is the notion that at one time the shamans of Latin America were capable of levitation and flight, and did not merely "fly" in the hallucinatory rites that they still conduct today under the influence of herbs and drugs.

There has also been a great deal of scholarly investigation of the lines. Carrying on the work of Paul Kosok, who started the modern study of the lines, Maria Reiche has spent over forty years on the Nazca plain trying to prove that the vast designs are aspects of a calendrical system of the ancients. But when Gerald Hawkins, the controversial American astronomer whose investigation at Stonehenge is legendary, applied his computer methods to the lines, he found little support for the astronomy theories. "The animal figures, disappointingly, do not reflect the constellations with which their images might be associated" (Lippard 1983).

There is no reason to neglect the possibilities of a pragmatic explanation for the Nazca Lines, but there is also no reason to neglect the possibility that they had a quite distinctive and non-pragmatic function in Nazca society. Their meaning may be metaphoric rather than utilitarian. When S. I. Hayakawa, then based at the Illinois Institute of Technology, wrote an introduction to Gyorgy Kepes's landmark book (which is the source of the title of this book), he urged us to experience vision as vision and to relinquish our tendency to see all things in a literal or representational context. "To a Chinese scholar," he wrote,

> the pleasure to be derived from an inscription is only partly due to the sentiments it may express. He may take delight in the calligraphy even when the inscription is meaningless to him as text. Suppose now a singularly obtuse Chinese scholar existed who was solely preoccupied with the literary or moral content of inscriptions, and totally blind to their calligraphy. How would one ever get him to see the calligraphic qualities of an inscription if he persisted, every time the inscription was brought up for examination, in discussing its literary content, its accuracy or inaccuracy as statement of fact, his approval or disapproval of its moral injunctions?

What Hayakawa was suggesting is the dilemma we face when researchers insist upon a representational or utilitarian purpose for the Nazca Lines and resist their significance as metaphor and myth.

Trying to set this obtuseness straight, Robert Morris, writing about the Nazca Lines in *Artforum,* suggested that they had a metaphysical and abstract raison d'être. They were made, he suggested, by a society obsessed with "space as a palpable emptiness." He saw the lines as a reflection of the minimal art that greatly preoccupied him in the 1970s.

Earlier in the century Hermann Kern pointed out another possible distinctive motive behind the creation of the Nazca Lines. He claimed that there is abundant evidence in various parts of the world that tribal peoples have long regarded *invisibility* as a common denominator of the sacred. This premise of "the ineffable as invisibility" has a wide-reaching potential for explaining the staggeringly complex array of massive earthworks created by peoples throughout history. Their arduous efforts make it impossible for us not to surmise that they upheld a belief in the spiritual importance of vast earthen patterns, though the makers themselves could never see fully—nor did they ever intend to be able to see—what they created. Such a possibility forces us to consider a radically new motive for the creation of "art" with a *conceptual* and, therefore, an intangible—rather than a *tangible*—existence, which appears to be the same premise that defined the efforts of both minimalist and conceptual artists in our own century. Such artists have often spoken of the impact of ancient Earth Art on their works. They looked back through time and space and were deeply influenced by what they saw, including: the magnificent Serpent Mount, dating from 1000 B.C.—the effigy of a serpent devouring an egg, one among thousands of other earthworks created in the valleys of the Mississippi and Missouri rivers; the sprawling White Horse of Uffington, a late Iron Age "hill figure" that still survives in Berkshire, England; the Giant of Cerne Abbas, dating from the first century A.D. and located in Dorset, England; the medicine wheels of the North American Northwest Plains; the giant copulating figures drawn on the earth near the town of Blythe on the California-Mexico border; the tomb of Yamatotohimomoshohime of Japan, dating from A.D. 300–700.

There is no known connection among these massive earthworks except the nagging fact that they were produced by people who could never see the full result of their herculean efforts.

Such "pointless" dedication and "unrewarded" labor should not baffle us. In our own time it has become apparent that human beings have always devoted themselves to things unknown, unseen, and unheard by them. All of religion and metaphysics are celebrations of the unknown and unknowable; and, as we have seen, a great deal of the deliberation of postquantum physics is devoted to the Einsteinian realization that we can speculate about the working of a "cosmic clock" but we can never actually look inside of it and observe its mechanism. We can only observe its outward effects. Our grasp of reality is as "blind" as the capacity of the ancients to see the mighty and mysterious earthworks they created. Perhaps those massive and invisible structures were the symbols of a prolonged mythology of human limitations as contrasted with the inexpressible grandeur of nature. As Amos Vogel has pointed out,

> What we know of the world comes to us primarily through vision. Our eyes, however, are sensitive only to that segment of the spectrum located between red and violet; the remaining 95 percent of all existing light (cosmic, infrared, ultraviolet, gammas, and X-rays) we cannot see. This means that we only perceive 5 percent of the "real" world; and that even if we supplement our primitive vision with our equally primitive senses of hearing, smell, and touch, we are neither able to know everything nor even realize the extent of our ignorance.

It is possible that even if the people who created these vast earthworks could not see them, they were able to *comprehend* them in a conceptual, if not in a perceptual, manner. Lucy Lippard (1983) has suggested that "they probably did so through the fundamental concept of mapping. Just as maps are fusions of the real and the abstract, so are such para-visual monuments." It is also possible that the invisibility of huge monuments provided an experience not vastly different from what Patricia Johanson attempts to elicit in her own earthworks: "mediations between human scale and the undifferentiated vastness of nature."

As Lucy Lippard (1983) suggests, "These [invisible] shapes were undoubtedly as well known to the people who built them as the shapes of their own bodies, and were as recognizable as the Christian Church's [ichnography] of the Cross and Christ's body, or the prehistoric temples, shaped like the body of the Great Goddess in Malta." The arduous efforts it took to make images on the scale of the Nazca Lines might be explained by rituals that enacted sacred or secular reconciliation between the unthinkable vastness of time and the equally unthinkable vastness of space; that is, ones that offered a slowing down of time and compressing of space in direct proportion to the difference between what Johanson has called "human scale and the undifferentiated vastness of nature" (Lippard 1983).

Our limited "human scale" may be a description of a comprehensible microcosm of the incomprehensible macrocosm of "the undifferentiated vastness of nature." We do not know how, but we do experience the unimaginable wholeness of nature—which is an aspect of the invisible—by slowing down time and, thereby, compressing space into a microcosm. That microcosm becomes a metaphor of ourselves and of our finite, human scale, and therefore, it is an expression of the limits of our ability to grasp things infinitely smaller or infinitely larger than ourselves.

The idea of invisibility was developed long before the invention of the telescope and the microscope, instruments that verify our long-standing awareness that things exist that we cannot see with the naked eye. Invisibility may be the human context of the unknowable and, as such, when we create something beyond our visual grasp, the resulting "invisible art" may be an expression of our passionate hope of touching upon the unknowable.

This process is not as enigmatic as it may seem. For instance, we do not "see" New York City unless we are in an airplane, and yet we can have an existential experience of the entire city when we are located in just one small part of it, in terms of what we know and what we imagine about its complex topography. From our limited vantage on one street corner, New York is as "invisible," in terms of our experience of its totality, as the Nazca Lines are for a person with a limited vista standing in just one spot along the lines.

The whole, which we cannot grasp, is the background of our lives. Experience can only be defined when it exists against a background. An axiom of optical science is the notion that we cannot see things in motion unless we see them against a background. But one need not be aware of the entirety of the background in order to grasp its existence and thereby to grasp the things that can only be seen in relationship to it. The gestalt is a bit like Platonic reality: It is the insinuation—the shadow—of a whole we cannot imagine. The gestalt is more than the sum of its parts because, ultimately, it is an idea and not an object. It is a metaphor of an unthinkable wholeness. Therefore, invisible art might be understood as such a gestalt. Its power rests in its insinuation of an entirety beyond our grasp, an enormity that provides us with a sense of sacredness at the same time that it rebukes our deluded self-importance.

Perhaps invisible art is a legacy of a time when we could still intuit "the secret of the world that is the tie between person and event." In our ceaseless efforts to define persons and events and objects as singular and separate entities, we seem to have lost the experience of the "background"—that metaphoric gestalt which is the secret of the world. As S. I. Hayakawa has told us,

> The reorganization of our visual habits so that we perceive
> not isolated "things" in "space," but structure, order, and

the relatedness of events in space-time, is perhaps the most profound kind of revolution possible—a revolution that is long overdue not only in art, but in all our experience. (Kepes)

XIII.

The Wheel of Fortune

Iconography as Destiny

[Artistic] experience is more than the experience of pure sensory qualities. Each configuration contains a meaningful text, evokes associations of things, events; creates emotional and conscious responses.

Gyorgy Kepes

A sphinx holding a sword is seated at the summit of a gigantic, turning wheel. On the left side of the wheel is a descending figure with a human face and a lion's tail; on the right is a rising figure that probably represents the mythic Greek serpent Typhon. This Tarot card is the symbol of destiny and inevitability, with all of the attendant possibilities of gain and loss, growth and decay, fortune and misfortune. The Wheel of Fortune serves as the gateway to the exploration of iconography: forms of meaning that are the outward aspects of a symbolic language, arising not only from images, but also from gestures, structural shapes, calligraphies, actions, and sounds.

Language can also have an iconic impact. As Max Scheler notes, "By creating new forms of expression the poets soar above the prevailing network of ideas in which our experience is confined by ordinary language; they enable the rest of us to *see*, for the first time, something which may answer to these new and richer forms of expression, and by so doing they actually *extend* the scope of our *possible* self-awareness."

Iconography exists as symbolic forms in every type of art and every aspect of social communication, from the gratuitously violent and sentimental imagery of the nightly news and the negative advertisements of political candidates to music's use of the soaring themes, emotive minor keys, and contrasting fast/slow heartbeat rhythms, and the use in theater and dance of kinesthetic configurations and body language. But the most vivid and influential icons are those that dominate our visual experiences. The iconic process of art can be seen as "a series of expeditions against the intuitable world, within and without, to subdue it for our comprehension" (Scheler). That subduing of the intuitable world results in symbolic forms that allow us to allude to objects that are not present and to feelings and ideas that are not objective. They are analogies that bear witness to the unsubstantial and idealized things we wish to express both as individuals and as social beings. They are responses that Austrian art historian Alois Riegl called "heptic" expressions: dictated by inward sensation rather than by outward observation. Iconographic mannerisms are often incarnations of noumenal experience, heightened and exaggerated both by imagination and the impulse to express deeply felt sensations and feelings. For instance, in purely visual terms, we find that running figures, whether in prehistoric art or in the bathers of Picasso's "primitivist" period, are often elongated—not as a result of realist observation but because the act of running elicits the sensation of protraction. This iconographic process—of reordering experience in terms of heptic sensation—is what André Malraux called a fundamental humanizing mechanism: "How man would have made the world had he been God."

> It is only in so far as the artist establishes symbols for the representation of reality that mind, as a structure of thought, can take shape. The artist establishes these symbols by becoming conscious of new aspects of reality, and by representing his consciousness of these new aspects of reality in plastic and poetic images. (Read)

Icons are not necessarily abstract or stylized. They can be found in a wide variety of forms: naive images that illicit a highly predictable reaction; ambiguous images that are allusions to things more universal than literal images; or highly designed images that require a good deal of orientation before we become aware of their intent.

Rudolf Arnheim proposed three functions fulfilled by iconic images: picture, symbol, and sign.

The *picture* renders relevant qualities—shape, color, movement—of the objects or activities it depicts. The picture is not a replica of a natural object or action. It

> can dwell at the most varied levels of abstractness. A photograph or a Dutch landscape of the seventeenth century may

be quite lifelike and yet selective, arranged, and almost unno-
ticeably stylized in such a way that it focuses on some of the
subject's essence. . . . A child may capture the character of
a human figure or a tree by a few highly abstract circles, ovals,
or straight lines. (Arnheim)

A *symbol* is referential, suggesting something other than itself.
It is frequently a heptic image, expressing inward sensation rather
than outward observation. "A symbol gives particular shape to
types of things or constellations of forces" (Arnheim). It can be
entirely abstract or it can be representational. But its function is
found in its capacity to insinuate rather than to "quote" reality.
For instance, the image depicted in a painting may be an object or
a person, but, essentially, its symbolic intent is to be neither object
nor person. It is a symbolic form that builds upon a vast repertory
of learned and intuited visual elements capable of evoking a wide
range of human responses. As such, the painted object is more
than a reference to something familiar, as evidenced by Belgian
artist René Magritte, who made a famous little painting showing
a tediously rendered tobacco pipe on a blank background, with the
inscription: *"Ceci n'est pas une pipe . . .* This is not a pipe."
　　Such an inscription is unsettling to the observer who sees
only the recognized object: a pipe. But what Magritte is telling us
is that discursive recognitions are not the purpose of paintings. The
pipe is not a pipe because *it is a painting.*
　　In his delightful essay about Magritte (1982), French philosopher Michel Foucault reminds us that there is a separation "between linguistic signs and plastic elements," between "equivalence
of resemblance and affirmation." In short, a painting is not a pipe.
　　A *sign* is an image that designates, but it requires foreknowl-
edge if its designation is to be significant to us and thereby serve
its largely practical purpose. Unlike a symbol that alludes to its
meaning or a picture that qualifies what it represents, signs are
substitutes for words, which attempt to be the exact equivalent of
what is signaled, whether idea or object or behavior. Thus, a sign
such as a swastika does not possess a self-contained meaning; it is

a discursive reference to something other than itself—Nazis or Native Americans. But the swastika does not automatically evoke the idea of Nazis (if its configuration is clockwise) or the idea of Native Americans (if its configuration is counterclockwise). We must be aware of the implication of a sign before it can have the kind of specific meaning it is supposed to convey, whether it is the patriotism aroused by national flags, the authority implied by traffic signs, the ownership signified by trademarks and logos, or the information imparted by signs on restrooms and emergency doors. "It may take a powerful and prolonged effort to endow a simple design with a particular meaning" (Arnheim).

In all art there are also three basic iconographic concerns that achieve symbolic meaning: one is the way space is used; another is the forms made in space; and a third is related to the way time is suggested in nontemporal arts such as painting, architecture, and sculpture. These distinctions can be illustrated with a few examples: geometric divisions of a surface with hard-edge lineation and solid, unshaded distribution of color is an example of the way space is used; a jaguarlike linear motif repeated successively over a surface is an example of forms produced in space; and depicting consecutive and multiple images of a nude descending a staircase or rendering a succession of gun bursts that seem to hang in the air exemplifies the manner in which time can be suggested in nontemporal art.

The way these three basic graphic elements are treated constitutes the mannerisms that give rise to a sense of "cultural style," a recognizable visual character that usually differs vastly from era to era and from society to society. This cultural style is the major basis for our recognition of the difference between a Hopi kachina mask and a Javanese dance mask. It is also the basis of our comprehension of the messages of iconography. If the style of representation is alien to us, we cannot "read" the picture, symbol, or sign, and, as a result, the icon baffles rather than informs us of its message.

There are iconographic variations among all cultures, as well as within a single culture. There are also similar iconographic styles in widely separated parts of the world. Certain visual motifs (and verbal, musical, and ritualistic dance motifs) are diffused from one culture to another or they are invented simultaneously by different peoples. Such iconic and stylistic similarities in widely different cultures have prompted the question asked by Jan B. Deregowski in an essay in *Scientific American:* "Do drawings offer us a universal lingua franca?" In other words, is there something about human beings that provides them with the capacity to inherit ideas? Is there something about Homo sapiens' mentality that gives rise to the same forms of expression and communication in widely different societies? Despite the inclination of many idealists, who ardently believe in something that approximates Jung's collective unconscious, the answer Deregowski (and, for that matter, Jung himself) gave to this question is an unqualified NO.

In *Symbols of Transformation* Carl Jung stated, "It is not a question of a specifically racial heredity, but of a universally human characteristic. Nor is it a question of *inherited ideas,* but of a functional disposition to produce the same, or very similar, ideas. This disposition I later called the *archetype.*"

According to Deregowski, "There are significant differences in the way pictures can be interpreted. Their differences are more prominent than their similarities both in style and in function. The task of mapping out these differences in various cultures is only beginning."

And yet, as Jung suggested, certain archetypal techniques of dealing with visual space seem to dominate the thinking of many different peoples. For instance, the Northwest Coast Indians of America solved the

> problem of how to present the side view and the frontal symmetry of an animal at the same time by splitting up the body into two side views, which were combined in a symmetrical whole and kept in precarious contact with each other by sharing either the middle line or the back or the head or by cohering at the tip of the nose or the tail. Morin-Jean has

shown that very similar forms occur in Oriental decorative art, on Greek vases and coins, and again on Romanesque capitals. (Arnheim)

Deregowski puts a great deal of emphasis on the so-called split image.

Although preference for drawings of the split type has only recently been studied systematically, indications of such a preference have long been apparent in the artistic styles of certain cultures, for example the Indians of the Northwest Coast of North America. Other instances of split style in art are rock paintings in the caves of the Sahara and the [primal] art found in Siberia and New Zealand. It can also be found in the drawings of children in all cultures, even in those cultures where the style is considered manifestly wrong by adults, . . . [yet in] all societies children have an aesthetic preference for drawings of the [cubistlike] split type. In most societies this preference is suppressed because the drawings do not convey information about the depicted objects as "accurately" as perspective drawings do. Therefore, aesthetic preference is sacrificed on the altar of efficiency in communication.

But if the split image is a universal form of imagery, it is an inclination that is manifest in drastically different cultural styles. Recent developments in the field of the psychology of perception make it possible to describe this artistic process more adequately. As Arnheim indicates, in the past

an oversimplified concept of this process was based on a double application of what is known in philosophy as "naive realism." According to this view, there is no difference between the physical object and its image perceived by the mind. The mind sees the object itself. Similarly, the work of the painter or the sculptor is considered simply a replica of the precept. Just as the table seen by the eyes is supposed to be identical with the table as a physical object, so the picture of the table on the canvas is simply a repetition of the table the artist saw. At best the artist is able to "improve" reality or to enrich it with creatures of fantasy by leaving out or adding details, selecting suitable examples, rearranging the given order of things. This theory encountered puzzling contradictions in the field of the arts. If spontaneous perception corresponded to the projective image, it was reasonable to expect that naive pictorial representation at early stages of cultural development would tend toward completeness and perspective distortion.

It could be expected, in other words, that naive realism would be the preferred and singular preoccupation of artists. "The opposite, however, was found to be true," Arnheim continues. "Representation started genetically with highly simplified geometric patterns, and realism was the late and laboriously accomplished product of such sophisticated cultures as Hellenism and the Renaissance."

A major theory, for instance, for the origin and subsequent preference of the split style was formulated by the anthropologist Franz Boas. His hypothesis proposes the following sequence of events: solid sculpture, created in the mode of naive realism, was gradually adapted to the ornamentation of objects such as boxes and bracelets. In order to decorate a box or a bracelet the artist had to flatten the sculpture to conform to the surface to be decorated, including, in both the bracelet and the box, an opening in what had originally been a solid, sculptural form. When the sculptured, in-the-round object was flattened out, it became an example of either a split image or an atomized image, which is a bit like what an orange peel or a globe of the earth looks like when it is carefully split and flattened on a two-dimensional surface. Naive realistic relationships as seen in the object in-the-round are greatly changed by the splitting or atomizing of the image. According to Boas, this is the explanation for the widespread use of split image.

According to Hilary Stewart,

Northwest Coast art owes its structure to a general system of design principles. Depending on how these are used, the crest or motif being portrayed can vary from realistic and easily recognizable to involved and somewhat difficult to figure out—or the identity of the figure can become totally abstracted through the rearrangement of its anatomical parts.

The bilateralism usually associated with this kind of iconography is apparently a fundamental element of formal balance used by the artist to give abstract cohesion to the figurative realism that has been sacrificed in the process of manipulating a figure anatomically so it fits a given surface. The process is exceptionally complex and is anything but primitive. The visual thinking implied by this process is at least as rarified as the mathematical process that gave rise to linear perspective in early Renaissance art.

Another important element of the visual arts of many tribal peoples is the inclination to portray the essential but unseen aspects of subject matter: The artist portrays all that he or she knows about the subject, whether these qualities are visible or not. The resulting "X-ray image," like split image, is one of the fundamental ways in which artists have dealt with representation. But in the case of X-ray imagery, the representation includes the internal, unseen structural aspect of animals and beings at the same time that the external forms are portrayed carefully, with a good deal of realistic detail. Thus the knowledge of the object being painted or carved may be the basis of an emphasis (or, from the naive realistic point of view, "overemphasis") of certain features of a particular subject. The knowledge of a thing may inspire the artist to show it from many more viewpoints (angles) than could ever be seen by one person in one position at one time. For these artists, all that is known about an object is more important than what can simply be "seen" at any given moment and from any given point in space. Knowledge of an object, including knowledge of its internal structure, can result in condensation through selectivity as readily as it can inspire mythic elaboration, such as X-ray imagery or the multiplication of external limbs. Condensation—the minimalization of the image—results in varying degrees of abstraction, as in the simplified structural planes of the Mezcala effigies of pre-Columbian Mexico or the Cycladic figuration of the ancient Aegean; elaboration often results in a futuristic approximation of animation and motion, as in the multiplicity of "moving" arms of Hindu deities.

And, finally, there is among many tribal and Asian artists the classical *horror vacui*—the almost compulsory necessity to fill all blank spaces. For such craftspeople a vacant surface in a composition is undesirable and unaesthetic. The entire surface must therefore be filled through an intricacy of design that produces an "all-over" result. Doodling is a half-conscious effort to fill space with a complex maze of details, all interconnected or related in an elaborate spatial orientation. The same impulse to cover the entire surface is found in Nazca textiles and in the pottery of ancient Peru, and in the architectural reliefs of India and Southeast Asia, like the Gopura of Rameshwara and the Angkor Wat in Cambodia.

Whatever the origin of *horror vacui*, X-ray imagery, and atomized or split images, all of these techniques are found in a great variety of global cultures and are also the graphic styles widely used by children in their depiction of objects, persons, and landscapes. But these visual techniques, for all their prevalence, do not constitute a universal form of graphic representation, for their variations are far greater than their similarities. Just as naive realism is by no means a universal lingua franca, though the conditioning in Western art since the Renaissance makes us think of pictorial illusionism as a human norm, so *horror vacui*, X-ray imagery, split images, and all other iconographic styles do not represent a universal visual language. The only truly transcendent aspect of human cultures seems to be a remarkable and unlimited diversity.

Neither the techniques nor the symbolic references of iconography are universal.

In the study of art, the relation between form and content is not often enough considered; the tendency is to place undue emphasis on one or the other. Most works of [primal] art show a highly satisfactory combination of form and content. However, it is true that contemporary observers are more likely to derive enjoyment from the form, since the content is lost in the symbolization of the culture in which the work was created. (Inverarity)

What this observation affirms is that iconography is highly localized and not truly transcendent in its impact and symbolism. Its localization is unique because it is built on regional custom. As such, much iconography is allegorical, with its meaning unapparent unless the viewer is part of the culture in which the iconography and its symbolism are a fundamental aspect of cultural orientation and general education. For instance, the Iroquois of the American Northeast create false faces—masks carved from a living tree. As Paul Wingert has pointed out,

> The Iroquois face mask, with the crooked nose, distorted mouth, and deep folds of flesh above the brows and around the mouth, represents the Great One, who, in mythical times, entered into competition with the Creator for mastery of the world. In the course of this struggle his nose was broken, but as a consequence, he was given the privilege of instructing humankind in the making and weaving of a mask in his likeness, together with certain ritual procedures to help people combat the evil of disease. The meaning of the mask is a dramatic expression of these circumstances, interpreted by the sculptor's rendering of the facial features to convey pain as he understands it. As a result, there are many variations in the treatment of this aspect of the subject matter.

But all the variations are based on a central mythic theme that is familiar only to people fully immersed in tribal custom. Those outsiders or insiders who are unfamiliar with the cultural context of the false faces would not be capable of grasping their aesthetic form or their iconographic messages.

Likewise, in Balinese dance dramas like the Wayang Wong, which incorporates stories from the Ramayana (the great Hindu epic dramatizing the triumph of virtue over vice), all of the performers wear masks that possess powerful iconographic significance. Those people—Balinese or foreigners—who are not aware of the mythic basis of the masks would not understand their dramatic significance.

This predicament is intensified by the fact that a Balinese ritual is an invitation to cosmic forces to "come down" and listen to human requests for protection and forbearance. Therefore, the dancers enter what Westerners call "trance," a vulnerable state that allows cosmic powers to "enter" the performers and act and speak through them. The masks are seen as aids not only in visualizing divine powers but also in providing them momentary material manifestation (Slattum). To flatter and attract the divine powers, these masks must precisely illustrate ineffable deities through the depiction of highly symbolic details: cannibalistic demons with gaping mouths, protruding tusks, long curling tongues, and large, round, glaring eyes. Such masks are marvelously grotesque. And yet the most honored characters of the dramas, like the white monkey Hanuman, must be depicted with many of the facial characteristics of demons, requiring a great deal of cultural clarity on the part of the spectator who wishes to grasp the moral and mythic intent of the masked characters. Iconography may be archetypal as a human communicative impulse, but specific iconographic meaning is not self-evident, for it is the result of cultural context and localized aesthetic traditions.

Among the Kwakiutl artists of the Northwest Coast of America there are allegorical tales that are a highly important part of the people's worldview. The Nulmal, or "fool dancers," are much concerned, for ritualistic reasons, with the nose and its mucus, and so they carve Nulmal masks with a great emphasis upon the nose and the splayed and decorated upper lip. Likewise, the famous transformational masks of the Kwakiutl dramatize mythic history by having "articulate parts"—an outer mask (for example, of an eagle) which can be opened by pulling strings to reveal an inner mask (for example, of a human face)—thus recounting a specific event in tribal oral tradition.

Among the Australian People of the Dreamtime (the Aborigines) and among the Kiowa Indians of the Central Plains of North America, there has been wide use of pictographic images. For instance, Kiowa women used only nonfigurative, geometric designs on objects employed in everyday life, while the men kept history in figurative art, the so-called winter counts: radial patterned "storyboards" made up of pictographic images painted on animal skins by tribal historians. On the other hand, the Aborigines use only geometric signs and symbols in their rock art, which they have painted and repainted for at least forty thousand years. After European contact, however, figurative forms began to appear: crocodiles, emu birds, and kangaroos. But the change seems to have been influenced by the European presence. As the Aborigines say, "The Europeans have no power to visualize" (Lawlor).

Even today, iconographic images—in the form of signs and words that "name"—have an integral relationship to the most fundamental aspects of Aboriginal life. As Robert Lawlor notes, the greatly revered ancestors created separate, definite things by naming them. "Therefore, the symbols and language of sacred art can touch the otherworldly ancestral powers. The ancestors' consciousness was so wide, powerful, and concentrated that it could swallow great multitudes of the incomprehensible plentitude of the experiential world," transforming them into a single word or image. Symbolizing or naming is a central aspect of the Aboriginal notion of devouring the experiential world.

> The experience dies . . . as soon as it becomes word or image. The naming mummifies the experience, converting the . . . actual into a reflection suspended in the veiled mirror of language. Reality and meaning escape the entombment of experience—they fly through the grid trap of sign and symbol. Their fearful desertion permits the inner vision to catch only a glimpse of them fleeing. (Lawlor)

Thus, for many peoples, the ineffable is never replaced by signs and symbols. At best, such iconography can only allude to the indescribable.

Of a much more secular mode are the pictographic books (codices) of ancient Meso America. Histories were recorded in allegorical iconography painted on fanfold "books" made of animal skin. In one of these surviving books, called the Nutall Codex, warriors are seen crossing a lake. They appear to float on the waves, while beneath them the watery depths are indicated with a series of serpentine lines, in the midst of which appear strange aquatic creatures. Iconic elaborations are used as naming devices for both the individual warriors and for the place name of the land they are approaching. The stylization is complex, combining highly detailed profile depictions of the warriors in full regalia, a hillock that designates the land upon which they are advancing, as well as sky symbols above the scene and water symbols below the invading warriors—all composed on a two-dimensional plane.

In numerous codices, speech is also represented, but in the manner of speech balloons in comic books, by the use of a volute emerging from the mouth of the speaker—which is an elemental form of ideographic writing, an approach that had already been developed into a highly evolved calligraphy by the Japanese.

In the "ledger art" created by imprisoned Plains Indians during the late nineteenth century, tribal and personal histories were recounted through elaborate iconographic conventions. Unlike iconography that depends upon cultural context, however, the allegorical intentions of much ledger art are clear to us because of the coexistence of more than one view of the events depicted in the art, providing a curious kind of Rosetta stone. As it happens, the events drawn by Indians are the same events that were also recounted (from a strikingly different perspective) in the nineteenth-century histories of white men. Despite radically different points of view, this Western history provides a basis for understanding the

185

context of the Indian ledger art, both in terms of its manner and the meaning of its distinctive iconography.

"Reading" ledger art can be an engaging effort. For instance, the Lakota (Sioux) artist Kills Two produced many historical drawings filled with allegorical iconography. One such painting (on fabric) depicts the warrior Red Walker and his companion fleeing from Crow Indian enemies. The iconographic interpretation offered by Kills Two himself is that Red Walker has a broken leg and that his horse is also wounded—as can be seen from the blood issuing from the horse's nostrils and from the wound in Red Walker's left leg. Meanwhile, his unharmed companion turns back toward the pursuing enemy and fires three shots, a temporal image that would not normally be seen in a painting in the naive realistic tradition, but which is made possible in this example of ledger art by showing—in comic book fashion—successive temporal events in one static image: three visual blasts hang in the air, as if they had burst consecutively from the warrior's outstretched gun.

The visual history of Kills Two comes to life with the help of the artist's instructive narration. And, because Kills Two employed an iconic form vastly different from the Western iconographic traditions, there is a good deal of satisfaction in comprehending with certainty not only the content but also the non-Western technical procedure that the artist used to convey his story. This assisted interpretation, however, should dramatize the puzzlement of a person alien to Plains Indian iconography. At the same time it should dramatize the puzzlement of a person alien to Western culture when that outsider is confronted by the image of a man and a woman covering their groins as they stand beneath a tree in which a serpent is coiled; or the equally pervasive image of a man who seems to be fastened to a cross; or the picture of a forlorn woman holding the dead body of a man in her lap. Without a context or an explanatory narration, such familiar Western religious images would be confounding to a stranger. When confronted by such Judeo-Christian religious art, someone who is at a great remove from Western mythology may recognize the agony of the Crucifixion and the sorrow of the pietà, but is unlikely to grasp the cause or purpose of such expressive forms without a cultural context. Even the emotional aspects of the art might be misunderstood by non-Westerners, if the visual stylization alienates them and, therefore, makes empathic response to the images an impossibility. This resistance to icons created in styles that are unfamiliar can baffle people of all cultures, Western and non-Western. In our own world, for instance, the "grotesque" has a rather negative connotation, whereas it has been a central aesthetic aspect of the arts of the pre-Columbian Aztec and Nazca peoples as well as the art of Bali and much of Asia, like the famous temple guardians and the witches portrayed in Kabuki theater. The Western observer cannot easily grasp the "beauty" and expressive power of art that seems gratuitously grotesque, while to the native eye grotesque imagery is an aspect of the mythic power of art.

It should also be emphasized that non-Western (Asian and tribal) people who are out of touch with their own cultures are as ignorant of and as baffled by their society's iconography as foreigners, at the same time that they may have the experience allowing them to grasp Western iconic representation. I can think of a great many composers, musicians, and artists of Japan who are intimately aware of the subtleties of Euro-American art, while they have virtually no comprehension of the arts of Japan. For instance, the celebrated Japanese composer Toru Takemitsu admitted that during the first years of his career he was deeply influenced by Western music but had little interest in or knowledge of traditional Japanese music.

Clearly, except in the view of racists, the comprehension of a society's iconography is not inborn.

On the other hand, a great many people of the West are alienated equally by the iconic context of the art of non-Western societies and their own. For instance, Westerners who are out of touch with Euro-American modernism usually fail to grasp the textual or emotional context of twentieth-century art, even though it is an outgrowth of their own society. In a like manner, many

187

Western observers cannot see the religious intent of the art of Christianized Ethiopians, who portray familiar biblical themes in an iconic style sufficiently different from traditional Western styles of religious art to perplex people of the West, even when prominent biblical characters and events are depicted. Apparently, both the style and the content of an iconographic context can create a sense of confusion and alienation.

Yet, for all of its diversity, iconography is destiny. It is such a central aspect of culture that we are virtually excluded from the life of our community if we do not grasp at least some of its iconographic contexts. Icons are so cardinal to our relationship with the people in our society that we tend to take social signs and symbols for granted and are rarely aware of their importance in our lives. The media and politicians constantly play with these deeply conditioned images, pressing motivational "buttons" that automatically illicit a wide variety of responses in the public, not unlike the effect of Pavlov's famous dinner bell on his faithful canine colleagues.

Iconography is destiny because it is a powerful and essential communicative tool that can be used for the best and the worst purposes, as a form of revelation and as a form of mind control. In the hands of artists like propagandists Albert Speer and Vladimir Kozlinsky or in the hands of individualists like Robert Rauschenberg and Andy Warhol, a vast array of commanding iconic images have been used to achieve both creative and destructive power, depending entirely upon the motives of the artists.

Iconography is destiny, but it is not transcendent or universal. And it does not possess the ubiquitous significance that many who manipulate symbols and signs would like to ascribe to it.

As Erwin Panofsky, the leading scholar in the field of iconography, has cautioned, we must be aware of what has been aptly called the "principle of disjunction," a concept that debunks the notion that specific icons are universal. Panofsky implies that forms of iconography that are continuous do not guarantee continuity of meaning. Icons may persist while their meanings change drastically from era to era and from place to place. The continuity of form does not necessarily imply a continuity of cultural meaning. So, as an example of the limits of iconographic meaning, we may not use descriptions of Aztec rituals of the sixteenth century to explain murals painted at Teotihuacán a thousand years earlier. Iconography may be destiny within a given society at a given moment, but its claim of being the voice of the collective unconscious or the axis of the Wheel of Fortune is greatly limited by both time and place.

A major aspect of socialization is the cultural instruction that gives us a grasp of the iconography of our community—and which results in our capacity for cultural literacy. But that essential aesthetic education must not encourage us to believe that our iconographic visions of the world are inborn: fixed, absolute, and universal. To the contrary, we urgently need to become aware of the tenuousness and localization of our icons, recognizing that they are only one possible manifestation of an archetype with an unlimited potential for variety. When we recognize the limitations of our own society's iconic visions of the cosmos, we are encouraged to acknowledge the existence of other styles of iconography, which reveal other realities. This crucial recognition allows us to look outward from our limited worldview and to see other peoples in terms of their own realities and their own monumental repertory of iconography. Like our own iconography, theirs is a unique vision that gives them their sense of identity and purpose, and ultimately produces that fertile ground from which ascend their own mysterious gods and their own heroic songs of destiny.

XIV.

The Hanged Man

Homosexuality as Metaphor

There is no clearer proof of the artist's doubt about his role than when he shows himself as entertainer or fool. The artist identifies the outcasts with himself: he is not using the world of the circus and the street players as subject matter, he is using it to symbolize the role of the artist and the entertainer in the world.

Hans Hess

A young man hangs upside down, usually tied by his ankle to a horizontal beam supported by two leafless tree trunks. The man's unbridled leg is bent at the knee, forming a triangle. The hands of the figure are tied behind his back, so his arms form another triangle. Despite his precarious situation, the young man is relaxed and smiling, appearing somewhat playful, as if he sees himself as being free while the rest of the world is fettered; seeing himself as upright while the rest of the world is upside down. This fascinating Tarot card has many interpretations, but for our purposes the most relevant is the theme of life in suspension, signifying the approach of a new age in which there will be a reversal of the human state of mind.

Like the Hanged Man, Oscar Wilde was a person in suspension—a curious combination of social climber, artist, fop, and verbose missionary of deviation. John Lahr (1993) notes that Wilde's "gospel of art was also a destiny of self-destruction."

Wilde's sardonic point of view attempted to repudiate his sense of living a life "in disgrace with fortune and men's eyes." His wit was both combative and compensative, intent upon indulging personal calamity with an endless string of roguish, bitter, and terse comments. "The artistic life," he once observed, "is a long and lovely suicide."

At first this remark seems flippant and melodramatic, the sort of complex and brilliant camp found in the black comedies of Joe Orton. But on closer scrutiny, Wilde's remark turns out to express a viciously precise social observation about the predicament of the outsider. And it is this subject of the outsider that graphically brings to mind the image of the Hanged Man: suspended upside down, but somehow smiling, as if to assure us that his inverted position is his natural state.

The mordant association of art and suicide in Wilde's statement alludes to the interminable process of alienation and longing in the life of the outsider. Anton Ehrenzweig helps to place Wilde's peculiar comment in an aesthetic context when he notes, "Up to a point any truly creative work involves casting aside sharply crystallized modes of rational thought and image making. To this extent creativity involves self-destruction." A ritual act of metaphoric transgression. A process of casting off the world of "crystallized modes of rational thought" in favor of a world of irrationality. But, by his linking of art and suicide, Wilde was inferring something far more radical than the process of artistic rebellion. He was addressing all the ramifications and crucial issues of a deviant life lived outside mainstream society—a society that aggressively invents and enforces its standards of norms. Wilde comprehended the nature of his antisocial point of view and his variance from codes of normalcy, an attitude that Jonathan Dollimore has called a "transgressive aesthetic." According to Wilde, this transgressive mentality is "a disobedience [that] in the eyes of anyone who has read history, is man's original virtue. It is through disobedience [through transgression] that progress has been made, through disobedience and through rebellion." Such a statement is an insightful but timid rationalization for deviant behavior, even for the puritanical England of 1891. A near contemporary of Wilde, philosopher Alfred North Whitehead, was far more precise when he said: "It is the business of the future to be dangerous." And several decades later, in the 1960s, sociologist Howard Becker summed up the centrality of transgression in the twentieth century:

> Deviance is not a quality that lies in behavior itself, but in the interaction between the person who commits an act and those who respond to it. . . . Whether an act is deviant, then, depends on how other people react to it. . . . Most important for the study of behavior ordinarily labeled deviant, the perspectives of the people who engage in the behavior are likely to be quite different from those of the people who condemn it. In this latter situation, a person may feel that he is being judged according to rules he has had no hand in making and

does not accept, rules forced on him by [the majority, which he, as an outsider, believes to be the real] outsiders.

In discussing Edmund White's biography of Jean Genet, Gregory Woods writes,

> Like Wilde, Genet felt that his relationship with language was profoundly affected by his sexuality. In his view, homosexual writers could not simply use language in a straightforward manner as a transparent medium. They were forced to comment on it—"alter it, parody it, dissolve it"—from a marginal position at a fixed distance. The [modern] literature of homosexuality was, therefore, stigmatized with involuntary irony.

But for all of Wilde's verbal outrageousness—such as his famous maxim "What is abnormal in Life stands in normal relations to Art"—he remained a stylish clown anxious for public acknowledgment, the "naughty delight" of a self-absorbed and bourgeois society, often endured and seldom adored and, finally, despised when he was tried publicly and imprisoned. In contrast, Arthur Rimbaud was an outcast and proud degenerate with no interest in modish respectability. He was a raging adolescent who had already vanquished the immoral implication of disobedience by making rebellion a moral act. Wilde's self-contradictory body of work hedged and lurched back and forth on matters of respectability and morality. But Rimbaud had no constraints. He would not allow himself to be distracted from the urgency of his own quest by social niceties. His feelings about the insolent demands of society were not unlike the attitude of the rebellious patients of psychiatrist R. D. Laing, when they insisted that "a common reaction [of the world] has been to forget *our* questions, and then to accuse us of not going about answering *other* questions."

Rimbaud seemed to grasp the need for outsiders to ask their own questions. Unlike Wilde, he did not justify his homosexuality or his artistic rebelliousness; he did not search for causes for his behavior, because he did not feel that his actions required explanation, apology, or justification. Rimbaud thought that life was monstrous, and he was determined to live it outrageously.

This defiance of society's demands for explanations of acts and objects it perceives as "odd" or "deviant" recalls a cartoon that appeared in an art magazine during the height of abstract expressionism. The cartoon showed an angry man pointing at a Jackson Pollock painting and demanding: "What does that mean?" The next frame of the cartoon shows the painting pointing back at the man and asking: "What do you mean?"

Rimbaud's life was a paraphrase of that confrontation between the man, who took for granted the absolute validity of his question, and the painting, which negated the man's question with its own equally valid question. For an epoch when God and natural law are no longer the bases of causation, the cartoon suggests that a reasonable answer to the often asked question "What causes homosexuality?" is the equally perplexing question "What causes heterosexuality?" God and natural law may have little to do with either answer.

Questions that insist upon justifications of idiosyncratic persons and actions do far more than confront controversial social issues. They also bring to the surface the covert motives of those who ask such questions. Inquiries into "norms" inevitably dodge profound issues that are both larger and less ethnocentric than questions that, in their very asking, presume answers that are built upon expectations of normalcy.

Rimbaud would not be sidetracked by explanations that were expected of him. He did not try to answer other people's questions about the causes of his behavior because such questions took it for granted that his behavior was abnormal and therefore required extraordinary explanation. Instead, he epitomized the crisis of the outsider in words wrenched from the mundane grammar of syntax and normalcy: *"Je travaille à me rendre voyant"* ("I am laboring to become a visionary") . . . *"Je est un autre"* ("I is another"). And finally he uttered the ultimate mystic statement about the suicidal implications of a life in art: "I had to give up my life in order to be."

Long before Rimbaud and Wilde, the outsider's voice had been alternately jubilant and self-effacing, but had rarely been defiant. In the lyrics of Sappho and Ibn Al-Abbar, in the sonnets of Michelangelo and, as here, Shakespeare:

When in disgrace with Fortune and men's eyes,
I all alone beweep my outcast state,
And trouble deaf heaven with my bootless cries,
And look upon my self and curse my fate,
Wishing me like to one more rich in hope,
Featured like him, like him with friends possessed,
Desiring this man's art, and that man's scope,
With what I most enjoy contented least,
Yet in these thoughts my self almost despising,
Haply I think on thee, and then my state,
(Like to the lark at break of day arising
From sullen earth) sings hymns at heaven's gate,
For thy sweet love remembered such wealth brings,
That then I scorn to change my state with kings.

André Gide was the last of the reluctant and self-effacing literary homosexuals who struggled against his identity, believing that his Catholic scruples were engaged in a cosmic battle against the willfulness of his desire. In his *Journals,* Gide wrote, "Will he [Wilde] force me to think that homosexuals have more imagination than the . . . others? No, but they are more frequently called upon to exercise it."

Despite his conflicting reverence for and fear of Wilde, Gide was sufficiently possessed by the French preoccupation with reason to speculate at length about something he and others call "homosexual sensibility" in candid books published anonymously or privately *(If It Die* and *Croydon)* as well as in less than candid books published openly *(The Immoralist* and *Strait Is the Gate).*

This inquiry into gay sensibility has occupied a great many

twentieth-century writers, who want to identify a realistic view of homosexuality, rather than mindlessly accepting the archaic notions of a religious dogma or the obsolescent medical paradigm that once concluded, without much reflection, that homosexuality is either an abomination in the eyes of God or a psychotic deviation, resulting from the prolongation of homoerotic adolescence and/or mother fixation. Example: "God didn't create Adam and Steve." Then who created Oscar Wilde? Example: "Homosexuality is the result of the trauma of broken homes." Far more heterosexuals come from broken homes, so is the dysfunctional family what causes heterosexuality?

In 1966 Susan Sontag completely overlooked the immense contribution of Hispanics to visionary literature and African Americans to gospel music, jazz, and rhythm and blues when she wrote that

> Jews and homosexuals are the outstanding creative minorities
> in contemporary urban culture. Creative, that is, in the truest
> sense: they are creators of sensibilities. The two pioneering
> forces of modern sensibility are Jewish moral seriousness and
> homosexual aestheticism and irony.

George Steiner (1978), with no intention of flattery, was far more emphatic about homosexual influence. "Since about 1890," he wrote, "homosexuality has played a vital part in Western culture." He goes on to assert that whereas heterosexuality is the very essence of classic realism, a radical type of homosexual mentality is the essence of modernity: in its narcissism, solipsism, and self-referentiality. "Homosexuality," continues Steiner, "could be construed as a creative rejection of philosophic and conventional realism, of *mundanity* and extroversion of classic and nineteenth-century feeling." Furthermore, homosexuality, Steiner insists, helped lead to "that exercise in solipsism, that remorseless mockery of philistine common sense and bourgeois realism which is modern art."

Steiner contends that two major historical events splintered the foundations of Western tradition and precipitated the crisis of modernity: "one epitomized in Mallarmé's 'disjunction of language from external reference,' and the other in Rimbaud's 'deconstruction of self'—*je est un autre* (I is another)" (Dollimore).

Again, the name of Arthur Rimbaud surfaces as a force in the history of both twentieth-century modernity and homosexual sensibility. His role as cultural and sexual outlaw has become a romantic legend that he himself fabricated and that he lived to the fullest. He idealized the mythology of the outsider—visionary, saboteur, deviant, and desperado. His origins, however, were far from bizarre. He was born in the north of France, the unlikely son of a pious and domineering countrywoman and of an army officer who, during the years of his campaigning, paid sparse attention to his wife and children and eventually abandoned them without apology. Rimbaud's childhood, under the domination of his willful mother and three self-absorbed sisters, suggests the stereotypical image of the sensitive and intelligent youngster without a male role model who is "driven" to become a homosexual. But it is a familial situation that is experienced by a great many heterosexual males and is not experienced by a great many gay men.

By the age of nineteen, Rimbaud was a prize scholar and an accomplished, if traditionally romantic, unpublished poet. He was highly cultivated, having already consumed the whole canon of nineteenth-century artistic and philosophical knowledge. A reading of Darwin revolutionized his thinking. He repudiated his mother's religion and embraced a vacillating atheism as well as Buddhism and tribal paganism, a metaphysical mentality that would dominate the course of his life.

As Wallace Fowlie points out,

Without always realizing it, Rimbaud explicated by the example of his life and by the far less mysterious example of his work, an aesthetic doctrine which had been slowly formulat-

ing in France during the nineteenth century. Baudelaire had
made the most significant contribution to the doctrine.
. . . He had become what Rimbaud justly acclaimed him, the
first visionary. . . . During the 1860s Mallarmé wrote his first
poems which were efforts toward the perfecting of this poetic
theory.

Rimbaud's life as a poet lasted only four years—a fire storm
of unprecedented intensity, virtuosity, originality, and wild inspiration. Most of his poetry was written between the summer of 1871,
when he composed "Le Bateau ivre" ("The Drunken Boat"), and
the summer of 1873, when he completed his final work, *Une
Saison en Enfer (A Season in Hell)*. This remarkable literary
achievement has been described as a concept "intimated by Baudelaire, perfected by Mallarmé, and given by Rimbaud its most
explosive expression. . . . We might say that it [is a concept that
derives from] a belief in the relationship which necessarily exists
between a poem and witchcraft or magic or *sortilege*, as the French
call it. A poem comes into being due to a process which, like
alchemy, is magical and therefore foreign to the rules of logic and
even the rules of instinct" (Fowlie).

With Rimbaud, the term "irrationality" became the major
designation for both the source and the shape of artistic modernity.

The young Rimbaud eventually made the acquaintance of an
older man, the twenty-seven-year-old poet Paul Verlaine. Verlaine
encouraged the boy, took him into his house in Paris, and introduced him to the Parisian literary world. In return, the youthful
Rimbaud had a great influence on Verlaine's poetry and an equally
immense impact on his private life. Verlaine had just been married.
His wife was expecting a baby. But despite his respectable family
situation, Verlaine became obsessed with Rimbaud, who apparently had a profound sense of his power as a cultural outlaw,
impelled by the daring of his own willful imagination and by the
provincial fortitude he had learned from his domineering mother.

Rimbaud did not fit into the domesticated art world of

Paris—which, for all its nonconformity, was tame by comparison to the creative ferocity of the young poet. He quickly ran afoul of the literary circle to which Verlaine introduced him. And after disrupting Verlaine's domestic life, he carried the older poet off on a series of perilous adventures in Belgium and England.

Rimbaud, like Wilde, was a missionary of deviation; but, whereas Wilde's assaults were cultivated and droll, Rimbaud was capable of nothing less than passion and savagery, fired by his "uncanny, animal-like sensitivity to atmosphere" and his rare ability to grasp immediately the impression he was making on others (Starkie).

Speaking of Verlaine, he said, "I had undertaken to restore him to his primitive condition of child of the Sun . . . and we wandered, fed with the wine of thieves' dens and the hardtack of the road."

It should be understood, however, that Rimbaud was hardly an infantile debaucher.

> Verlaine had escaped from the meshes of conjugal discipline long before the coming of Rimbaud to Paris. He was after all ten years older than his young friend; he had knocked about the Latin Quarter since his adolescence; as a youth he was alleged to have practiced sodomy, and he was already a confirmed drunkard by the time of his marriage. (Starkie)

As for Rimbaud, he was apparently unrehearsed in the art of indulgence, a mere adolescent in the rarified Parisian world of moral and sexual ambiguities. But he possessed a commanding imagination that provided him with the sophistication of a far older man. He doted upon his disenfranchisement. Like Jean Genet, Rimbaud had always pictured himself in the romanticized role of "outlaw." For the young Rimbaud, subversion was one of the highest callings. Crimes were not what fascinated him; it was the criminal's life as an outsider that captivated his imagination. Now, as the quintessential outsider, he guided the elder Verlaine into his outlaw imaginings, a seditious game reminiscent of the wicked amusements of the brother and sister in Jean Cocteau's novel *Les Enfants terribles*. On one occasion Rimbaud and Verlaine were both arrested in the railway station at Arras for discussing their imaginary robberies and murders. They delighted in living—metaphorically—on the brink. They were obsessed with each other at the same time that they were engaged in constant sexual and emotional combat. Eventually, after numerous quarrels and separations, Verlaine and Rimbaud parted in Brussels, but not before Verlaine had been sentenced to two years in prison for shooting Rimbaud in the wrist. The stormy relationship did not end there. As the story goes, Rimbaud rejoined Verlaine in Stuttgart after his friend's release from jail. Rimbaud was outraged when he discovered that, during his confinement, Verlaine had returned to the Church and disavowed his homosexuality. Rimbaud took vengeance by getting Verlaine drunk and making him blaspheme his faith, and then, while walking in the Black Forest, confronted Verlaine with abuse, knocked him down with a club, and left him unconscious.

A Season in Hell was published by Rimbaud himself in the fall of 1873, but no one read it. He could not afford to pay the printer, so the books remained in the cellar of the print shop for twenty-eight years. Rimbaud bids farewell in the final lines of *A Season in Hell:* "My great advantage is that I can laugh at old love affairs full of falsehood, and shame those deceitful couples—I saw the hell of women back there—and I shall be free to *possess the truth within one body and one soul.*"

By the age of twenty, Rimbaud's career as a literary outlaw was over. Like many rebels who came after him—such as the hippies of the 1960s—he grew up and eventually vanished into the mainstream. The remainder of his life was spent as a trader in Africa. He died at the age of thirty-seven in 1891, a year after the death of Oscar Wilde and four years before the posthumous publication of Wilde's homosexual apologia *De Profundis*.

Rimbaud had made one last halfhearted effort to contact

Verlaine, not with a proposal of renewed love but with the threat of blackmail. Ultimately, Rimbaud wanted nothing more of Verlaine and nothing more of poetry: "His concerns are now with other things, grownup things: making money. He was no longer a child. How then could he still be a poet? Together then they died, the child and the poet, abandoned, passed over, swallowed up in practicalities. And Rimbaud went off, a man half-grown, to wander through the world" (Schmidt).

Rimbaud is, debatably, the most dramatic example of the outsider, more provocative than Wilde, more mystical than Orton, more truly alienated than Genet: businessman, poet, prankster, sexual desperado, and homosexual. He lived an incredulous and paradoxical life that clearly had an immense influence on the mentality of modernity. With the possible exception of the Marquis de Sade, Rimbaud has been one of the most provocative and effectual influences on twentieth-century writers. But what does the openly gay life of his early years tell us about "homosexual sensibility"? Not very much. As Jonathan Dollimore contends, there is little question that homosexuality has been a central force in the creation of modern culture. In fact, it is difficult to discuss many aspects of the modern arts or twentieth-century popular culture without reference to gay underground activities and styles that became mainstream trends. But there is good reason to doubt that there is, as both Steiner and Sontag contend, something truly transcendent that may be called "gay sensibility." That stereotypical generalization, flattering or otherwise, is frankly sexist, if not outrightly homophobic.

> Questions abound: is this sensibility transcultural, or histori-
> cally rooted in the (varying) histories of the presentation of
> homosexuality? Is it a direct expression of homosexuality, or an
> indirect expression of its repression and/or sublimation? Is it
> defined in terms of the sexuality of (say) the individual or artist
> who expresses or possesses it—and does that mean that no
> non-homosexuals can possess/express it? (Dollimore)

How does the notion of a homosexual sensibility relate to drastically different societies with drastically different views of sexuality? Is there the slightest evidence in classical Greek literature that supports the notion that Socrates and Plato, Aristotle and Alexander, expressed themselves socially in anything like the camp mannerisms found in some New York, Paris, or Amsterdam gay bars at the end of the twentieth century?

Why do so many people wish to think of homosexuality as something more culturally and socially specific than the matter-of-fact assertion of a form of sexual conduct—a mode of behavior often identical to heterosexuality except for same-sex partners? Is homosexuality really a "lifestyle," or is it simply one of many ways in which human beings live out their very ordinary lives? In societies past and present, where same-sex partnering has not been regarded as a form of renegade sexuality, what has been the homosexual's attitude about himself or herself? Surely the answers to this question are so various that they provide nothing remotely resembling a transcultural and transtemporal "gay sensibility."

In America and Europe (and wherever Judeo-Christian evangelism has had an impact), homosexuals have necessarily become part of a subculture of sexual outlaws with certain recognizable attributes, but only in certain places and at certain times. The notion of a homosexual sensibility is a political concept, but it fails to account for the fact that homosexuals are every bit as diverse as heterosexuals in their moral values, religious attitudes, political persuasions, professional talents, familial attitudes, and social and sexual behavior. The notion of a homosexual sensibility hardly explains the diversity of attitudes of gay and lesbian people about their own identity and sexuality.

There may very well be a certain continuity of homosexual (and heterosexual) sensibility in a given culture, but in transcultural and transtemporal terms, there is little basis for formulating a universal profile that "explains" so-called gay and/or straight temperament. In short, there is no gay lingua franca.

Even the icons of gays in relatively homogeneous American

and European cultures are not as cohesive and pervasive as the straight and gay media would have us believe. And such icons have almost no parallels among homosexuals of vastly different cultures. For instance, it is virtually impossible to explain camp to homosexuals who live in rural Thailand; even when they are aware of many of Sontag's examples of camp—Bette Davis in *All About Eve*, Bellini's operas, Tiffany lamps, *Swan Lake*, Tallulah Bankhead in *Lifeboat*—still they cannot provide similar examples of camp in their own lives, because, apparently, their sexual and cultural experiences do not require the kind of travesty, impersonation, theatricality, and exaggeration found in the gay subculture of the West. Among non-Christian and traditional Zuni Indians, who have a long history of undifferentiated attitudes about sexuality and gender, it is impossible to explain or to find a parallel of Oscar Wilde's delicious comment "In matters of great importance, the vital element is not sincerity, but style." Likewise, among the sexually ambivalent men of Bali, it is unlikely that an American gay male, using the hackneyed practice of referring to males with female pronouns and female names, could get as much as a snigger from a gay Balinese youth. In short, camp does not travel well. The difference among gays of varied cultures are so enormous that they preclude the "translation" of gay humor. Whereas transvestism is usually regarded as high camp in the West, in other cultures, especially Asian cultures, it is considered to be a highly prized talent and, often, a powerful and sacred form of behavior. Even the basis of signifying gender differs greatly from place to place. In Mombasa the relationship between gender identity and sexuality is closer to that of the ancient Greeks than to that of Anglo-Americans. Gender is assigned solely on the basis of biological sex, not sexual behavior. Therefore, in Mombasa lesbians remain women and dress as women, though they are actively homosexual. In nearby Oman there is just the opposite view of sexuality. A male homosexual is looked upon as a "transsexual" and may change his gender and effectively become a woman. Here, it is the sexual act and not the sexual organs that determine gender.

What we want and what we do, in any society, is to a very great extent what we are made to want and what we are allowed to do. Perhaps the best explanation for camp is that it is, for many homosexuals living in the West or in societies influenced by the West, a mechanism for coping with their status as outsiders, and an attempt to deal with the exclusive mentality of those who make the moral rules that keep them outsiders. But camp is conditioned by the circumstances that create it. It is not a transcendent aspect of homosexuality any more than something ethnocentrically called "human nature" is a universal aspect of Homo sapiens. Camp is simply a Euro-American variation on the theme of what we are made to want and what we are allowed to do, openly or subversively.

To regard camp as a central aspect of a historic and global homosexual sensibility is virtually the same as identifying a heterosexual sensibility with *Leave It to Beaver* or *The Cosby Show*. It is a banal and culturally bound notion that fails to embrace the immense diversity of the very people it claims to epitomize. As gays have become more visible in Western society, it has become clear that there are as many gay muscle men and fragile lesbians as there are ninety-five-pound weaklings and masculine women; that there are as many gay jocks and construction workers and military leaders as there are hairdressers, costume designers, and librarians. The only overriding trait that one finds among gays in the West is their historic predicament as outsiders. And in that capacity homosexuality is a powerful metaphor of alienation and complicity. It has given rise to secret languages, outrageously overcompensative attitudes about the sexual majority, equally outrageous exaggerations about gay identity, and a unique, tragic sense of life that idealizes alienation as clandestine camaraderie and converts pain into a passion that gives some small compensation and some sense of significance to the lonely experience of outsiders.

The search for the nature of the distinctively gay sensibility can be productively redirected as an exploration of the limita-

tions of the aesthetic as conventionally understood. . . .
Rather than seeking such a sensibility in an "inner condition," we might more usefully identify it outwardly and in
relation to other strategies of survival and subversion, especially the masquerade of femininity, and the mimicry of the
colonial subject. (Dollimore)

With superb insight, Homi Bhabha argues that sexual mimicry may be viewed as a powerful strategy used against colonial
subjection—an appropriation of gender roles and a way of menac-
ing colonial influences through mockery. As such, gender mimicry
becomes, in Bhabha's memorable phrase, "at once resemblance
and menace," a political act that mediates social dominance
through extravagant theatricality and impersonation, whether it
takes the form of racial or sexual drag: white face, dutiful home-
making, corporate she-manliness, female impersonation, and that
form of gay machismo called "male impersonation."

"In imitating gender, drag implicitly reveals the imitative
structure of gender itself. . . . [Thus] gay is *not* to straight as copy
is to original, but, rather, as copy is to copy" (Butler).

Richard Dyer argues that gay machismo does much social
mischief by taking signs of masculinity and "eroticizing them in a
blatantly homosexual context." Conversely, Leo Bersani is skeptical about the subversive claims for gay machismo, regarding it not
as a mockery and repudiation of straight machismo, but as an
obsessive respect for it: Narcissus peering into the pool and desiring himself—his idealized and macho self.

Narcissism is a central aspect of both the gay and straight
male's obsession with masculinity. But whereas the straight male is
not pressured by society into justifying his imitation of exaggerated
masculinity, the gay male is faced with Western society's association of homosexuality with effeminacy, and therefore his male
excessiveness is often seen both as a disguise of his homosexuality
and as a vivid demonstration of his masculine desirability.

Narcissism may be the basis of the gay man's obsession with

male beauty and male impersonation, but, in a similar manner, Narcissus may also be a metaphor for artists as outsiders, many of whom search for a focus of their obsession with beauty in their own images, attempting to transform themselves into what they believe to be ecstatic desire, and trying to become the embodiment of that desire.

Artists transform themselves through imagination and invention. *(Je est un autre!)* The male impersonator transforms himself through emulation. *(I am what I desire!)* Both efforts, however, are a search for an experience of ecstacy.

> I would wish to emphasize that our "normal" "adjusted" state is too often the abdication of ecstasy, the betrayal of our true potentialities, that many of us are only too successful in acquiring a false self in order to adapt to the false realities [of our societies]. (Laing)

R. D. Laing would instruct us to reclaim the ecstasy and to reject the society that denies our realities. Foucault would have us take back the society by disinheriting the rulers with their own rules.

> Rules are empty in themselves, violent and unfinalized; they are impersonal and can be bent to any purpose. The successes of history belong to those who are capable of seizing these rules, to replace those who had used them, to disguise themselves so as to pervert them, invert their meaning, and redirect them against those who had initially imposed them . . . so as to overcome the rulers through their own rules. (Foucault 1977)

But I must ask: In the course of this sexual insurrection, do we lose ourselves? What becomes of the outsider—the Hanged Man? Do the strategies of subversion and confrontation deprive us of a hard won, if separate, identity? What, then, becomes of the pearl born of the afflictions of the oyster? Do we lose the child and the poet in the same instant? Does the painfully acquired metaphor of the outsider—which persistently challenges the rules—now turn into a dreadful conformity . . . an updated version of "sexual busing"? Does the empowering of sexual émigrés become just another way of getting into politics?

In *The Thief's Journal* Jean Genet says: "I am steeped in an idea of property while I loot property. I re-create the absent proprietor." The enemy transforms himself into his enemy.

In his study of R. D. Laing, Edgar Friedenberg cynically contends that "being Jewish, being Black, being gay—all these used to work wonders in establishing marginality, for those who were able to afford it. Today, they avail very little; they are just different ways of getting into politics." Friedenberg goes on to summarize Laing's decisive view of social outsiders:

> Freedom and self-realization have always been, and must remain, the concerns of an elite of some kind, self-defined by its very nature as an enemy of the people. If it is not to become merely another group, obsessed and corrupted by the demands of its own defense, then clearly it must be relatively invulnerable. . . . Wealth helps, but capitalism has done a superb job of defining wealth so that nobody ever seems sure he has enough and can keep it, especially in a state made fretful by an uneasy social conscience.

Meditating on much the same subject of politicizing and, consequently, deflecting the power of the idiosyncratic individual, T. S. Eliot put these mordant words into the mouth of Thomas Becket in his play *Murder in the Cathedral:*

> . . . *those who serve the greater cause may make the cause serve them.*

Still doing right: and striving with political men
May make that cause political, not by what they do,
But by what they are.

The Hanged Man persists as a talisman of marginality and as the metaphor of the most fundamental form of rebellion in the West, the one that arises out of the unlimited possibilities of human sexuality and passion. It is a passion generated by the intensity of mind and the voracity of body. Unfortunately for us, the miraculous body has a terrible reputation in our world. The mythology that created our repressed society has outlived the society it created. Until we are profoundly aware of that mythology we cannot change it. And until we change our myths we cannot change our minds and we cannot change our society. We must continue to repeat all of the atrocities of our interminable self-contempt.

Desire will always bear the history of its oppression. It cannot escape its reputation, because it cannot overcome its mythological past. It cannot disgorge itself from its disgust for itself. It cannot repudiate itself. But it also cannot quell its animal ferocity, because that ferocity is the marvelous and fearsome power that drives the process of life and produced us. Whatever else we may be, we are surely a momentary emanation of natural process, which embraces every possibility of life without pity or malice or moral consternation. We may wish to be angels, but we cannot be angels because angels are the echoes of a fabulous innocence we have never possessed. There was no Eden except an Eden of the mind. And there was no paradise lost, except the paradise of our animality. We are inimitable beasts who have miraculously dreamed ourselves into our little existence.

That dream is greater than our constraints. Homosexuality outrages many people because it defies their tenacious religious myths about naturalness and normality. Homosexuality haunts the public conscience because it is feared as a latent and contagious matter of choice. Yet, through all of this, homosexuality remains a profound metaphor of the unbounded possibilities of desire, just as homophobia persists as a symbol of the limits of the capacity of human beings to cherish one another.

> All desire bears its histories, the desires of the exploited and the repressed no less than the desires of those who exploit and repress. . . . In Western culture the "tragic vision" has been one of the most powerful means of containing and sublimating desire. (Dollimore)

But desire will never be completely contained or vanquished. It prowls through the shadows of all our days. It secretly groans in our languid sleep, when our bodies have dominion over our minds, resurrecting sensual images from our savage childhood. Its long memory has left its footprints in our minds. And, if we listen, it speaks to us of delights that know nothing of renunciation and evil.

Our bodies remember. Only our minds forget. And we cannot change our minds until we change our mythologies.

XV.

Death

Transformation and Identity

We are what we imagine. Our very existence consists in our imagination of ourselves. . . . The greatest tragedy that can befall us is to go unimagined.

N. Scott Momaday

The figure of a skeleton, holding a scythe, stands in a field. He is a benign character, revealing neither malice nor aggression. In most Tarot decks he simply stands and patiently awaits the endless procession of humankind. His symbolism has a surprisingly positive meaning: transformation. Given this symbolism, it is interesting to note that permanence and youthfulness are central fixations of Americans, while the most terrifying and naive fears surround the mysteries of change and death.

It was in America that the almost preposterous notion of the "individual" came into its own. The United States quickly became the symbol to Europeans and, eventually, even to tribally oriented Asian peoples, of how liberal democracy is driven by the power of individualism. Alexis de Tocqueville wrote at length about this European view of America in his famous analysis of the 1830s. To depict the effects of American liberalism on the population of the United States, Tocqueville employed the then rarified French word *individualism,* and the term was thus introduced into the English language through translation of Tocqueville's *Democracy in America.*

Americans had long prided themselves upon their sense of independence and personal identity without having a word for it, and so Tocqueville's term was introduced at an ideal time. In the decades before the Civil War, romantic connotations of dynamism and ambitiousness infused new meaning into the concept of the emancipated individual, different considerably from what the republican founding fathers of the United States had understood or meant by "personal freedom." The largely invented idea of individuality allowed Americans to be capable of far more than uncoerced options to have freedom; they also had the opportunity to develop their natural talents without regard to social rank and wealth. Eventually, even race (commencing in 1833 with the organization of the American Anti-Slavery Society) and gender (starting

215

with the suffragette movement of the turn of the century) were theoretically disavowed as barriers of the individual American's right to equal opportunity. Such equal opportunity became an ideal of individualism as it was understood in America; of all the access to equality, the most valued was education. It was education, however, of a very special kind, for it envisioned that "barbarism" and all the other deviations that separated peoples could and should be obliterated by the Western notion of knowledge—which was, by and large, capitalist and programmatic. It therefore became mandatory to be an educated individual, and all good Americans were expected to take advantage of their opportunities to become the same as everyone else and, thereby, to become as good as everybody else.

The romantic American scheme of individualism lost much of its validity as it was tested by the realities of sexual, racial, and class distinctions, and as it gave way to the consensus that some people are more equal than others. Though progress and change are high ideals of democracy, Americans typically feel somewhat uncomfortable if they are told that their attitudes or behavior has changed. Perhaps this reaction is a residue of the mythology of the Middle Ages, when it was believed that change was the work of the devil. Thus, the hidden agenda of individualism is the ideal of being uniquely and *permanently* the same person. For this reason, people are persistently urged to be individuals; and then, at every turn, they are punished if they act in an individual manner. Even the success of the individual has not been judged by the intentions or aspirations of people themselves but by bourgeois standards of success that are every bit as devastating and alienating to the individual as the mandates of behavior in nations that do not celebrate freedom and individualism.

As Paul Zweig suggests, democratic society is only the latest variation on a millennia-long fascination in the West with the cult of the individual. In the shadows of this fascination is the greatly denigrated mythic persona named Narcissus, a figure not unlike the Tarot figure of Death. Narcissus stood for a danger that has fascinated as well as repelled us for centuries: the danger that the individual will become so enamored of his mind and flesh, that society will go untended and God go unloved; or, perhaps more secretly, that each of us will go unloved. For Narcissus is never ourselves, he is always the other one who cannot see us.

We deplore his inhuman solitude, yet furtively admire him as a figure of youth, fulfillment, and personal transformation.

In the speculative fantasies of the Gnostics, in the programmatic self-indulgence of the Medieval Brethren of the Free Spirit, in the almost objectless love poem of [the troubadours of] Provence, in Adam Smith's theory of self-interest, in the radical social criticism of the nineteenth century, we find the same cult of self-love, along with the same foreboding that self-love will undermine the teetering fabric of sociability. (Zweig)

It is against this background of a contradictory individualism that artists must define themselves and must now be defined by the values of democratic societies. Those definitions are exceptionally difficult to form because America is built upon a facade of good intentions and impossible ideals—a society without access to its intrinsic consciousness. For the artist, who deals with the interior world of imagination, self-invention, and transfiguration of inner experience into outward form, America is a foreign land. And, in return, for the great majority of Americans the artist is both an alien and a narcissist, because art seems to them to be self-indulgent in its explorations of the interior world of "Self." And Self is not a conscious aspect of American individuality, because it is dismissed as morally improper egotism.

Nietzsche, along with Schopenhauer, Kierkegaard, and Burckhardt, was among the first philosophers to describe the romantic malady of the nineteenth century. "The most characteristic quality of modern man," Nietzsche said, "is the strange contrast between an inner life to which nothing outward corresponds, and an outward existence unrelated to what is within." This severe dichotomy is not a conscious part of the American mentality, because the inner life of the Self has been largely forfeited for the pragmatism of an outward existence of the individual. And without this cognizance of an inner/outer life, the arts of the twentieth century make virtually no sense, for it is essentially to this dichotomy that artists have addressed themselves.

Nietzsche did not know the works of Keats, nor was he aware of that poet's renowned celebration of Greek pottery, but his philosophical stance was antithetical to Keats's famous axiom: "Beauty is truth, truth beauty." After all, Nietzsche was a lion at the gates of Western civilization with enough "dynamite" (a term he once used to describe his philosophy) to shatter far more than a Grecian urn. "The truth," he proclaimed, "is catastrophically ugly. And as for beauty, we make it, and make it our shelter and hiding place from the ugliness of reality. We have Art in order not to perish of Truth."

In a curiously contradictory way, the idealistic delusions of American democracy are an unconscious invention—a shelter and hiding place from the ugliness of reality. But America is entirely unaware of itself as artifact. It believes itself to be the natural result of an evolutionary political process, almost a creation of God. And failing to understand that it is an artifact—an invention of fancy— it has little awareness of the inventive worth of its artists, because it believes that all things in the world are manufactured rather than created.

In the industrial world of the twentieth century, when American democracy is such a pervasive global prototype, it has become exceptionally difficult to exist as an individual with an interior vision. Every aspect of life has been externalized and rationalized in terms of a pragmatic mythology of commerce and utilitarian values. In order to vitalize a visionary imagination, artists, like mystics, must reimagine themselves—must transform themselves from "individuals" into "selves"—cognizant persons with access to an interior consciousness, and not simply a person with a political identity. But this act of transformation is exceptionally difficult, because almost none of the alternative identities available to people in nonindustrial societies are accessible to the people of the West. The stereotypes of individuals in the West are so much taken for granted that it is extremely perplexing to realize how differently other peoples see themselves. For instance, many tribal groups do not understand the concept of "identity" as something that is permanent or individual. They see themselves as part of a communal being: a *mana* or *orenda,* which is somewhat like a "group soul." They look upon dreams, hallucinations, and rituals as sources of personal and communal transformation. Such transformation is an essential aspect of tribal life. What is called "art" in the West is often viewed as the vehicle for such transformation: the song carrying the singer out of the body, the dance opening the portal through which the ineffable descends into the body of the dancer.

With rare exceptions—like the religious transformations of Catholic initiates, the metamorphosis brought about by a civilian wearing a uniform, and women who change their names, family ties, and loyalties when they are married—no personal transformations are acceptable in the West. I am reminded of *Arsenic and Old Lace* by Russell Crouse and Howard Lindsay, in which a character believes he is Teddy Roosevelt. Someone asks his sister: "Have you ever tried to tell him he isn't Teddy Roosevelt?" and she answers: "Once we tried to suggest that he was George Washington, and he just laid under his bed and wouldn't be anybody."

In a democracy that emphasizes the individual without an inner Self, a great many people are inclined to refuse to be anybody. They celebrate individuality, but they refuse to be individuals, because such a persona requires an act of the imagination. They want to discover a source of power and inspiration that will help

219

them escape the drabness of their immutable world, but what they really hope to find is some kind of science fiction that duplicates their accustomed tedium but does so with a dash of mysticism. They do not want revelation because they are afraid of all forms of change—with the exception of a cosmetic transformation of their bankrupt world into a fantasy hiding place like Disneyland, the ultimate artifact of American artifice.

Without a transformation that makes a person capable of revelation there cannot exist the incredibly simple entity we call art. For the politicized individual without the capacity for vision, art is very difficult. It is a bit like an apple. Cut it in half and it seems to be the most mysterious of objects. Yet, as the story goes, for the apple tree an apple is easy.

In the absence of a visionary sense of the interior Self, the sublime trickery of American artifice often passes as art. Contrivance replaces invention. Fashion subordinates idiosyncracy. Popularity supersedes achievement. And narcissism (because of the psychiatric overtones of the term) becomes a diagnosis rather than a metaphor of the sinuous conflict between the Self and society that has been the signature of Western cultural history (Zweig).

Yeats once said that "out of the argument with ourselves we make poetry, out of the argument with others, rhetoric." It is little wonder that there is so little poetry and so much rhetoric in America.

As Paul Zweig points out, since the time of Rimbaud, the heroes and the poets have become inseparable in Europe and America.

> Divided from the world by the violence they dream of committing upon it, heroes need new languages—styles of expression appropriate to what they have shaken loose from their own inner lives. . . . It is surely no accident that our civilization, obsessed with material progress, engaged in perpetual warfare with "nature" and thereby became isolated from it as few civilizations have been, should also have pro-

duced a repertory of languages for self-discovery, a "poetry"
on which its very politics have [presumably] been founded.

But the destiny of the heroes and poets is unclear. The poetry
of modernism has lapsed into a devouring of Self by self, and the
rise of an egotism that is infatuated with the interminable romance
of alienation and isolation. It is a mentality that bears far more
relationship to diagnostic Freudianism than it does to the process
of art. It is, as Susanne Langer declared, far more concerned
with therapeutic outbursts than it is with crafted forms of self-
expression.

At an earlier time, when James Joyce elaborated upon the
stream-of-consciousness as a novelistic technique, he achieved a
transformation of external realism into a palpable poetic style capable of describing "contours of the inner landscape, telling us what
the characters cannot tell each other because there is no way of
saying, perhaps even of knowing, such things socially" (Zweig).

But the danger of modernism and the peril of its focus upon
the neglect in the West of the interior Self has been the inclination
of art "to slip all too easily from the Self into the self; from the clear
transparency of which Kierkegaard writes, into the rehashed memories and obsessions which lie like a tangle of roots along the under
surface of experience" (Zweig).

So now we foresee a future that will be overwhelmed by the
conflict between superficial individualism and artistic egotism. We
are uncomfortable with the conformity of political individualism,
with the censure of authoritarian religion, and with the double-talk
of both conservative and liberal social justice. At the same time, we
are distrustful of the sentimentality that now surrounds the poetry
of alienation. We are dismayed by the immense artistic digressions
of ego, which have so little resonance that they betray a scope and
vision even smaller than the archaic American notion of the externalized and unchanging individual.

We are faced with a government and clergy that have been all
but oblivious to art for two hundred years, but now are making

moral judgments about it. And we are equally confronted by artists who, lacking a vision of their own, delight in antagonizing the censors by producing political art that condemns politicians in art. And all the while, the figure of Death patiently watches over the endless procession of humankind, pointing the way toward a crucial transformation into a new world we cannot yet imagine.

XVI.

Temperance

Myths of Morality

You have to imagine how the fellow in the loony bin who thinks he's Jesus feels on meeting an inmate who agrees with him because he thinks he's Pontius Pilate. They may be enemies, but they're also co-conspirators.

Henry Louis Gates, Jr.

The winged female figure of Temperance pours water from one urn to another meticulously, making certain that none of the water is spilled. Usually one of her feet stands on earth; the other stands in water. As a symbol of abstinence and restraint, the Tarot card depicting Temperance introduces the uneasy relationship between social morality and artistic freedom, and epitomizes the battle of free expression against the barriers that moralists erect around the arts.

Such barriers are a prevalent and contradictory aspect of America, a nation renowned for both its respect and violation of individual liberties. Nothing is a better analogy of these struggles between freedom and artistic restraint than the inevitable intrusion upon the American landscape of unsightly fences, railings, and barriers that mar every scenic vista.

Here we stand in the land of some of the most spectacular natural scenery on earth, and yet we are confronted with endless miles of obstacles that are erected to protect us from falling off cliffs and slipping down pathways because, apparently, we are too clumsy and too stupid to protect ourselves and our children from perfectly avoidable accidents.

There are treacherous cliffs and precipices on the Greek Islands, climbed and donkeyed by millions of tourists each year. There are bottomless lakes in the grottoes of Croatia, fearsomely hot geysers and mud pots in Iceland, ferocious fishes and caimans in the Amazon River, precarious slopes high above the fjords of Norway, and steep, jagged promontories on the coastline of Cornwall—yet there are no fences.

We can only speculate about the reasons for the lack of barriers and the apparent "neglect of public safety" that we find beyond the borders of the United States. It seems to be based on several factors, not the least of which is the absence in other nations of the American obsession with civil suits. But the fundamental rationale for open rather than confined spaces is an aesthetic priority that favors access to the spectacles of nature rather than a social atmosphere akin to the cautionary design of a playpen.

The analogy of social barriers raises an inevitable question: Does such openness result in occasional mishaps? Of course it does, because danger is an intrinsic aspect of an open society, and risk is the essence of liberty. Laws only facilitate safety and limit degrees of risk and danger, but laws cannot entirely eliminate risk and danger from any society without depriving its citizens of freedom.

In America, however, there is a dumbfounding preoccupation with both fences and prohibitions, motivated, apparently, by the paternalistic inclination in the United States to protect us from ourselves. And here we come upon a central problem of the arts in a nation with a vocal dedication to liberty as well as a fixation about censorship and repression that lingers from its historic links with the notorious Puritan purges under the rule of England's Anglican King James I.

That dissenting puritanical tradition of England became an implicit aspect of the American mentality from the time of the founding of the colonies. In 1620 a small body of Puritans boarded the *Mayflower* and sailed for America. In New England they ruled with stubborn, humorless authority, enforcing fines, public flogging, and the stocks for any resistance to their rules against levity. America's future would be forever influenced by that Puritan mentality, which, among its many strictures, disavowed sensual pleasures and amusements, constellating the American neglect of artistic imagination and clouding the differences between art and entertainment.

Though Puritan repression remained a strong influence in New England, in the rest of the ever-widening American territories, rustic melodramas and dances were the staple of American entertainment. Artistic dance forms were practically nonexistent, even in the cultivated eastern cities of America, until the 1900s. In painting, the emphasis was on religious subject matter and military and high-class portraiture.

226

> The seventeenth-century mind in New England was wrapped up in "a deep sight into the mystery of God's grace, and man's corruption, and large apprehensions of these things," as the Reverend John Norton, pastor of the First Church in Boston, said of his colleague, John Cotton. To these men the world was evil and transient. (Richardson)

There was no art of landscape based upon a sense of the sublime in nature, nor of genre studies, based upon delight in daily life. Such sensual imagery was not possible for the semimedieval mind of Puritan America. "The Puritan vision of the ideal world of faith was embodied only in stern words, in religious books, or sermons. To embody it in the mere concrete images of painting was distrusted as 'papistical,' " and any inference of the authority of the Vatican was a considerable threat to Puritan ideas, which were staunchly anti-Catholic (Richardson).

Eventually the Puritan moral influence was felt throughout America. Until the midnineteenth century, games and sports were considered sinful unless they were associated with some kind of utilitarian function, rather than being a matter of diversion and sensual delight. For this reason, the amusements of most early Americans were activities like barn raising, corn husking, log-splitting contests, and other "sports" that seemed to "achieve something" (Mandell). So it is not unexpected that, even today, in the United States it is taken for granted that the "authorities" have the paternalistic obligation to make rules that restrict acts of pleasure, even when those rules impede the rights of adult individuals in making their own moral judgments and conducting themselves in privacy as they wish to conduct themselves.

That inclination to interfere with our private lives is only one aspect of the American mentality. At the same time that authorities are trying to legislate morality, they are giving patriotic speeches about the inalienable rights of the individual. This contradiction affects our lives at every turn. As travelers we should be appalled by the presumption that we are not smart enough to stay a respectful distance from the brink of the Grand Canyon. As artists we should be revolted by the attitude of Kafkaesque politicos and bureaucrats who wish to place limits on the themes, images, language, and styles of our creative efforts.

There is, of course, the inevitable "other side" in this debate about regulation. It, briefly, insists that *some of us* are not equipped to make decisions about what is best for us, especially in a free society where certain unsavory people use their freedom of expression to poison the national consciousness with prejudice and bias, whether that prejudice and bias is a matter of sexism and racism, on one hand, or atheism and sexual diversity and explicitness, on the other. According to this argument, which comes equally from the right and the left, freedom of expression in the arts, like freedom of movement in scenic landscapes, is dangerous and must therefore be "fenced."

This debate about morality and art declares, variously, that a masterful film like *The Birth of a Nation* should not be shown because of its offensively racist attitudes and images; and a commercial film like *Terminator II* should not be shown because of its sexism and gratuitous violence; and a provocative film like *My Own Private Idaho* should not be shown because of its explicit and implied homosexuality.

Each side of the debate insists that such control of the arts and media is intended to protect society from those who would reenforce unsavory and antisocial points of view. But what will be the basis of this obstructionist control? The answer, of course, is that these limits should be based on the biases of the politicos, bureaucrats, and evangelists who profess to know what is best for us.

Robert Hughes (1993) makes quick work of the issue of censorship in the arts: "If someone agrees with us on the aims and uses of culture, we think him objective; if not, we accuse him of politicizing the debate. In fact, political agendas are everywhere."

In the broadest sense of the word, such political agendas are the expressions of paradigms—social mythologies that are the basis of our various belief systems. For instance, liberals (at least among extreme factions) promote an agenda no less aimed at imposing controls and limits of expression in the arts than extreme conservatives. Every political and moral position seems to want to erect a fence around a favorite enemy.

In the arts, these debates about correctness are nothing new. They have been under way for centuries, ever since "art" became an activity separate from the ritualistic and religious infrastructures of societies, and ceased to be the expression of communal values that were largely or entirely unchallenged by individuals or factions within the community. But a new philosophical element has arisen since the turn of the twentieth century, when, in America particularly, the entire basis upon which moral judgments are made was radically explored and contested by anthropologists.

The result of this exploration is a philosophical stance called ethical relativism. It is a principle first suggested by the German-American anthropologist Franz Boas, who introduced the concept that all experience is interpreted by people in terms of their own backgrounds, frames of reference, and social norms, and that these factors will influence perception and evaluations, so that there is no single scale of values applicable to all situations and all societies. "It proposes a theory of value according to which we should respect other ways of life. Behind this value in turn is the basic moral belief that people ought to be free to live as they choose" (Hatch). The relativist position is admirable, but it also opens the door to a tremendous moral dilemma.

> Boasian thought does not provide suitable grounds to justify the assertion about the intrinsic worth of all people and all cultures. We are left without a response to the question why we should be tolerant, hence we face the dilemma of having a potentially worthy moral theory but no good reason for adhering to it. . . . To say that values vary from [person to person and from] culture to culture is to describe (accurately or not) an empirical state of affairs in the real world, whereas the call for tolerance is a value judgment of what ought to be,

and it is logically impossible to derive the one from the other. The fact of moral diversity no more compels our approval of other ways of life than the existence of cancer compels us to value ill health. (Hatch)

In the 1930s, anthropologist Ruth Benedict tried to clarify these problems in her classic work *Patterns of Culture*. Among many other subjects, she dealt with large moral issues, attempting to stick to relativist attitudes, but inevitably reaching conclusions built on the kind of value judgments that the relativists abhor. In evaluating cultures, Benedict used a variety of criteria, such as happiness. For instance, she proposed that the Zuni Indians of the American Southwest were what she called "mildly happy," whereas the Puritans of colonial New England exhibited a strong "sense of guilt." Another of Benedict's criteria was the presence or absence of coercion in a society. The Zuni Indians, she contended, are relatively free of coercion, so the people enjoy "freedom from any form of social exploitation or of social sadism, . . . a society willing to live and let live, . . . but they have few outlets for personal initiative and consequently lack vigor as individuals" (Benedict).

On the other hand, the rivalry among the Kwakiutl Indians of the Northwest Coast of North America contributed a "vigor and zeal" to their lives that the Zuni lacked. "But this was bought at high cost—a limitation of the peoples' freedom" (Hatch). The Kwakiutl engaged in a highly competitive ritual called potlatch, in which they vied for rank by giving away and by destroying vast amounts of personal property as ostentatious proof of their wealth. The potlatch literally bankrupted the tribe and was socially ruinous as a contest of power.

Another approach that Benedict used to explore ethical relativism was the discussion of the abnormal in societies.

By the abnormal she meant the person whose natural inclinations or abilities run in a different direction from that in which the culture is moving, and who therefore is unrewarded, unsuccessful, and frustrated. An example is the homosexual who lives in a society in which homosexuality is regarded as a perversion. Benedict wrote that the homosexual's "guilt, his sense of inadequacy, his failures, are consequences of the disrepute which social tradition visits upon him, and few people can achieve a satisfactory life unsupported by the standards of their society." Here it is culture that does the tyrannizing—or more accurately the "normal" members of society do so in expressing their culture's values. And Benedict was not neutral about this tyranny, for she recommended tolerance toward those who deviate from the cultural standard. She even speculated that "it is probable that social orders of the future will carry this tolerance and encouragement of individual difference much further than any culture of which we have experience." (Hatch)

What Benedict anticipated was a time when the tyranny of tradition would decline. But, for all the benevolence of her ethical position, she offered no rational basis for it beyond the kind of value judgments that relativists—with their live and let live stance—are not supposed to make about other cultures and other persons.

The credibility of ethical relativism shifted drastically with World War II, which was a bitter experience pervasive in the lives of virtually all the peoples of the world, providing the greatest lesson in cultural difference the world had ever known. World War II was a moral embarrassment to ethical relativism for two reasons. First, it was necessary to face the question of reasonable limits of the tolerance of one culture for the standards of another culture. Second, the ghastliness of the war and of its war crimes aroused a widely held belief that it was urgently necessary to attempt to arrive at ultimate, international, and transcultural values, such as those of freedom and humanity (Hatch).

Absolute ethical relativism insists that its agenda of "live and let live" means that no person or society has the right to intrude upon the activities of another person or another society, no matter how immoral or inhumane we may consider the activities of that person or society in terms of our own ethical standards. At the turn of the twentieth century, the relativism precept had been a welcome change from the colonialist attitudes that denigrated tribal cultures and placed Europeans and Americans at the crown of creation. But after World War II, the relativism position was no longer endurable, because it seemed to have no means of repudiating global aggression. So several humanistic alternatives to absolute relativism were suggested: It is good to treat people well; we should not do one another harm; people ought to enjoy a reasonable level of material existence (Redfield).

The obvious virtues of such humanistic principles are self-evident until we begin to test them against experience, by asking both philosophical and practical questions about how, exactly, these noble principles are to be applied. How does the belief that people ought to enjoy a reasonable level of material existence affect societies that are capitalist? How does the premise that people should not harm one another affect cultures in which head-hunting and cannibalism are intrinsic ritual acts? If the definition of ethical behavior is not god given or the result of provable and universal and transcultural values of good and evil, how can we justify any specific code of behavior? Apparently we cannot. And that leaves us in the dilemma of accepting any judgment as a value judgment with no claim to universality. Morality becomes an ethical procedure not unlike the legal process by which we create traffic regulations: rules admittedly without divine sanction or social permanence; built, necessarily, upon an unprovable humanistic alternative to anarchy. Without the assistance of divinity or some other source of absolute truth, morality becomes a very dangerous business, and that takes us back to the analogy of a world without fences. So once again we must ask: Does such openness result in occasional mishaps? Does it mean that some bluntly obscene and politically offensive arts and entertainments will find their way into public? Does it mean that mercenary producers will create television programs that exploit voyeurism and violence? Of course it does, because danger is an intrinsic aspect of an open society, and risk is the essence of liberty. Laws only facilitate safety and limit degrees of risk and danger, but laws cannot entirely eliminate offense and jeopardy from any society without depriving its citizens of freedom. Ultimately we must take responsibility for our own values—deciding what things we will and will not allow ourselves or our children to experience—rather than asking our government to legislate decisions that should be made by individuals.

Beyond this brief history of anthropological paradigms that govern social regulations and cultural interactions is the large and controversial issue of art and censorship. And I can offer only one response to that quandary. It seems to me that, despite innumerable possible social perils, the artist must be defended against fences. Like all moral positions, my position is not an emanation of absolute truth, but it does have credence as an interpretation of the humanistic principles that, in the wake of the collapse of religious and political mythologies, seem to be the only basis available to us for living with some degree of sanity in a tumultuous world.

For the artist, the world is a model. So at its most naive, censorship in the arts is a bit like one of Picasso's models looking at the way he painted her and exclaiming, "That's ugly and grotesque. That isn't me. I don't want to be represented like that. So I want the painting destroyed or, at the very least, I want it withheld from public view."

The model may feel that the painting maligns and defames her, that it misrepresents and slanders her. But the model is not the work of art. She is only its point of departure. The world cannot dictate to the work of art. Only the artist can determine how he or she is going to represent the world. *That is what the artist does.* And if the artist is not allowed to do that, then he or she cannot do anything. If there are any constraints about the way in which artists may represent the world, then censorship becomes a relentless, unstoppable social mechanism, because censorship is not quantifiable: There is no such thing as *limited* censorship. Either there is censorship or there is *no* censorship. Rules may qualify the openness of a society, but they do so at great risk to our freedom. We can set up regulations that limit audiences by fencing the entrance without fencing the arts, by excluding unattended infants and unaccompanied minors from activities that we believe confront them with potential confusion or harm. We can outlaw forms of entertainment and art that exploit children, simply because we have a certain international consensus about both the definition of who is a minor and how minors should be treated. But the risks become insurmountable if we attempt to delimit the arts beyond such fundamental concerns for young people and for the reasonable privacy of people who do not wish to be *confronted* by what offends them. (And here the word *confronted* specifically means the action of *forcing* an experience upon someone who does not have the capacity to turn away, to stay away, to change the station, or to close the windows and pull the blinds.)

What I am saying is that art is responsible to nothing but the imagination. Yet I do not want to seem to support the nineteenth-century preoccupation with art for art's sake. To the contrary, I believe that art has a wide range of responsibilities, but they are responsibilities quite different from those that we identify, for instance, with governance. A major problem in the arts in the 1980s and 1990s has been the inclination of people (especially people with little or no artistic experience) to impose the values of governance upon the arts. Such values—social relevance, political correctness, responsibility, and communal and global involvement—are essential to governance and social doctrine, but, no matter their great importance in human affairs, they are not and should not be artistic issues. Democracy is a grand ideal that has attained almost universal approval in the twentieth century, but our devotion to democracy has tempted us to democratize fields that are diminished by democratic precepts. *The Yellow River Concerto* was composed by a committee of Chinese composers. It was an effort of Chinese communism to communalize or democratize music—to eliminate its emphasis upon the creative power of the individual and to abolish artistic elitism—yet it was an artistic disaster for all the very obvious reasons. Art by committee cannot work in China any better than it worked in Stalin's Soviet Union. Governance is concerned with the relationship of the individual to the group. Art, like noninstitutional religion and conceptual science, is concerned with the revelations of an individual. Art is not group therapy. It is not a societal process. There is absolutely nothing democratic about the process of revelation or art. At least in the Western world (which is the only world preoccupied with the social implications of the arts), the "group" has no role in revelation, yet the group is often greatly benefited by the revelations of individuals. The basis of art is not morality but imagination and revelation. Art is a way of comprehending experience. It is not a way of acting out or prescribing experience. Art may imply morality, but it is not itself moral or immoral. Morality is the focus of those who can see nothing but the content of art. But in art the content is totally absorbed by the technique and conception of the artwork, and the technique and conception, in turn, are totally absorbed by the content. As Thomas Mann, a very socially responsible writer, said: Art is the place where thought and feeling merge. At such a place morality is implied, but it is not explicit. When art becomes explicit, it ceases to be art and becomes propaganda. Zola was apparently unaware of this danger, but somehow succeeded in creating works of art that ignored his own naturalistic theories of art. He became so intent upon penetrating the social fabric of his time that he superseded it and produced novels with profoundly nonsocial textures. There is evil art. There is such a thing as a deliberately moral art such as the conspicuously doctrinaire play *Everyman*. But neither good nor evil has anything to do with what makes art what art is.

Given the tenuousness of moral judgments about art and the distinction of art from morality, what then do we do with someone like D. W. Griffith, a brilliant American filmmaker who produced a film like *The Birth of a Nation*? The epic film was based on a thoroughly repugnant and insipid novel that glorified the Ku Klux Klan, depicting white men in blackface playing African Americans. The brilliant climactic scene depicts the Klan in sheets and hoods dashing on horseback to the aid of white women who are supposedly being savaged by a group of African Americans. It is a completely repulsive scenario, and yet it is one of the most important films of cinematic history, having influenced every major director since its release in 1915.

> From his opening titles in which he states that the "bringing of the African to America sowed the first seed of disunion" to his concluding sequences in which the Ku Klux Klan ride to save some besieged whites, his aim is to show the Negro as the greatest danger to the values he most cherished. Iris Barry, in her monograph on [Griffith], tried unsuccessfully to extenuate his racism by seeing it as a consequence of his [Southern] culture. . . . His racism comes over neither as some thoughtless reflection of views dinned into him since childhood nor as some imposed message that audiences can learn to disregard, but as a malevolence that suffuses the whole action; and allied as it is with his gift for persuasion, it results in a propaganda as noxious as the anti-Semitism of the Nazi film *The Swiss Jew.* (Rhode)

Writing in the midtwenties, H. L. Mencken, himself an avid anti-Semite and racist, was nonetheless outspoken in his criticism of Griffith. "In 1915," he correctly noted, "the Ku Klux Klan was unheard of, but [now] in 1925, it is one of the most powerful factors in American life," a situation that many attribute to the propagandistic impact of Griffith's *The Birth of a Nation.*

Given the power of art to influence public opinion, to confirm the terrible biases of fanatic groups, and to shape the mentality of the young, how can the continued exhibition of Griffith's film be justified?

It is justified because the film is a triumph of cinematic art, a dangerous cliff over which countless people may fall in the absence of a fence, but a vision so sublime that it must not be obscured by barriers. The merits of the film are worth its social risks. It is a masterwork that should be exhibited in a context that celebrates its achievements and deplores its social faults. It should be an example of the realities of moral duplexity in human beings, who are capable of both noble creation and obnoxious bias. The racism of the film should be actively challenged by debate and discussion rather than being shut away as if it did not exist—when, in fact, both the film and the ugliness it espouses do exist.

The Birth of a Nation is remarkable for its use of natural settings, its epic proportions, its innovations in editing and cross-cutting. The high point of the film is the Battle of Petersburg. The burning of Atlanta with lines of refugees on the roads, intercut with scenes of violent fighting, is handled superbly; the sequence concludes focused on a field covered with the dead, as night falls. It is positively baffling that such intense sympathy as Griffith exhibits in such poignant scenes could have been expressed by a man with rabid racist attitudes. In fact, one of the most fascinating extra-artistic approaches to the film is its exceptional contradictions and what it reveals about the artistic process in relation to individual psychology. For instance, Griffith was so distressed and confused by the demonstrations against the racism of the film in New York, Chicago, and Boston that in a subsequent film, *Hearts of the World,* he showed a white soldier kissing his wounded black comrade, and in a film like *Intolerance* (1916), where he was not dealing with his blind prejudice as a Southern racist, he showed himself to be both extraordinarily liberal and progressive in his social attitudes (Sadoul).

What does one say about a work of art that was one of the milestones of cinema—and that is absolutely repugnant in its treatment of African Americans? I don't think there is an easy answer to this question, and that lack of a decisive answer is why great caution is needed when we formulate our attitudes about *The Birth of a Nation.* I know, however, that the answer is not "Throw it away!" I am certain that the answer is not "Ban it! Confiscate and destroy it!" Because if those are our answers, then we are in great trouble. The momentum of censorship is uncontrollable. It takes on a life of its own. It facilitates equally social concern and social domination. If liberals insist upon banning *The Birth of a Nation* because they are offended by its racism, then fundamentalists must have an equal right to ban films that offend them, like the explicitly homoerotic *My Own Private Idaho* by Gus Van Sant or Martin Scorsese's revisionist view of Jesus in *The Last Temptation of Christ.* It is not a crime to contest or ridicule someone's beliefs. It is a privilege of liberty.

The possible offense that is generated by a work of art is often a matter of the viewer's failure to grasp the work in its entire context. The "messages" of art are only its lyrics, but the words alone are not the song. To understand the words out of the context of the song is like hearing the notes but not the music. There is a difference between journalism and art. To approach art journalistically results in the same confusion that results when we try to explain a metaphor in concrete terms. We miss the point and arrive at a great many mistaken conclusions. Journalism has its place. But art is not responsible to journalism. For art to be relevant does not mean that it has to turn into journalism. It can remain metaphoric—which is where its real power resides. Journalism is concerned with the relevant moment. Art has a wider focus that reflects a wider temporal mentality. That is why yesterday's newspapers are used to line garbage cans and art remains vital and experiential for centuries after its creation. One is entirely perishable while the other resonates beyond its own time and place. Beyond the facts. Beyond the issues. Beyond the moment. Even beyond the crises we think we will not survive.

There are a great many politically adventurous people in academia, in the African-American world, in the world of Latinos and Native Americans, in the world of women and gays, who are deeply resentful of the arts. They want art to abide by politically dictated attitudes. They say that they want art to reflect life as it is lived. Of course, what they really mean is *life as they believe it is lived* or as they personally experience it. But art is not responsible to such demands. If it were, it would be the equivalent of painting by numbers.

Art has a responsibility only to the imagination of the artist, and if we don't like what is produced, then we don't have to buy it or to look at it. Society and its various zealots have a great many appropriate ways of expressing their dissatisfaction with the arts. But for us to build fences around art is unthinkable. Too often in the past we have undertaken disastrous actions in the name of decency or faith or political creed. The whole world of the Maya vanished in 1562, when a self-righteous zealot, the Bishop Diego De Landa, piled hundreds of Maya "books" in the square of the city of Mani (Yucatán) and burned them. This was probably the single greatest loss of historical documents since the burning of the Library of Alexandria. Yet it was carried out in the name of God. Equally horrendous were the book burnings of the Nazis, carried out in the name of what was in the German context a politically correct action.

We are given not only the privilege to be free, but also the responsibility of freedom. And freedom is inherently dangerous. Most of us idealize it as a social paragon, but, at the same time, we want no part of it in our own lives, because it requires us to make constant political and moral decisions. If we still believed in the absolute answers to social questions that religious and political mythologies once provided, we would not be called upon to determine the political and moral course of our actions. We would have the exquisite comfort of an informing paradigm that automatically clarifies all of our questions about morality. But those absolutes are gone. And what remains is a highly transient and utilitarian frame of mind that tries to sort out the possibilities of the world—often erroneously and destructively.

Given the limits of our perspective and the long catalog of errors and atrocities we have been capable of committing in the name of morality and social justice, we must regard the inclination

239

to control ideas with great caution. Given the fact that the arts have persistently outlived political schemes and scientific truths, we must resist the proclivity to raise barriers around the freedom of expression. It is a devastating idea that any of us be allowed—whatever the basis of our political ideals and no matter how urgent they may seem to us—to determine what people in the present and future may and may not think or see or feel or read.

The future flows through the unfettered landscape of the present. We cannot imperil the lives of those who are not yet born by building barriers that impede the free flow of ideas and art from one generation to the next. We cannot build fences. We must face the risks of an open mind.

XVII.

The Devil

Play as Mythology

It seems highly significant that in none of the mythologies known to me has play been embodied in a divine or demonic figure, while on the other hand the gods are often represented as playing.

Johan Huizinga

The Devil of the Tarot deck is depicted as a grotesque creature that seems to be assembled from erratic and random parts: the horns of a ram and the breasts and arms of a woman on the body of a man. It has hairy legs and the hooves of a goat, a lizard tail and bat wings. It stands on a cubic stone to which are chained two small satyrs. The symbolism of the Devil includes such elements as controversy, shock, and bizarre influences, which provide an introduction to the subject of this chapter: a survey of nonverbal art forms that have merged so-called high art and low art to become the most influential aspect of youth culture.

Youth is associated with the spirit of play. The Greeks even had a specific grammatical ending—*inda*—designating the special kind of play that is undertaken by the young: *sphairinda*, to play at ball; *helkustinda*, to play at tug-of-war. But the Greeks also understood that play is not simply a childhood activity. It is serious business. And they had "no less than three different words for play in general. . . . And the Greeks do not stand alone in the matter of play. Sanskrit too has at least four verbal roots for the play-concept" (Huizinga).

To our way of thinking, play is the opposite of seriousness. Yet on close examination we find many forms of play that are undertaken with the utmost seriousness: chess and football are played with solemn concentration. "The players have not the slightest inclination to laugh" (Huizinga). In other words, play is not a laughing matter.

But as we have already seen, puritanism in America and England resulted in a negative attitude about "playing." To waste time is "to play around." To dally with someone without respect is to treat that person like a "play-thing." Play is also a form of trickery: "to play dumb" or "to play dead." It is also an act of imaginary transformation: "to play a role." In fact, the entire art of the playwright, devoted to simulating the personalities, emotions, speech, and events of life, is called "a play." The punsters and poets are skilled at something called a "play on words." We also "play" an instrument, which represents an action with some degree of dignity in the West; it is not usually considered merely a matter of "playing around." But, in general, play represents frivolity and indulgence, an activity unjustified by the only forms of endeavor that are morally acceptable in many cultures: namely, work and worship.

Perhaps play has this bad reputation because it is such a decisive link between human beings and other mammals—which universally engage in play. Even the most ferocious creatures engage in play, especially when they are young, but also when they mature. In human cultures, play is manifested in a great variety of activities: tournaments and masquerades, pageants, dance and music, theatrical and ritual performances, exhibitions, contests and races. It is characterized by a spirit of both engagement and liberation. It is, indeed, very serious business. Yet play is an activity that achieves nothing in a utilitarian sense. Undoubtedly that is why it is frowned upon by highly utilitarian societies that look upon it as childish action with no valuable consequences. And this is also at least one of the reasons that the efforts of artists are often regarded as pointless play that achieves nothing—except in those rare moments when an artwork, such as a painting, fetches an enormous price at public auction, a financial success that mystifies most people. Yet, incongruously, we also designate the efforts of artists as *works* of art—a term which seems to justify artistic effort by associating them with labor. In this way, art and play have much the same reputations in Western cultures: They are viewed as being pointless activities without mercenary, religious, or socially significant motive or effect.

Though the impulse to play may evolve into complex civic and religious forms, such as rituals and warfare, in its primordial form it is an activity uniquely without biological necessity or moral duty. It is not simply the result of animal energy. It is too complex to be merely an outburst of stamina. To the contrary, it is an activity of leisure.

Here, then, we have the first main characteristic of play: that it is free, is in fact freedom. A second characteristic is that play is not "ordinary" or "real" life. It is rather a stepping out of "real" life into a temporary sphere of activity with a disposition all of its own. Nevertheless, the consciousness of play being "only a pretense" does not by any means prevent it from proceeding with the utmost seriousness, with an absorption, a devotion that passes into rapture. (Huizinga)

So intense is the act of play, and so sublime the levels of consciousness it is capable of arousing in its participants, that we have created special terms like "spoilsport" to describe those who break the magic world of the game.

By withdrawing from the game [the spoilsport] reveals the relativity and fragility of the play-world. He robs play of its *illusion*—a pregnant word which means literally "in-play" (from *ilusion, illudere* or *inludere*). . . . The outlaw, the revolutionary, the cabbalist or member of a secret society, indeed heretics of all kinds are a highly associative if not sociable disposition, and a certain element of play is prominent in all their doings. . . . Inside the circle of the game the laws and customs of ordinary life no longer count. We are different and do things differently. (Huizinga)

This special game world reminds us of Rimbaud and Verlaine, those make-believe outlaws who fabricated imaginary murders and robberies. We are reminded of the brother and sister of Cocteau's *Les Enfants terribles* and their mischievous and tragic diversions. And we are also reminded of various amusements of today's youth: collegiate games such as "Dungeons and Dragons," media game worlds such as Nintendo, as well as seemingly pointless activities that generate tremendous concentration and skill, such as break dancing, voguing, playing pinball, or using a skateboard. What is fascinating about all of these activities is the fact that they were created out of unique American street styles taken from the worlds of urban Blacks, Hispanics, homosexuals, and the ever-growing subculture of homeless adolescents.

When social commentators wish to defame American society or denounce the decline of literacy and lament the death of canonical education, they inevitably point to the activities and amusements of youth, which they denounce as mindless and pointless. As it turns out, they are wrong.

It is possible that there is a far greater relationship between the use of a skateboard and experimental theater and dance than there is between the latter and traditional ballet. It is equally possible that MTV has a great deal in common with postmodern visual and performance art, because it represents an entirely new and radical way of comprehending time and space and depicting dramatic action, and it is having an immense experiential (and not merely an intellectual) impact on a huge audience.

A couple of decades ago it was possible to speak of something called pop art. Today that designation has become obsolete because the doctrinaire distinctions between so-called high and low art have been steadfastly blurred, and elements of street culture have entered every aspect of mainstream art at the same time that elements of mainstream artistic invention have found their way into street culture. The designation of something called pop art suggested a discrete style: the marriage of pop and art. In contrast, the work of someone like Larry Fuente (for instance, his 1975 piece called *Derby Racer*) makes no distinction between a sculpture and an automobile. Created of beads, buttons, rhinestones, costume jewelry, guitars, tennis rackets, ceramics, mirrors, feathers, and spark plugs set in epoxy resins over a fiberglass base on a 1960 Berkeley (a British sports car), *Derby Racer* transforms the "idol" of a costly automobile into a celebration of the street and a protest to our materialistic society of extravagant objects that provide a false sense of status and eminence. The street object is transmuted by Fuente's Latino baroque sensibility. "The transformation of cars into works of art," he tells us, "is a manifestation of my belief that art should be more accessible to the general public than is permitted by gallery and museum showings, and that the street provides a perfect format" (Lippard 1990).

The "junk theater" of Paul Zaloom also makes use of every-day toys and objects. He manipulates them in an infinitely imaginative and satirical manner during his uproarious performances commenting on contemporary society. He also uses technological devices, such as an overhead projector (inherited from 1960s light shows), and the pop techniques of standup comedy to forge a delightful but highly caustic and reflective theater experience.

In the spontaneity, nonchalance, and vernacular of the theater works of performers like Meredith Monk, Bebe Miller, Kei Takei, the Urban Bush Women, and Trisha Brown we find ordinary street movement as well as performing attitudes that were invented by break dancers, voguers, and other disco performers who excel in animal grace and energy without much reference to the careful "body line" and avowed discipline and grace of older forms of ballet and dance. The street has taken over the dance theater at the same time that much of the style of popular dancing has been derived from theater and television.

The wide distribution of music videos by MTV and other pop music television channels has revolutionized the way young people look at images and motion—and ultimately the way they look at cinema and visual arts in general. That radical change in perception has spilled over into all the other arts and entertainments, and, finally, it too has overflowed into life on the street, resulting, for instance, in the great popularity of images such as those created by Keith Haring that, a decade earlier, would have been regarded as incomprehensible and avant-garde. Even print and television advertising has been fundamentally transformed by this new spatial and temporal imagination of the young.

The point is that youth culture has had as extensive and subversive an influence upon mainstream society and the arts as the Dadaists and symbolists did during earlier decades of this century. One need only think of visual artists Salvador Dalí, Meret Oppen-heim, René Magritte, or later modernists such as Richard Hamilton, Roy Lichtenstein, Claes Oldenburg, and, of course, Andy Warhol to find endless parallels between the playfulness of the former avant-garde and today's youth culture.

Despite the almost universal attitude that young people are illiterate and uninformed and committed to mindless activities, the truth is that through their game world and the seriousness of play they have forged a revolutionary kind of intelligence that has never before been seen in the West. It is true that the great majority of high school students cannot and do not read and know very little about history or current events, and, surely, that is lamentable, but it is equally true that they have achieved levels of consciousness that cannot be found readily among adults. Surely, some kind of creative application should be made of that achievement, including a recognition of its new form of abstract expertise.

At the end of the twentieth century, we need to take a careful look at what once passed for "mere play." The skateboard is a toy, but it is also a wheeled dance stage upon which young men and women perform the most startling and expressive technical feats, with a concentration and imagination seldom encountered in the endless and clumsy community revivals of *Swan Lake*. In the technopop music that began in Europe in the 1980s and now dominates American dance sound, there is the use of a wide spectrum of electronic and natural sounds previously encountered only in the most rarified works of Steve Reich, Karlheinz Stockhausen, Edgard Varèse, and Morton Subotnick. In the exceptionally sparse lyrics of most pop music of the 1990s (often consisting of four or five words repeated constantly over mesmerizing rhythmical variations) there is a redundance and minimalism and abstract use of words reminiscent of the writings of Gertrude Stein. This same reductionist approach to language is found in the libretto of the Robert Wilson and Philip Glass opera *Einstein on the Beach*, which has been immensely influential in both concert and pop music and performance art. Another element of the impact of the street is found in director Peter Sellars's vernacular productions of the operas of Mozart.

In music videos there is a greater use of abstract time and space—in which cause and effect are entirely jettisoned in favor of an associative and stream-of-consciousness progression from image to image and from action to action—than one finds in the most daring films of David Lynch, Stanley Kubrick, Jean-Luc Godard, Luis Buñuel, Pier Paolo Pasolini, Michelangelo Antonioni, or Federico Fellini. True, the substantive content of music videos may be unimpressive, but their intellectual implications and innovative techniques and mind-bending forms and styles are both significant and artistically exquisite—unquestionably the most imaginative and daring images on the television and movie screens today. In fact, the kind of visual intelligence that music videos have fostered in an entire generation of viewers makes it possible for an immense new audience to look at major films, paintings, sculpture, and theater works that were once admired by only a tiny audience of devotees.

The world of the street has created a major shift in the paradigms that define and then redefine both art and artistic process. This shift amounts to a fundamental revision of the mythology that informs the sensibility of artists and makes it possible for them to discover the visions and revelations that are the basis of their arts. This new mythology is built upon attitudes and icons that are only now being fully defined; so it is possible to survey them only tenuously.

Because of its ability to parody and annihilate sexual attitudes and taboos, camp plays a central role in our emerging mythology, as do many other aspects of the homosexual subculture—everything from s/m leather and studded drag to gay pop icons such as "Bette Davis Eyes." Voguing, a term referring to the fantastic activities of gay dance parties in Black and Hispanic communities (often involving drag), is playfully explicit in its embrace of every sort of sexuality. Another element of the new mythology is the tendency to idolize women who act like men pretending to be women, such as the gender-bending and gender-excessive pranks of the Marilyn Monroe/Madonna/Bette Midler phantasms.

The cultural and political sensibility called multiculturalism is another persistent and informing aspect of a new social mythology, bringing together a vast variety of culturally distinct influences and points of view. The street itself and the arts of the street celebrate and exaggerate vernacular ethnic icons and activities. Political rage and unquelled lamentation find their way into much of this effort: from the tragic impact of the AIDS quilt to the outcry of ghetto murals; from the in-your-face music videos of MTV to the hilarious invectives of the Spiderwoman Theater's *Sun, Moon and Feather* (1989), a performance piece created and performed by three Native American sisters who grew up in Red Hook, Brooklyn, where their parents ran a tawdry touring "Medicine Show."

Political cynicism and disengagement are also aspects of the new mythology, and they lend an air of playful social satire to almost every expressive form of art with bittersweet allusions to deflated heroes such as John Kennedy, James Dean, and Martin Luther King or acidic denunciations of counterfeit upstarts who are demolished artistically with equal parts hostility, derision, and demented sarcasm. In the films of Monty Python, in the frolics of Ken Kesey's Merry Pranksters, in the bent satires of the Firesign Theater, and in the original episodes of *Saturday Night Live* there was a political disenchantment that was so pervasive that it permeated even nonpolitical vignettes and art forms.

What distinguishes the art of the street is playfulness. And from that playfulness has come a vivid new mythic basis for the arts of our time. The street has revived play in the twentieth century after its total eclipse during the rather solemn nineteenth century. The revival began, perhaps, with Marcel Duchamp's quirky exhibition of a real urinal that he entitled "Fountain." Or it may have begun with Duchamp's fur-lined teacup or his outrageous 1919 work *Mona Lisa's Mustache*—a reproduction of Leonardo's famous portrait with mustache and beard added in pencil. Following the lead of Duchamp and his fellow Dadaists' revolt against "serious art," the 1920s, 1960s, and 1990s became decades in which the spirit of play has been rampant in both society and the arts. For better or worse, play has been institutionalized and commercialized by the huge amusement parks that, like Disneyland, have spread throughout the world. Improvisational playfulness and reckless bacchanal also abound at events such as New Orleans's Mardi Gras, the Ft. Lauderdale spring break vacation, and the San Francisco gay pride march, all of which allow people to act out their most twisted and subversive impulses. But nothing is as vivid an example of the richness and vitality of play as the antics and games that were born in the street and have subsequently infused a truly populist element into our arts and entertainments. As Johan Huizinga points out, "Civilization today is no longer played." In fact, the rather grand and archaic idea of "civilization" has been submerged in the smaller but brawnier notion of *neighborhood*. And in that broadly democratic turf the street has become one of the most vital and inventive playgrounds of Western history.

Standing in a public square in Philadelphia and gazing rapturously up at a forty-five-foot-tall clothespin sculpted by Claes Oldenburg, we can have no doubt that here in Philadelphia we have, at long last, a monument embodying a divine and demonic figure representing play. Once again the gods are amused as they play with our world.

XVIII.

The Star

Reinventing the Past

Voices who mythologize the lives of the oppressed are voices we must

be wary of.

Kathryn Morton

A naked female kneels near the sea. She is holding two urns. From one urn she pours water into the ocean and with the other she pours water onto the land. Above the woman's head are eight stars as well as a central large star, which may represent Sirius. This Tarot card, called "The Star," is thought to symbolize the mixing of the past and the present as well as the accumulation of past knowledge for use in the present. For our purposes, the Star is the basis for a conversation about the efforts of artists with progressive social ideals to abandon traditional artistic forms and invent new techniques that better support their social visions.

This is a subject that greatly preoccupies art critic Christopher Knight, who must have taken a deep breath before he could summon the courage to write a searching and controversial piece called "Multiculturalism in Art" for the *Los Angeles Times*.

What Knight contends is that there is something askew in the relationship of iconoclastic art and its artistic forms. He asks pertinent and, some would say, impertinent questions. Multicultural art is an art that ideally draws its inspiration from ethnic diversity, but has it become so self-conscious, so cautious, and so politically correct that it has become the first cliché and the first casualty of the 1990s? Has it become part of the Establishment? Is it repressive or regressive or progressive? Is it art, finally, that matters or is it something like journalism: full of passionate rhetoric and auspicious ideas that don't hold their heat?

During the decade of 1975–1985, when I was writing about Native American visual art I was constantly asked to explain the fact that not a single "Indian painter" was represented in the permanent collection of any major museum or public gallery. I was being asked, ultimately, if Indian art is any good. I tried to find answers to the question of "quality," and I attempted to explain the irrefutable and embarrassing fact that identifiably Indian art is almost solely the province of galleries and museums of the American Southwest that deal in inane Americana and the type of Western art derisively called "boots and saddles." I attempted to mediate the neglect of Native painters like Fritz Scholder and Juane Quick-to-See Smith by coming down on their critics. I wondered why painters of Indian heritage, like Leon Polk Smith, James Havard, and George Morrison, who do not make an issue of that heritage in their résumés or in the visual elements of their works, have achieved a visibility denied their peers who call themselves "Indian painters."

A wide variety of art critics with whom I discussed these matters told me candidly, but anonymously, that nothing they had seen by "Indian painters" could stand on equal ground with O'Keeffe, Kahlo, Hartley, let alone Kandinsky, Picasso, or Matisse. They reminded me that the collectors of Western Americana are the same people who detest modernism and postmodernism. They cautioned that such reactionary collectors control the Indian art market and demand conservative and pictorial forms and styles that have more in common with interior decoration than with fine art. They also pointed out that social issues such as socialism and ethnic diversity have been recurrent themes in the works of many artists besides Native Americans. Such social forces, they pointed out, have often given impetus to the marriage of political progressivism and aesthetic conservatism. In the first decade of this century, for instance, there were the paintings of the Eight—Glackens, Henri, Luks, Shinn, Sloan, Davies, Lawson, and Prendergast—along with several other artists who were eventually dubbed the ashcan school by those who did not like their rebellion against the gloss of the national academy aesthetics and who were distressed by their unprecedented and realist portrayals of urban life.

> If their gritty subject matter was progressive, their aesthetic conceptions were old-fashioned, especially compared to the contemporaneous work of Picasso, Matisse, Marsden Hartley, Arthur Dove, and others. Dredging up Old Masters,

from Frans Hals to Gustave Courbet, they blended traditions
of painterly realism with popular styles of urban newspaper
graphics. (Knight)

Their work, by the standards of the day, was idea-bound, explicitly
pictorial, and politically illustrative. A good many critics told me
they admired the things in which the ashcan painters believed, but
they had modest regard for how those painters made their beliefs
visible in most of their art.

It is a difficult argument to fault, especially since it comes
from mainstream critics appraising the works of mainstream artists
of their own culture. But I was not so certain that these same critics
had a very good take on the artists of cultures distinctive from their
own. It seemed to me that they often missed the point of works
of art coming out of entirely different artistic mind sets. For
instance, a *New York Times* art critic betrayed both his naïveté and
his prejudice when he used the offensive term "Boy Scout art" to
describe a major display of nineteenth-century Plains Indian art. So
it was clear, I insisted, that mainstream art critics did not have the
background to grasp contemporary Indian painting and sculpture
in their cultural and historical context. There was some validity to
my argument, but there was also a good deal of rationalization. As
one critic confided when he and I walked through an exhibition of
contemporary Indian painting: "This is not exotic stuff. It's not
the continuation of some ancient Indian art tradition." When I
tried to point out certain native icons and techniques in the paintings, the critic smiled patiently and reminded me that Marsden
Hartley had done a better job of invoking Indian symbolism. "This
stuff," he insisted, "is a poor imitation of European and American
art of twenty and thirty years ago. It's not something so outside
my experience that I feel reluctant to judge it. This kind of imitation of modern masters is very familiar to me in the student work
of white kids. To call it Indian art rather than just calling it art is
like giving it immunity from critical judgment."

What I had overlooked is the fundamental question: forgetting all other considerations of identity and politics, is this art any good? Does anybody have the right to expect something from it in the way of quality?

I knew the answer that question would arouse in a great many people: Quality, they would insist, is a term that colonializes art, forcing it to stand up to standards that are culturally alien to its creators. Did that mean that art is not responsible to any standards of quality?

All art forms—jazz, tribal ceramics, ritual dancing, painting—have culturally forged standards by which achievement is recognized. The standards used by jazz aficionados may be very different from those used by classical music buffs, but still there are expectations and standards that are conscientiously applied to all artistic experiences. We don't expect of a break dancer the same things we expect of a ballet dancer, but we do know when we see someone who is skilled and talented in each dance form.

The point is that we must be careful not to apply the wrong standards to a work of art born out of different standards of perfection. But artistic standards do exist, and they exist in all cultures.

During my decade of defending Indian painting, I often suggested that the Anglo art market is elitist and excludes many artists simply because they are not part of the art scenes of New York and Los Angeles. Today I realize that that predicament is experienced by a great many regional artists, regardless of their heritage. But at the time I imagined something of a conspiracy in the exclusion of artists of color who were my friends. So I took a favorite stance of the day: Indian art, I maintained, is one of several forms of "ghetto art" that are willfully excluded from the Establishment art world.

In response to these arguments, liberal people wagged their heads to humor me, but persisted in asking the same question: But is it art of any quality or artistic merit? The question was so disarming that many people decided to discredit the question rather than attempt to answer it. They decided that words like "merit" and "quality" and "significance" were racist terms built on standards of the dominant culture that did not apply to out-siders—but were promulgated to keep them out of the main-stream world. Many people concluded that what is important about art is the ethnicity or gender or culture of its creator. As the popular political mythology contended: If an Indian paints a painting, that fact alone makes the work not only "an Indian painting," but it also makes it "Art" with a capital A. The Western concepts of *merit* or *quality* have nothing to do with such art.

This defensive metaphor of ethnic/gender privilege is still popular with some people who are not involved in the arts, but for the rest of us it has become more than a bit perplexing and embarrassing. Today the rhetoric about privilege and specialness tends to ignore the individual and aims, instead, at the dignity of the group. The effort to submerge the individual in the group has a great many advantages for those who wish to avoid the obvious problems that arise when we infer that an individual's race or gender provides him or her with special privilege. Somehow the collective notion that a group is privileged offers fewer problems, whether that privilege is attributed to so-called minorities or to those long privileged by dominance. For instance, in Afrocentrism there are troubling implications of efforts to submerge and surren-der the individual to the notion of "a group identity." And, ultimately, what art (and society) is attempting to sort out is the rationale behind the processes of tribalization as opposed to the process of democratization as opposed to the process of socializa-tion. The arts are uncomfortably balanced on the conflicts and concordance of these very different approaches to the relationship of the individual to society and the relationship of art to the individual and to the society.

I recall sitting with ten other people on a panel concerned with multiculturalism in literature at a conference organized by PEN, America Center, in New York City, while a young man railed endlessly about his calamitous mistreatment as a poet because he is homosexual and Puerto Rican. Though the group was composed of a splendid array of people of color and various sexual orientations, none of us had the nerve to point out publicly what at least seven of us later confided to one another: This angry poet's failure to succeed was not because of his sexual orientation or his heritage, but because, unfortunately, he is not a very good poet.

I had confronted most of these perplexing problems and formulated most of these tenuous notions when, in 1985, Edwin Wade of the Philbrook Art Center (Tulsa) asked me to contribute to an anthology of essays on Native American arts, entitled *The Arts of the North American Indian*. Times were a bit less politically frantic and ethnically partisan in the mid-1980s, so I fearlessly and naively wrote an essay culminating my decade-long meditations on the subject, called "Controversy in Native American Art." Even before it was published, that essay instantly produced all kinds of dirty tricks and pointless renunciations from the same friends and artists whose work I had ceaselessly celebrated and promoted for a decade. I had questioned the privilege of race and gender, and that was (and still is) considered treasonous by many of my colleagues. In the next few years the diatribes grew in frenzy, spreading from my doorstep to virtually anyone who dared to address the subject. Almost everyone remotely connected with issues of gender, race, or ethnicity learned that independent opinion had become "the enemy of the people"—the nemesis of the era. But *Los Angeles Times* art critic Christopher Knight must have overcome a great many premonitions about nasty letters and harangues when he wrote his insightful and candid article "Multiculturalism in Art," for he attempted to confront and understand some exceptionally sensitive and important questions about the relationship of style and content in arts that have a political agenda.

While discussing an installation by artist Pepon Osorio at the 1993 Biennial Exhibition at the Whitney Museum of American Art in New York City, he observed that

> artistically, Osorio's installation is starkly conservative. I
> don't mean that its pictorial style or technique of assemblage
> is antiquated or stale. I mean that Osorio has conceived of art

in a conservative way. The installation is merely a seductive vehicle for the delivery of commonly held ideas. "The Scene of the Crime" preaches to the converted, in a playful, homiletic manner that would do Norman Rockwell proud. The installation feels sharply at odds with itself. Its politics reach for the pointedly progressive, but the work is artistically conservative. In this, it's emblematic of our cultural moment. For the surprising dichotomy it embodies—political progressiveness happily wedded to artistic conservatism—has lately emerged as a dominant, recurrent motif in multiculturalism.

Knight asks where this seemingly odd couple came from and what it signals. As part of his answer, he associates the dichotomy of style and content in art with the populist passion of the Reagan era. Though Knight admits that multiculturalism represents "a politically progressive, not conservative stance," Reaganism and multiculturalism, he believes, have somehow ended up as "two sides of the same populist coin."

Classical populism promises equality and opportunity through a belief that the people are never wrong. Behind populism is the fundamental assumption that a collective wisdom flows innately from generation to generation. That collective wisdom is variously called horse sense and common sense and is supposed to result from training in the school of hard knocks. Whatever we call it and whatever its source, populism believes that all common people possess a clear and profound native wisdom. Through simplicity and sincerity they understand the things that confound intellectuals. Ironically, populists, for all their reverence for the sagacious "common man," intimate or even proclaim that native wisdom is found among American and European Christians to a greater degree than it is found among other peoples, such as Turks, Asians, or the tribal peoples of Africa. In other words, populism has never traveled well over national or religious boundaries. It is as ethnocentric as the elite social philosophies it abhors. And its most ironic character is its own brand of elitism, which amounts to the dictum that some common people are wiser than other common people.

The only consistent aspect of populism is its effort to be captivating, and, as Christopher Knight points out, that effort inevitably results in aesthetically conservative forms and styles. The multicultural mentality strives for a progressive message but cannot escape the populist inclination to be captivating and facile. The result is a dichotomy of technique and content that is profoundly unaesthetic.

There have been a great many iconoclastic artists who have espoused *ideas* of exceptional social and moral originality: Dostoyevsky's "invention" of the subconscious, Picasso's depiction of multispatial surfaces, Leslie Silko's orchestration of Native American majesty and tragedy, Toni Morrison's rapturous incantation of African-American experience, Samuel Beckett's debate with an absurd god, Martha Graham's evocation of the primal female, Bartók's and Stravinsky's conjurings of primal mysterious and forgotten ancestors. But in each instance of these brilliantly explored ideas there was an equally brilliant exploration of techniques and styles that were capable of supporting and amplifying the novelty and ardor of the artist's content, rather than using endless reiterations of moribund artistic mannerisms that submerge and decimate the very ideas that are to be glorified.

When ideas become more impassioned than vision, the result, inevitably, is ephemeral. Art posing as disposable instruction. *Hamlet* with explanatory footnotes that destroy the unanswerable mysteries of motive and meaning that have kept the indecisive Hamlet alive in our minds. When art serves ideas rather than venturing beyond them into the realm of metaphor, both the ideas and the art are devoured by time. In such idea-bound art the unabated effort is to communicate and to captivate. And such populist motives always result in homiletic displays rather than revelations and artistic experiences. We get the point and we get the moral, but what we don't get is the story. And it is in the story that the experience of art resides. Without the experience we cannot respond to art, we can only understand it.

The ardent but mundane novels of Upton Sinclair and Frank Norris, even the rather splendid plays of Elmer Rice and Karel Čapek, were greatly admired and then forgotten because their impact depended almost entirely upon their connections to social events that are of little or no importance to us today. Ibsen also wrote social dramas, but even his syphilis tragedy, *Ghosts,* which shocked several generations of audiences, continues to have substantial power as drama—despite the fact that venereal disease is no longer scandalous—because its form and its language transcend its social and pathological themes.

One of the trends of the Whitney biennial that distressed critic Christopher Knight was the persistence of texts.

> Illustrated text is everywhere in the Biennial. . . . In the dichotomy between progressive politics and conservative aesthetics, it isn't the politics that require words and illustrations. Rather, if art is expected to function within a populist milieu, discursive text and descriptive pictures are simply necessary.

The images become illustrations of the text because the images themselves do not communicate as metaphor but only as the insignias of political and social attitudes, like flags or stop signs. Flags and traffic signs may have inherent aesthetic power as visual icons, but that power is obliterated by the fact that they are pressed into pedagogical duties and thereby deprived of their force as images. They become billboards, referring to ideas at the expense of their communicative power as symbols.

There is no reason not to admire artists who devote themselves to the creation of billboards, but there is a great need to recognize the fact that many artists who celebrate social change are those who are committed to a personal vision rather than to the effort of making political ideas visible. For instance, there is a curious difference between the wholly personal works of homosexual artists like playwright and novelist Jean Genet or photographer Robert Mapplethorpe and the "movement" orientation of gay artists such as playwrights Larry Kramer and Tony Kushner. Though all four of these artists possess distinctive talents, they also represent a striking difference in motivation and, therefore, in artistic manner. Genet and Mapplethorpe made no secret of their sexual orientation, but their art is not confined to their sexuality; it is in the service of their totality as persons, erotically, socially, emotionally, aesthetically. Homosexuality was the stage upon which they played themselves, but by "themselves" I mean the largest context of their experience as persons and not merely their social and sexual experiences as homosexuals—which, for all of its potential adversity and gratification as a sexual orientation, is only one aspect of any person's life. For Genet and Mapplethorpe, homosexuality was not doctrine or creed or an agenda entirely in the service of the *idea* of homosexuality. Their idiosyncratic vision was not consumed by their sexual orientation; to the contrary, their homosexuality provided them with a metaphor with which they played out fully every aspect of themselves. They were not the voices of a movement but the voices of individuals existing in a life that other people made into a movement. Their work is about a life lived and not about a life defended. And that is what gives their work great power and persuasion, while the efforts of those who strive to be the voices of a movement and the defenders of an idea usually fail to capture that vulnerable part of us that resonates to the unique part of them that is tormented and enraged by injustice and brutality and castigation.

Picasso's *Guernica* is not a political manifesto. Nor is it a journalistic outcry or a protest poster. It is not a pictorial representation of a tragic historic event. It is not a picture that illustrates a text. *Guernica* is the highly idiosyncratic work of an artist who reinvented the world so it reflected his visions and experiences. *Guernica* may fail as a populist statement, because it probably escapes the comprehension of a great many Spaniards who survived the Spanish Civil War, but Picasso's painting speaks to anyone who is capable of revelation, even if it evades those who require explanation.

At the heart of the dichotomy of progressive content and

conservative technique in art is the issue of imagination as a political force. Nietzsche said: "The world does not revolve around those who invent new upheavals but around those who invent new values; it revolves *in silence.*" Progressive aesthetic forms are implements of newly invented values, and, like them, they revolve in silence. Their messages are experiences. They are not tautologies that must be heard.

According to Jean Cassou, in the moment of crisis out of which an artist's creation springs, imagination is the essential motivating force. Yet, for all his emphasis upon the revelation of the art of the individual, Cassou is no stranger to political fervor and communal action. He fought in the Spanish Civil War and in the French Resistance during World War II. But he sees the power of revolution in the individual rather than in the fabricated notion of "a movement" or "a group." It is again imagination, he insists,

> that is the driving force when the individual creation of an artist becomes the collective creation which we call a revolutionary movement. A confrontation with the existing society arises, but those who do the confronting are aware that their confrontation is only valid if it is accompanied by a creative upsurge—hence the appeal to the imagination. Thus one of the inscriptions spread over the walls of the colleges and the streets of Paris during the May 1968 student uprising was the slogan: *Imagination Takes Power.*

In America, by contrast, the populist slogan of 1968 was: *Power to the People.*

As I recall, "the people" (the majority) already had all the power, and most of the people were using that power in support of racial discrimination, homophobia, militarism, sexism, and anti-Semitism. Imagination had not taken over in America because imagination has little place in the lives of Americans.

> At times of crisis history stands still, and suddenly there is no more game, nothing plays, nothing thinks, nothing

happens; if there is activity it is a mechanical activity that leads nowhere. But imagination arises and intervenes. It takes power and is itself power. (Cassou)

Out of crisis comes the imagination of an individual who forges an interior response to calamity. Incongruously, that highly personal response becomes the voice of a community, a movement, even a crusade. The nation does not know the *words* of its national anthem, but it is stirred and carried into action by the *experience* of the melody. The imagination does not recall the urgent messages of politicians and iconoclasts, but it does remember the experiences that stir us into action and that shape and control what we have been and what we are and what we are becoming.

XIX.

The Moon

Deception as Doctrine

On both sides there is a tendency to see Western culture as monolithic and to overlook its complexity, its long history of responsiveness to other cultures, and its tradition of internal conflict and doubt.

Michael Benson

The full Moon is seen rising between two towers. A dog and a wolf bay in the night. In the foreground a large crayfish creeps from its hiding place in a pool. The Tarot card called "The Moon" represents deception and disillusionment, and, as such, it is the perfect symbol for a discussion of the mythology of the American melting pot.

The United States was the birthplace of a liberal democracy that became the basis of a unique political philosophy: the merging—melding—of countless different peoples into a single nation. It is an impossible ambition, highly dissimilar from the massive and heterogeneous Roman Empire, where assimilation was motivated by political rather than religious or cultural motives. The ever-increasing sprawl, diversity, and localized jurisdictions of the Roman world were some of the reasons that it eventually collapsed. But in the United States, at least for its first two hundred years, such a diversified and heterogeneous social order has somehow worked, despite the fact that its motivating theory of "the melting pot" has been exposed as a fraud.

In many ways, America is unique for its highly disparate religious, ethnic, racial, and cultural components. It also comprises one of the vastest land masses to be called a nation, with great divergence in its climates and landscapes. As the name implies, the United States is the result of rapid expansionism and integration of sovereign states and independent territories. As the new nation grew it absorbed these vast territories and populations: the Dutch, French, and British of the northeastern region, the Russians of the Northwest, the Spaniards and Mexicans of the Southwest. And everywhere, during this consolidation of colonies and territories into a nation, there remained dwindling islands of Native Americans striving to retain their own diverse identities. Then came waves of immigrants from Russia, Central Europe, Ireland, Scandinavia, and Italy. The regime of slavery brought vast numbers of

Africans, abducted from their native land. Another vast population of Asians found its way into America as coolie labor for the westward expansion of the railroads.

> In society as in farming, monoculture works poorly. It exhausts the soil. The social richness of America, so striking to the foreigner, comes from the diversity of its tribes. Its capacity for cohesion, for some spirit of common agreement on what is to be done, comes from the willingness of those tribes not to elevate their cultural differences into impassable barriers and ramparts. (Hughes 1993)

Diversity and multiculturalism are clearly the strengths of the United States, but "the willingness" of diverse peoples to sacrifice something of their individual identity for the common good is not as often a matter of willingness as it is a matter of political expediency—an expediency that has dissipated greatly during the last decades of the twentieth century, when differences of ethnicity, religion, and culture have become increasingly important issues of activism. The blindly patriotic bromides about America as a melting pot have been dismissed as euphemisms for a distressing reality: diversity smothered by conformity. With the disillusionment born out of national scandals and emergencies, the childhood and innocence of America ended, and its citizens began to take a long look at the bluster and aggrandizement of their deluded Norman Rockwell world. That self-examination revealed some ugly facts. Equality had been confused with conformity. Many people became enraged by the injustices of their idealized world: the defaming of African Americans, the sexualization and denigration of women, the slandering of gays as abominations, the absurdity of thinking that God, somehow, is on their side in all issues and during all conflicts. The slow recognition that when presidents like Ronald Reagan and George Bush refer to "God" they mean a very specific "God"—which has little significance to the many American citizens of non-Western origin. Americans also began to grasp the inherent contradictions of their high democratic ideals and the systematized inequality that is an intrinsic aspect of the ethos of capitalism. As Michael Foucault has said, "The politics of truth changed."

Karl Marx once observed that "the ideas of the ruling class are in every epoch the ruling ideas." But as Philip Green notes, the ideas by which the ruling class justifies itself to society as a whole somehow must also seem to speak to the needs of society as a whole if the ruling class is to be allowed to continue its rule. In short, the ideas of any era always contain their own contradictions.

> Whereas the ethos of capitalism per se is inequality, the ethos of liberal democracy is equality. Despite vast economic divisions we learn that we are all citizens and in some sense we are supposed to be equal citizens; every citizen should count for one and none for more than one; that government is supposed to be of, by, and for the people; and that the system promises worldly "success" to all of us who are not incorrigible idlers. Every man (if not woman) can be a king. Authority is alleged to result only from merit, not from wealth, and wealth itself is justified as only a reward for serving an important social function. (Green)

From the perspective of many social critics, American democracy is the province of the Moon of the Tarot cards: a deception, "a fraud, a betrayed promise, even if everyone knows that the promise was never intended seriously" (Green).

Against this background of social contradiction, inequity, and deception, it is difficult to accept Robert Hughes's idealistic vision of Americans' willingness "not to elevate their cultural differences into impassable barriers and ramparts." In reality, for two hundred years American cultural and sexual diversity has been methodically and steadily eradicated by the "well meaning" divisiveness of those who dominate authority. Their process of "unification" is actually a form of ethnic and gender cleansing, but they diplomatically call it "assimilation." Then—not surprisingly given the political climate—there has been in the last decade a reaction to the divisiveness of authority. Regrettably, this activist reaction is as extreme, cunning, and destructive as the dilemma it attempts to remedy. It is a bit like the French Revolution: Those who had nothing plundered those who had everything.

The revisionist stance that attempts to reinstate cultural diversity is usually called "identity politics": "a new label for an age-old phenomenon of mobilizing political allegiances around collective identities," like race or gender or sexual preference (Gates). As a social position this new form of militancy sounds admirable, but the hidden agenda of identity politics is to encourage disenfranchised groups to expend all of their political power in the service of a single issue, turning voters, who are supposed to deal with the whole spectrum of political concerns, into what is known as the "single-issue voter."

In this way, the subject of cultural diversity in America is divided between those whose cultural identity has been lobotomized by social pressures and those who are so intent upon resurrecting collective identities that they are anxious to take antagonistic positions that are quite the opposite of the conciliation Hughes presumes to be the implacable spirit of American society. One group has been forced to abandon its cultural distinctions, while the other group clearly wants to elevate cultural differences as "impassable social barriers and ramparts."

The social mythology at work in America is a brilliant fraud, the ruling idea in which we are supposed to "believe" that the strategy of the melting pot is actually the idea of the ruling class turned against the rest of the population. People are urged to betray their own identities in order to achieve social coherence. At the same time the assimilation required by the ruling class is reversed by activists into strategies of their own: namely, identity politics, which urges people to betray their own identities as persons and to assume the identity of a specific group. Clearly, such tactics are two negative sides of the same problem and are capable of the same malevolence.

E. D. Hirsch, Jr., who won attention with his controversial stance on cultural literacy, likes to celebrate the transformation of peasantry into nobility, an educational process he calls "a miracle." For instance, in a telling sentence Hirsch cites Eugene Weber's classic study *Peasants into Frenchmen* (1976), which records the transformation of a heterogeneous peasantry into what became the French nation. But as fine arts professor Mary Marien notes,

> The French experiment with cultural literacy, which Hirsch calls a "miracle," was a nightmare for the thousands of children who endured it. Weber's middle chapters ought to be required reading for teachers and administrators. They recount years of drudgery and abuse—something Hirsch fails to mention. In the last half of the nineteenth century, French children received crabbed lessons in moral rectitude, disguised as nuggets of French cultural achievement. They were taught to work hard, pay taxes, and perform military service. Children who persisted in speaking their own language (German, Basque, Flemish, Breton, and a variety of patois, were widely spoken at the time) were put on a diet of bread and water, made to clean latrines, or humiliated by having to wear a symbol of their offense. And there was no miracle—just a tendentious breaking of wills. And many children remained illiterate.

This malevolent process of enforced assimilation of diverse groups into an imaginary national unity has been particularly endemic in American history. Disguising itself as a humane social process—as the miracle of integration—well-meaning religious and cultural missionaries (calling themselves by various names: teachers, evangelists, social workers, Peace Corp volunteers, et al.) have undertaken the transformation of outsiders into insiders, assuming that the nicest thing they could do for others is to turn them into facsimiles of themselves.

There is no better example of this breed of evangelistic person than Captain Richard Pratt, who supervised Indian prisoners of war at Fort Marion (Florida) during the late nineteenth century—at precisely the same time that the French "miracle" of cultural experimentation was underway. At the turn of the century, during the last years of organized military resistance by Indians to Anglo incursions, Captain Pratt, an unyielding assimilationist, opened the Carlisle Indian School in Pennsylvania, with the aim of stamping out all Indian cultural traits that Pratt felt impaired the Indians' entry into mainstream society. The humiliating and disorienting process that had been practiced in the French transformation of peasants into Frenchmen was used by Pratt's school, which became the prototype for Indian education in America. The founding of Pratt's school marked the birth of the Indian boarding school system that has taken Indian children away from their families, tribes, and cultures. That system continues to operate today. In 1905 the Carlisle Indian School enrolled one thousand students. It closed in 1918. During its years of operation its major purpose was to discourage Indian children from speaking their own languages, from practicing their own religions, from grooming and dressing as Indians, and from perpetuating their unique cultures. Pratt's aim for Indian education was to convert the children into farmers, cooks, servants, and maids. They were not urged to aspire toward positions of social or intellectual significance in Anglo society; so when Charles Eastman (a Sioux Indian originally named Ohiyesa) became, first, a graduate of Boston University and a physician in 1888 and then a renowned writer at the turn of the century, he was regarded as an oddity at the same time that he was held up as an example of what the Indian mission-school system could accomplish, though Eastman was virtually terrorized as a mission-school student.

In my experience, nothing speaks more poignantly of the decimation of the process of cultural assimilation than the saga of a young Cheyenne Indian named Bear's Heart. In May of 1880, Bear's Heart spoke before a large audience in the school auditorium of the Hampton Normal and Agricultural Institute in Virginia. He was one of seventeen young men from Plains Indian tribes accepted at Hampton in 1878 as students in the all-black institution. Prior to entering Hampton, Bear's Heart had spent three years imprisoned at Fort Marion, as one of seventy-two Indians confined without the benefit of trial or due process as an aftermath of Indian wars on the Southern Plains. He became one of the first Indian artists while a prisoner. A correspondent from the *Boston Journal* took down and printed Bear's Heart's speech. It is a rare and sad account, the autobiography of a buffalo-hunting nomad who was never confined to a reservation, recorded without the interventions of interpreters, and seen sharply with the memory of youth and not through the vague recall of old age and the unconscious compromise of partial assimilation that marks so much of the narrative of Indians whose words were published in subsequent years. These, then, are Bear's Heart's own words:

When I was a little boy, I got out of bed, maybe six o'clock every morning. I got out wigwam, wash face, go back to wigwam. My father comb my hair and he tie it then he paint my face good. Then my father said you go shoot; my little friend come and I said to him let us go and shoot. When finish cooking, my mother say Come here, Bear's Heart, breakfast. Then I told my friend after breakfast you come again we go shooting again. I had buffalo meat just one [?] for breakfast. I will tell you how my home look, Indian bed just on ground. My father and my mother have a bed one side of the wigwam; I and my brother other side, and my sister another side, and the door on one side. The fire is in middle. My people sit on bed, and my mother she give us a tin plate and cut meat, we have one knife no fork hold the meat by hand, eat with knife. After breakfast I go shooting with my friend. I eat three times every day. Sometimes two times when not much meat. All the time meat, that is all. I no work. I play all the time. After a while I big boy. My father he said, Bear's Heart you try kill buffalo now. I say yes. When Indians went buffalo hunting I go too. One time I shoot twice and kill buffalo. I skin buffalo and put skin and beef on my horse. I took to my wigwam. My father he say Bear's Heart, how many times you shoot. I say one time. He say good. When I big boy my father give me gun and I shoot deer. All the time I shoot. I done no work. When my father died I was a bad man [a depth of sorrow which traditionally requires pacification by taking a life]. Bye and bye about twenty Indian young men went to fight Utes [Indians]. I told my mother I want to fight, and she said yes. I go and fight all day, we killed one Ute and four Cheyenne. Sundown we stop. In Texas I fight again. In Texas all time fight no stop. In summer I fight, in the winter no fight. I fight then I got tired, I say my two friends let us go back to [government] agency. My friends they say yes. We went to agency [tribal centers created by Anglo supervisors], the captain [talk] to us, he say, Bear's Heart what you want to do, fight or stay here. I said stay here, all right say he "go to wigwam." About one month after, Cheyenne chief he tell agent Bear's Heart had been fighting so he is bad, then the captain put me in the guard house. Bye and bye the captain he sent my two friends to tell all Indians to stop fight and come to agency. All Indians come back then Cheyenne chief he look at all Indians and told captain what Indians fight, the captain put bad Indians in guard house, and colored soldiers put chains on their legs. One man he got mad and run, the soldiers shoot but no kill him. Bye and bye good many soldiers come from Fort Sill and took us to Fort Sill [Oklahoma Territory], where I saw Captain Pratt. Good many Kiowas, Comanches, and Arapahoes, Cheyenne all together with soldiers and Captain Pratt take us to Florida. When I ride to Florida all the time I think bye and bye they kill me. When I been to St. Augustine [Fort Marion prison] some time and womans and mans [Anglo journalists] come to see me and shake hand, I think soldiers no kill me. After a while Captain Pratt took off all Indian chains, but not too quick. Captain Pratt he see boys no have money. He got sea-beans, he say make sea-beans shine, he told us how and when we make sea-beans good we take to him, he give us money. First time we made sea-beans, then bow and arrows, then paint pictures. Bye and bye teacher she come with pictures of dog, cat, cow, and tell us every day nine o'clock morning we go to school stop at twelve o'clock, afternoon just make sea-beans. Before Indians went to school, Captain Pratt he gave Indians clothes just like white men, but Indian no want hair cut. Sunday Indians go to church St. Augustine: down from head, Indians same as white men, but head, long hair just like Indians. Bye and bye after Indians go to church, they say I want my hair cut; my teacher say very good. Two years I stay at St. Augustine, then come Hampton School. At Hampton I go to school and I work. I like school and work. I don't want to go home just now. I want learn more English, more work and more of the good way. When I finish my school here, I go home to teach my people to work also. I want my mother and sisters to work house, and I and brother to work farm. When they put chains on me to take me from my home, I felt sorry. But I glad now. For I good boy now.

The endemic process of cultural assimilation uses every possible device of mind control, subtle and otherwise, in order to prompt individuals to betray both their individual and group identities. The intensity of this brainwashing agenda is often overlooked by both those who are targeted by it and those who target them. Advertising, slang, popular entertainments, and the news media bombard us with messages, making it clear that it is better to conform than to be different, that it is better to be heterosexual, white, male, tall, slender, athletic, inartistic, and not too smart. This assault on gender, sexual orientation, race, ethnicity, and physical appearance is unrelenting, making people feel a sense of humiliation if they reveal any hint of otherness: young people are embarrassed when their grandparents speak a foreign language in the presence of their friends; youths are abashed if their peers note that their single parent has a same-sex partner; people of color are so shamed by or uncomfortable with their physical features or regional accents that they undertake all kinds of radical measures to change their appearance and speech into an imitation of their white counterparts.

The metaphor of equality is easily distorted and turned into a ritual of exploitation and abuse, all in the name of assimilation and equal opportunity. Psychiatrist R. D. Laing has said that when you destroy a people's experience, they become destructive. When you make people ashamed of who they are, when you turn their diversity into adversity, when you engage in ethnocide—destroying the very elements that give people a sense of identity—then you instill in them such self-contempt that they become destructive—usually self-destructive. The pain and confusion that is inflicted by those who wish everyone to be the same is devastating. The response to this kind of ethnic cleansing inevitably explodes in a militant counteraction that expresses not only years of pent-up rage and resentment, but also a profound need to reaffirm a lost or compromised identity. It is a motive that has been felt by Native Americans and African Americans, by Hispanic people, and many other ethnic and religious groups that comprise the American population. It has also been the motive of women who have fought their exploitation and defamation steadfastly, and by homosexuals who have been so censured and emotionally assaulted by heterosexual expectations that they have agonized over their true sexuality and have long confined themselves in closets lest they be found out and victimized.

The aim of the protests of society's victims is to create a society that celebrates rather than denigrates differences; a society that recognizes that the greatest distance between people is not space but culture. That idealistic movement has been named multiculturalism.

When Robert Hughes looks upon the triumphs of this "rainbow society," as Jesse Jackson calls it, he is deeply impressed.

Multiculturalism asserts that people with different roots can co-exist, that they can learn to read the image-banks of others, that they can and should look across the frontiers of race, language, gender and age without prejudice or illusion, and learn to think against the background of a hybridized society. It proposes—modestly enough—that some of the most interesting things in history and culture happen at the interface between cultures. It wants to study border situations, not only because they are fascinating in themselves, but because understanding them may bring with it a little hope for the world. (Hughes 1993)

But this marvelous vision, so handsomely articulated by Hughes, is in jeopardy. As Henry Louis Gates, Jr., has frankly observed:

The real battle to rescue some reasonable and healthy form of multiculturalism isn't with psychology; it's with "identity politics." . . . If the rhetoric of multiculturalism has reached something of an impasse, it's because it has become so embroiled with this thing called identity politics that few observers are able to disentangle the two. To be blunt, the invocation of "multiculturalism" is quite often a ruse, used to provide respectable cover for political enlistment of racial and ethnic solidarity. Increasingly uneasy with talk of descent-based identities—like race and ethnicity—we seek to redeem them in the shiny currency of "culture." And so the culture of "culture" is born.

Cultural differences are intrinsic aspects of America. They are everywhere visible, though most of their visibility is built upon festive niceties that have a potential consumer spin-off, what Gates calls "recreational ethnicity"—like the buttons worn at the Saint Patrick's Day Parade that read "Kiss Me, I'm Irish" or the bumper sticker that reads "I'm Proud to Be Italian!" Having an "apparently" Italian or Jewish or Asian name in America has its advantages and disadvantages in terms of identity politics: One automatically wins the widespread support of a particular ethnic community or the ire of an equally widespread society of bigots. The problems with both ethnic cleansing and assimilation are obvious: They destroy the cultural diversity that animates the world and that brings about change and discovery. The problems with identity politics are less obvious: They silence the dissenting voices of individuals like Anita Hill, who was chastised for unveiling dirty laundry, for making public a problem that many of her compeers considered "an internal affair." Identity politics destroys the diversity brought by unique individuals to any ethnic or gender group, and it requires people to submerge themselves in the reign of somebody else's notion of an "appropriate" group identity. They defy a basic principle of liberal democracy by insisting that the good of a specific "group" is more important than the good of the individual; while humane societies are moving in quite the other direction as they try to find the means of protecting the individual against the tyranny of the group. Whether faced with identity politics or cultural assimilation, people find themselves in exactly the same predicament: In either case they are required to abandon themselves to someone else's definition of both the self and the group.

But as Gates suggests, a humane multiculturalism can be mobilized against both the melting-pot illusion of the assimilationists and the illusion of group solidarity that dominates the thinking of identity politics.

> A vision of America in which every individual has an "identity" and every identity a "culture" serves certain rhetorical purposes, especially if you're writing poetry for a Presidential Inauguration, but it bears little resemblance to the country we actually live in. (Gates)

For all his reservations about the Inauguration poetry of Maya Angelou, Gates neglects to mention that ideals and visions—

like myths and nations—are born not of actualities but out of imaginary *possibilities.*

Before we can live it, someone has to *imagine the possibility* of freedom.

XX.

The Sun

Cultural Piracy

Some of the most interesting things in history and culture happen at the interface between cultures.

Robert Hughes (1993)

Two naked figures stand in a garden. Above them shines a radiant sun with golden tears streaming down its face. This is the Sun card of the Tarot deck, and it is the symbol of favorable social relations and human engagement. Such an icon may be a strange introduction to a subject such as cultural piracy, which is charged with hostility and discord. But in exploring the borrowings of cultures from one another, I am inclined to believe that such cultural appropriation is not only universal but also the source of grandeur in every society in history, with the rare exception of those that were so insular that they declined and vanished for lack of essential alien influences.

When I was invited to the highly activist campus of New York's City College to take part in a symposium called "Transformations of Ethnic Content in Contemporary Art," I was aware that my host expected me to recite the celebration of cultural diversity that he had admired in my book *The Primal Mind*. I also knew that the conference would feature the familiar diatribes of some very accomplished people who regularly assail artists whom African-American social critic Del Jones calls cultural pirates: namely, both living and dead white men and women whose artistic efforts were greatly influenced by various non-Western ethnic traditions. Believing that in such a partisan forum someone really should play devil's advocate, I decided to risk presenting to the group an extensive catalogue of Western influences that are unmistakable in the arts of tribal people. My aim was to make it clear that "piracy" has been working in both cultural directions between Western and non-Western societies since the founding of the ancient trade routes.

At first the audience seemed annoyed and puzzled by my remarks, but as I moved through an extensive list of ways in which tribal arts have been drastically changed by Western influences, people looked rather shocked and amazed. Everyone, that is, but

Amiri Baraka, who had apparently not heard a word I said, but instantly launched into a fire storm of repudiation. Clearly, he did not want to know the things I was saying, yet he could not refute them because they are transcultural facts of African, Native American, and East Indian history.

The most famous of those "facts" concerned with cultural exchange is, unfortunately, untrue: namely, the anecdote about Marco Polo bringing wonton back to Italy from his Asian journeys, resulting in Chinese noodles being instantly transformed into what we now call spaghetti. It is a fine story, but, unfortunately, it is not true.

But there are countless other forms of cultural appropriation by tribal and Asian peoples that are. For instance, in the nineteenth century a British ship foundered off the coast of India. Its cargo of crates filled with baby dresses spilled into the sea and washed ashore. The inhabitants did not know what to make of the little, frilly garments, so they put them around their necks like fanciful collars. And to this day the famous Kathakali dancers of northeastern India wear frilly little "baby dresses" around their necks as part of the regalia of their highly traditional ritual performances.

There is also an interesting example of cultural exchange in Southeast Asia, where Bali remains one of the most culturally tenacious societies at the close of the twentieth century. And yet, since the 1920s, a long succession of European artists have visited and lived on the island, leaving their strong influences on the arts. Many artists have functioned as genuine and welcomed members of Balinese society with the full consent and enthusiasm of the people. One such artist was the Russian-born German painter Walter Spies, who came to Bali in 1930s and stayed on until the Japanese occupation during World War II. At the time of his arrival, traditional Balinese visual art was stagnating. The revival of the visual arts came about through the influence of Spies's own paintings as well as his introduction of Western materials—precut pads of paper, ink, watercolors, and tempera. Traditional Wayang painting was completely changed within ten years, and yet it retained a distinctive non-Western texture. Gone was the use of flat surfaces and the depiction of ritual subject matter; instead, there was a new emphasis upon scenes of daily village life. Sculpture also changed radically. Rather than a decorative craft in the service of temples, palaces, and household objects, wood carving became an independent art form. Through all of this artistic transformation, Spies didn't impose his ideas upon the Balinese; to the contrary, the artists of Bali actively sought his criticism because they had great admiration for him, and they realized that he had an ardent respect for them.

Spies's most remarkable influence on Balinese culture was his participation in the invention of a dance drama called *Kecak* (the "Monkey Chant" or "Monkey Dance") that is now considered one of the most traditional of Balinese ritual dramas, though it is a hybrid built entirely on Western theatrical and choreographic influences and was not even performed until 1932.

Kecak, a name indicating the "chak-a-chak" sounds, evolved out of the male chorus of the ritual *Sanghyang* trance ceremony. Through a coordination rehearsed for months prior to a performance, elements of dance merge in a startling assembly of motion and voices. Many words and gestures have no meaning other than as derivatives of incantations to drive out evil, as was the original purpose of the *Sanghyang* chorus. But there is also a narrative aspect of the ritual. *Kecak* includes high drama, in which the center of the circle created by the male chorus becomes a stage, and its periphery of men become living scenery, moving and making incredible sounds that give intense dramatic effect to the dramatic action taking place in the middle of them. Accompanied by the bizarre music of the human voice imitating percussive instruments, the storytellers narrate the events enacted by lavishly costumed mythic characters drawn from a major epic of India and Southeast Asia, the *Ramayana* (Hoefer).

Then dance techniques and styles were drawn from two popular dramatic Bali rituals: *Wayang Wong* and *Parwa*. The *Chak* chorus underwent remarkable transformations with greatly expanded varieties of sounds and the inclusion of group choreography that allowed the men's voices and actions to comment on the action of the drama performed in their midst, much as the ancient Greek chorus interpreted and responded to the action of drama with choral verses. When the first performance of *Kecak* was given in 1932, in front of the temple at the Gua Gajah, it was an instant sensation, and many other enthusiastic Balinese groups were formed throughout the island. *Kecak* became a truly native ceremony of Bali, though its entire premise was born of the influences of Walter Spies, a Moscow-born painter of German parents.

Such elaborate Western influences are found everywhere among tribal cultures. Of Native American arts, few are admired as much as the monumental totems and ritual masks of the Northwest Coast, yet the ability to produce these marvelous forms was vastly influenced when metal tools, which had not previously existed in the region, were introduced in the nineteenth century by European whaling ships.

The greatly admired squash blossom necklace of the Navajo is another result of European influences: the silver itself was secured by the Navajo Indians of the nineteenth century by stealing Spanish coins and melting them. It is probable that the Spaniards taught Indians the technique of casting metal, which was essential to the creation of the squash blossom. The design of the necklace owes little to Native American iconography: the pomegranate shapes are Moorish fertility symbols unknown in pre-Columbian America, with the possible exception of ancient Mexico, but widely used as icons in pre-Christian Europe; while the crescent pendant (or *najahe*) of the necklace derives from a Moorish symbol that wards off the "evil eye"—useful to the Navajos, who traditionally believed in witches and bad magic.

The renowned paintings created by the Kiowa Indians in the early part of the twentieth century were largely the result of the introduction of tempera and illustration board and the influences of Persian miniatures shown to them by their Anglo teacher Dorothy Dunn, an art historian from Chicago who founded a studio at the Santa Fe Indian School dedicated to encouraging rather than obliterating the artistic expression of young Indians. As noted Chiricahua Apache artist Allan Houser told me in 1975:

> What Dunn did was this—and I can tell you because I was right here at The Studio when it was beginning. Everyone was encouraged to search their background for traditional things. That's all she permitted us to do. If you did a landscape or something else she wouldn't accept it. She told us that it wasn't Indian. . . . "You either paint like this, Mr. Houser," she would say, "or it's not Indian art." (Highwater 1976)

So, once again, Western influence was an essential element in the development of twentieth-century Indian visual art.

The highly esteemed glass beadwork of the North American Indian tribes of the Great Plains was an industry largely developed after the introduction of glass beads from Venice and Prague, about 1675, which replaced the arduously hand-ground and -shaped shell and stone beads, as well as almost obliterating the traditional use of the split, boiled, colored, and sewn beaver quills that had decorated most Plains Indian objects and costumes for centuries. There is also good evidence that the floral designs widely used in Woodland Indian beadwork derived from embroidery patterns provided by French mission schools attended by Indians.

The fact that tribal peoples were susceptible to Western influences is not the point. What is important about these examples of cultural appropriation in India, Bali, and Indian America is the fact that tribal artists demonstrated an inscrutable individuality even when clearly basing their efforts upon typical European influences. Even when the imitation of Western ideas and motifs or the use of Western technology and materials has been apparently countercultural from the viewpoint of Anglo purists (who want tribal peoples to remain unpolluted), nonetheless the products themselves, for better or for worse, are totally tribalized, transformed into something ethnically unique and significant.

An excellent example of the extent to which borrowed ele-

ments are merged with tribal mentality is the fact that the borrowings are often given mythological explanations—which attempt to
assert their aboriginal rather than alien origins—though such
myths obviously postdate the actual introduction of the Western
motifs they mythologize. For instance, many Woodland Indians
claim that the floral designs so famous in Woodland beadwork
were not borrowed from French embroidery motifs but were
revealed independently to an Indian in dreams, an important
source of Indian revelation.

Innuit (Eskimo) artistic goals and values are also a blend of
traditional and European-introduced elements, especially in the
creation of modern soapstone sculptures and balsa masks, which
grew out of the Innuit heritage but were also the result of alien
inspiration and technologies. As Nelson Graburn has pointed out,
"The bolder sculptures, even when made entirely for sale to tourists, are important to the Eskimos and have become integrated into
their modern culture. Although I agree that carving is an introduced art form, the Eskimos do make their own selections of
stones, tools, and subject matter, often in contradiction to market
demands." Clearly, the Innuit craftspeople have used European
ideas and tools to their own advantage and have thoroughly amal-
gamated alien influences into their own culture through a strongly
centered Innuit aesthetic. But the fact remains that before the
introduction of the concept of sculpture by Westerners, the Innuits
were not carvers of large, representational figures.

There are a great many examples of cultural piracy in both the
Western and non-Western worlds, though, in these times of Western self-consciousness, we are usually given a long list of dead and
living white artists who appropriated tribal elements while we are
provided with little information about tribal piracy. For this reason
the list of Western "pirates" is quite familiar, commencing with
the startling use by Pablo Picasso of the example of African masks
in his seminal painting, *Les Demoiselles d'Avignon*. Picasso himself
declared that when he created this great painting in 1907 he still
did not know African art. But Picasso apparently forgot the Afri-

can sculptures he had seen in 1905 at the studio of his friend the painter André Derain, which clearly influenced *Les Demoiselles,* even though the ostensible influence of pre-Christian Iberian sculpture predominates the forms of Picasso's revolutionary painting.

The work of Paul Gauguin is clearly influenced by the arts of Polynesia, a fact that he happily acknowledged in his conversations and writings. Amedeo Modigliani made no pretense that his painting of 1910, *Caryatid,* was not directly influenced by the wood carving of the Luba people of the East Congo, specifically a chief's seat with caryatid.

The work of Paul Klee has many parallels in tribal arts, from the impact of the Incaic mummies of Peru to the visual influences of the fertility idols of the Ashanti tribe of Ghana. Sculptor Jacques Lipchitz was equally enamored of tribal arts, including both the totems of the American Northwest Coast and the copper figures of the Kota tribe of West Africa. Jean Dubuffet's intense interest in the art of children and, particularly, the art of the mentally afflicted (which he called *l'art brut*) gave rise to his visual references to paleolithic petroglyphs and the drawings of children and patients of mental hospitals. Hundertwasser (Fritz Stowasser) shows clear interests in the designs of fifteenth-century Tanta paintings. Brassaï evokes the paleolithic female fertility figures called Venuses. And Constantin Brancuşi owes a great debt to the remarkable and ancient sculptures of the Cyclades Islands.

It is not an overstatement to suggest that the entire movement called modern art was a twentieth-century awakening to tribal and prehistoric arts that proved to be as important as the Renaissance reawakening to the classical art of Greece. In many cases, such as Picasso and Brancuşi, the impact of tribal and prehistoric arts brought about revolutions in Western artistic forms and ideas, producing much of the seminal art of our century. The impact of the primal mentality is found in the arts of most Western nations, from the paintings of American abstract expressionist Jackson Pollock (influenced by Navajo sand painters), to the dances of American modernist Martha Graham (influenced by Pueblo Indian rites), and the sculpture of British sculptor Henry Moore (influenced by the reclining Choc-Mool figures of the Toltec-Maya world of Yucatán).

This appropriation of tribal art has roused a great deal of concern and consternation during the past twenty years. The use of tribal and prehistoric art forms are the basis of a huge controversy argued by identity politicians who regard the arts as "copyrightable" possessions; by indulgent art critics who are always anxious to get on the multicultural bandwagon; by progressive sociologists and political militants who know and care nothing about art; by cultural reactionaries and purists who believe that tribal cultures do not and should not change but should remain in a perpetual backwater; and by just about everybody else who is cranked up by the plight of hula hoops, Studebakers, and, of course, the "beleaguered savage."

Beyond this heated and rather pointless argument about ethnic plagiarism and cultural possessiveness are historical facts that make it clear that cultural exchange has always been a vital and persistent aspect of human growth and development, even the source of human diversity, because every influence—even the Pueblo Indian adaptation into their ritual pantheon of a "Santa Claus Kachina"—represents the transformation of a borrowed and alien influence into a profoundly assimilated aspect of the borrowing culture. To say otherwise is simply to deny the historical records of both the victors and the victims, the West and the East, the tribal world and the industrial world.

When the lessons of history manage to cool down the accusations of Western piracy, then the discussion turns to a very interesting and reasonable assertion: that the artists of the West who appropriate forms and ideas from prehistoric and tribal cultures fail to understand the mythic context of what they appropriate, so their art becomes not only a matter of theft but also a matter of desecration. There is, in fact, some basis for this argument. Yet those who indulge in such a fierce debate never address the equally puzzling fact that tribal peoples also fail to grasp the intent and context of the elements of Western culture that they emulate. And, if desecration is what concerns critics of appropriation in Western art, because they believe the use of tribal religious images by outsiders is a blasphemy, then they should take a long look at various Christian sects—such as the Christians in Ethiopia, in Japan, in South America, and in Africa—and take a careful listen to the marvelous variety of forms in which Mass is celebrated: *Misa Flamenca, Missa Luba,* or the *Misa Criolla,* to name just a few of them. These devout Christians of other lands deviate lavishly not only from the orthodox doctrine of Europe and America, but they also take great, imaginative liberties in the representation of Christ in many ethnic guises and in unlimited non-Western art forms and rituals, often in a marriage of pre-Christian and Christian motifs. Such manipulation of European Christian iconography and ceremonies of the Middle Ages (the time when the West reinvented a deviant Christian imagery from its original Near Eastern forms) can be seen as religious degradation by those who are always looking for transcultural blasphemies. In fact, I recall visiting a Catholic church in Ecuador as the guest of a cultural attaché of the American consulate in Quito, who happened to be a Catholic. He was unbridled in his disparagement of local Catholics for what he called "their distortion and savaging of Church decorum." As far as he was concerned, the Indians of Ecuador had appropriated his religion and he didn't like the way they practiced it. Therefore, it would seem that both Western and non-Western peoples can be equally accused of cultural piracy and religious blasphemy, if we must persist with the debate over cultural appropriation.

But it does not seem likely that the debate will end very soon. According to Dutch art historian Charles Wentinck, "The quest by European artists for originality in the art of the South Sea Islands, Africa, and other civilizations borders on aesthetic exploitation. Such foreign exploitation and influences had already largely destroyed primitive civilizations. Their art cannot be used as a model: it cannot be copied, and where imitation occurs it is based on a misconception."

By seeing Western modernism as merely a matter of empty

manipulation of art forms without any concern for content, Wentinck is able to conclude that "herein lies the fundamental distinction between primitive and modern art, despite a resemblance in form. Those elements which in modern art are merely aimless devices and variations in form, in primitive art are a formal necessity arising from a religious sense and guided by an inner compulsion."

Despite the raging romanticism and banal invocation of the "noble savage" in such a statement, Wentinck's point is clearly drawn from the ethical relativism of the Boazian school of anthropology: i.e., Live and let live and don't mess with other people's cultures. For instance, Wentinck insists that "primitive art is a religious art; for the religious artist, the 'canon' of his art is divine revelation. But a religion cannot be rediscovered at will, just as myth cannot be manufactured." Wentinck also declared, with some justification, that after the Middle Ages, the possibilities of a religious art in the West virtually vanished because of the secularization of society and the rise of a rich and manipulative middle class with purely profane interests in the arts. He also points out, with a good deal of accuracy, that when twentieth-century Western artists sensed the spiritual bankruptcy of their own society, they reached out into other cultures for something they felt keenly lacking in their own world. The fact that people of the West went in search of themselves in cultures they had overrun greatly antagonizes old-guard Boazian anthropologists, who are particularly enraged by the notion that the West, having won everything and, in the process, having lost itself, has now reinvaded other cultures in search of what was lost. Admittedly, there is a good deal of irony in such a transaction. And, if the situation makes Boazians irate, one can only imagine the disdain of identity politicians who can understand culture only as a matter of ethnic property.

But long before identity politicians began their attack on artists like Pablo Picasso, the renowned French anthropologist and structuralist Claude Lévi-Strauss was particularly hostile to both Picasso and the whole field of modernist art. In Picasso's art Lévi-Strauss saw the inner spiritual mentality of the primal person replaced by what he called "a kind of pulverization of artistic canons." He asked if that which had possessed a metaphysical significance in primal art had been reduced to what he called an "inner decoration" in Western appropriations of primal forms. But Lévi-Strauss, we must remember, understood visual art as a system of signs, quite literally as a language of syntactical marks. He supposed that a language is a system with meaning. According to Lévi-Strauss, a language that is dependent upon aesthetic emotion—as in abstract art—is only the poetic expression of an individual, rather than the expression of a community, and, therefore, as far as Lévi-Strauss was concerned, it has nothing to do with true language (Wentinck). Lévi-Strauss called such art a "pseudolanguage" because it lacks common symbols and, therefore, it cannot communicate syntactically. But what Lévi-Strauss failed to understand is a far more central aesthetic idea. Art as a discursive language is the kind of art that is itself a pseudoart, because the very essence of art is its independence from syntactical forms of meaning, and its power of communication derived from its existence as a "language of metaphor"—not of readable signs.

Wentinck eventually exonerates modern art from his charges of being devoted to nothing but empty manipulation of formal elements when he admits that in the face of spiritual bankruptcy Western artists succeeded in creating interior and personal mythologies that are capable of a subtle kind of communication that has no reliance on occult notions or the Jungian collective unconscious. "The Western world was trying to find the primal experience, the sphere of the miraculous, the foundation of all things. On its way it encountered primitive art. A shock was the result, a shock of recognition. The imagination of the West was kindled by the bizarre works of these primitive forerunners, and from 1907 on an undeniable affinity of form emerged" (Wentinck).

So it would seem that there is some vindication for the modern arts of the West when history is researched carefully and when some degree of reason prevails over dogma. We can now agree that the Western artist undertook a profoundly imaginative process when borrowing elements from tribal cultures. But how about the things that tribal peoples took from the West? Did they profit from them and did they use them to create vital elements of their own cultures? The answer seems to be a resounding "yes."

For many tribal peoples the incursions of Western technologies, materials, and ideas revived obsolescent and even obsolete art forms. For instance, during his years of work with the Pueblo people, archaeologist and anthropologist J. Walter Fewkes provided the entire basis for the rediscovery of the lost traditions of Sikyatki pottery both through the examples of his archaeological finds and through his abiding inspiration and encouragement. In 1895, the pioneer Hano Indian potter Nampeyo willingly expressed her debt to Fewkes, who had introduced her to ancient pottery from his digs at Sikyatki (present-day Yellow House in the Hopi province of Tusayan). She had never before seen such pottery, and its example guided all of her subsequent creation of pottery. Yet, for all we really know, today's Pueblo Indians may have little or no historical connection with the people who lived at Sikyatki and produced such grand pottery. And the celebrated modern pottery of today's Pueblo people may be a complete misunderstanding of the context in which the pottery was originally created and used by the long-vanished Anasazi people, who occupied Pueblo lands long before the appearance of Pueblo culture as we know it today.

But does any of this uncertainty really matter? I don't think so.

What Wentinck and Lévi-Strauss fail to recognize is that, from a creative perspective, the misinterpretation of one culture by another culture can be both significant and productive. Some of the great windfalls of science and culture have been built on misunderstandings and accidents. In the arts, misreading has been a boon. It was because the Kathakali dancers of Southern India *failed* to understand baby dresses that they were able to step away from a Western cultural context and create a highly original and productive context of their own. Pioneer American dancers Isadora Duncan and Ruth St. Denis totally misunderstood the culture and dances of ancient Greece and India, and yet they created their own dances, presumably built on Greek and Indian models, which revolutionized world dance. There are countless similar examples of such creative misconceptions, like the famous cargo cults of the South Pacific, which totally misunderstood the context of military aircraft transporting supplies to American troops, and saw, instead, those mysterious planes as gift-bearing aviary deities for whom they industriously built altars in the form of torch-lit landing strips, in the hope that the magic birds would return and bring them benedictions and gifts.*

When this kind of misunderstanding occurs in language, we face a breakdown in communication or, at best, the creation of puns and satirical twists of the facts. But such discursive "understanding" is not an aspect of art. Art is born of experiences that can transform anything—agony, bliss, anxiety, or peace, the richest metals or the worst urban trash—into revelation.

What Lévi-Strauss reasonably suggested is that primal people are able to infuse their borrowings from the West with an active spiritual paradigm that transforms whatever they produce into an aspect of themselves while, at the same time, he insisted that Western artists lack an active spirituality, and thus all they can do is elaborate on borrowed, empty forms. But the accusation that modern art is devoted to form at the expense of content, while primal art is overflowing with contextual meaning, is a romantic delusion. As art critic Michael Benson has pointed out, "From the Parthenon to Poussin to Manet to Mondrian, content, not form, has guided European art." The primacy of content over form is a fundamental aspect of Western artistic tradition. Form was subser-

---

*Interpretative errors are not limited to tribal folk. There is also an object lesson to be found in David Macaulay's *Motel of the Mysteries*, which brilliantly satirizes the creative nonsense archaeologists apply to their interpretation of ancient sites.

vient to content in the rebellious Dadaist movement, which revolutionized twentieth-century artistic philosophy by satirizing the inbred "seriousness" of academic, representational painting and sculpture. And content was certainly an essential element "in the Christian catacombs and other underground meeting places where persecuted sects communicated their religious messages in the most direct visual way possible" (Benson).

But beyond the obvious iconic aspects of religious imagery, there is also an aspect of artistic content that grows out of the purely formal aspects of art and that invokes an enigmatic and splendid response called "aesthetic emotion," which Lévi-Strauss was apt to impugn as pointless fluff. But despite reams of contention and intellectual argument, it is difficult to dismiss such a deeply human experience, because almost all of us have had the fortune of encountering an amazing experience that seems to have no connection with one's specific background or predispositions, like being Greek or Mexican, Christian or Jewish. It is an experience that simply summons and envelops something within us that is more fundamental than the conditions that make us specifically who and what we are.

> Aesthetic emotion has something to do with what people have felt climbing Greek and Mexican temples, or standing inside a French cathedral or the Hagia Sophia or gazing at the paintings of Piero della Francesca, Matisse or Tao-chi, or feeling the ferocious intensity of sculptures by Michelangelo, the Aztecs or the Egyptians. It is an experience at once personal and impersonal, specific and general. It is rooted in the object but it also suggests something beyond the object. It suggests the depth of feeling and knowledge of which human beings are capable. It brings with it an intensified awareness of life and death. It is related to the experience of revelation and love and is ultimately just as resistant to theory and language. Indeed it suggests that what is most profound can never be analyzed or held in words. (Benson)

Aesthetic emotion also invokes a sense of continuity in the human experience. Greek art was an heir of Egypt. Christian art was shaped by the idealizations of Greece and the mystic and disembodied spiritualism of the East. Even tribal arts are often the flowering of a native imagination made possible by Western materials, technologies, and artistic concepts. In turn, modernism resonates with the influences of Africa, China, Egypt, ancient Greece, and Mexico as well as prehistoric European art. Postmodernism reflects the impact of numerous popular and folk traditions from every global culture.

In the unexpected and in the unknown we are able to imagine ourselves. What this seems to mean is that *impersonation* is the means by which we find out who we are. Culture is a living process; it is not simply a self-contained abstraction, an immovable monument that withstands the assault of time. Culture lives and dies. It changes and grows. It is the act of a group of people imagining themselves, because cultural and individual identity is not innate but created and invented out of mind and spirit and aesthetic emotion. And though there are a great many people who play at ethnic and intellectual Halloween, assuming the costumes of exotic peoples while neglecting the mentality of their various cultures, there are also a great many creative people who succeed in discovering themselves in mirrors that reflect *otherness*—the unimaginable and unexpected rather than their own familiar persona.

Jean Cocteau told us: "The artist is a mirror. When you look into an artist you are likely to find out more about yourself than you will about him or his art."

XXI.

Judgment

The Mythology of Exclusion

Where there is a work of art, there is no madness; and yet madness is contemporary with the work of art, since it inaugurates the time of its truth.

Michel Foucault (1977)

A winged angel floats in a cloud, blowing his trumpet. Figures of the dead rise from their tombs and ascend toward the angel. This is the Judgment card of the Tarot deck, and it represents atonement, the metaphoric moment when we are called upon to account for the manner in which we have lived. It also signifies rebirth and rejuvenation. For the purpose of this essay, Judgment is the basis of an illusive cultural and ethnic inclusiveness that the world is in great need of during a time when the terrorist concepts of ethnic cleansing and the extremist strictures of Muslim, Jewish, and Christian fundamentalism advocate and excuse a deadly and retrograde mythology of exclusivity.

We live at a time when there is persistent revision of public attitudes about the most basic issues of life. In the process of meeting the challenge of such shifts in ideology, many of us are discovering that we are often better at changing our minds than changing our myths, those metaphoric concepts and standards that underlie our evaluation of other peoples.

There is probably no mythology as persistent and destructive as the almost universally held vision of our own people as a "chosen people": more blessed, more protected from our enemies, more exonerated from our atrocities, more favored by whatever god presumably condones our most heinous behavior toward those who are not one of us. Closely allied to that exalted myth of a superior and chosen people is the equally Machiavellian myth of the power of ordinary people made possible by their god-given, innate wisdom. The populist image of the "common man" is just another version of the collective notion of any ethnic group that considers itself the beneficiary of god-given privilege, won without edification or exertion or motivation.

What results from this exaltation of one group above all others or the veneration of any group above the individual is a repetition of the French Revolution: the furious desire to destroy anything, the best along with the worst, if it evokes the memory of a real or imagined enemy. This inclination is nothing new. Throughout history, empires have celebrated the destruction of outsiders by methodically executing them, while outsiders themselves have commemorated their victories over repression by imitating the methods of those who subjugated them, fighting not for equity but for dominion. Those who have been dominant are well known for their cruelty, which is second only to the cruelty unleashed upon the slavers by slaves, retaliating with a ferocity and ruthlessness equal to the ferocity and ruthlessness that once oppressed them, rather than inventing social reforms that rectify the social injustices of deposed regimes and despots.

Today we are attempting to avoid the destructive mania of the retaliatory mentality of the French Revolution at the same time that we are trying to find ways of breaking the political and cultural domination of one group of people over the lives and minds of all other peoples. A central issue of this social transformation is an effort to reinterpret art and culture in a nonelitist manner. This populist impulse began in the 1890s as a political movement that embodied an ideal that envisioned the "common man" as possessing wisdom as a gift of God—resulting, the populists would have us believe, in a condition that makes all people capable of astute judgment and ethical behavior that was once the exclusive province of those privileged by rank or wealth. The concept, at face value, seems highly utopian and deeply indebted to a romantic "return to nature" envisioned by philosopher Jean-Jacques Rousseau. But the inevitable implications of this populist stance suggest that we all spring fully grown from the head of Zeus, like the goddess of wisdom, Athena, and that intelligence and skill are, therefore, inborn and god given rather than the result of arduous effort. Populist philosophy also suggests that biology is democratic, despite all we now know to the contrary. It supposes that we are all born with perfect health: no inborn defects, no asthma, no colon cancer genes, no predisposition for sickle cell anemia, schizophrenia, or multiple sclerosis. Ultimately, populists equate conformity (we are all the same) with equality (we may be different but we have equal rights). They make the celebration of the "common man" the source of special social empowerment as autocratic as the elitist notion of the "privileged few."

Nineteenth-century populism didn't really take hold in America until after the Second World War, when it assumed an important place in the political arena. Believing that the grand colonial traditions of the past had no relevance after the war, artists, among many revisionists, searched for a populist mentality that might serve as the foundation for a new and less class-oriented and -segregated society—a society centered upon egalitarianism. This cultural process gradually assumed an American emphasis built on the growing belief that virtue and merit are not limited to a racial, financial, and educational elite.

The emergence of the civil rights movement and the struggle of minorities for social justice provided populism with new momentum in the 1960s, a time when many people were trying to discover the means by which art and society could better reflect the long struggle of common people against imperialism, sexism, and other forms of bigotry. At the time, the exclusively empowered white middle class was the major target of criticism, and little attention was given to the unfortunate fact that racism, sexism, and all other forms of bigotry are lavishly perpetuated by all kinds of people, including "common" people.

Political philosopher Philip Green would have us believe that the reason ordinary "defenseless" people are so often procapitalist or profascist or procommunist is not because their naïveté allows them to be misled and hoodwinked by cunning political leaders into wrongly espousing what is for them a self-destructive inegalitarian social order, but "because they are *driven* there by the activities of those ruling groups against whose power many people genuinely *are* defenseless." The fact that people are driven by ruling groups may very well explain the rise of organized labor and the escalation of the civil rights movement of blacks, women, and gays, but Green does not help us understand how the "collective wisdom of ordinary people" *drove* them into the stupendously popular Nazi regime with its sickening killing machine or how it induced them into supporting the revolting history of racism in South Africa and the American South (and North); nor how it encouraged them to back the widely supported Serbian homicides called ethnic cleansing in the former Yugoslavia or to bless the calamitous bloodshed in Northern Ireland or to approve an almost endless list of other atrocities committed with the apparent consent or acquiescence of ordinary people.

In an article in *Newsweek* (June 28, 1993) entitled "The Puzzle of Genius," the authors note that "as long as egalitarianism rejects the mystique of genius in favor of the notion that *everyone* has it in him to be an artist, there will be no successors to Picasso or Mies van der Rohe."

Populism wants us to dismiss the so-called great person theory and support the extreme egalitarian notion that a great idea is born of the people, so if one particular person does not discover and voice such a great idea then someone else will surely do so. One cannot avoid thinking that this concept parallels the familiar suggestion that, given enough time, a great novel can be created by a monkey at a typewriter. But the sad truth pronounced by scholars of just about every persuasion and background is that most of us will not be exceptional no matter how many opportunities we are given. Neal Thornberry, a management professor at Babson College at Wellesley, tells us that the message of our society is to excel. "Stand out in the crowd! Do more than the other person so that the boss, your peers, or the attractive man or woman at the health spa will notice you!" But unfortunately, Thornberry notes, "most of us are average and mediocre." When he stands before a seminar, Professor Thornberry knows "that sixty-eight percent of the class is average. They will remain average, no matter what I do to make them excel." The professor laments that statistic, but as most statisticians, popular psychologists, and social critics, from Erick Fromm to Rollo May, have informed us, the great majority of us are deeply fearful of being exceptional and urgently want to be ordinary.*

Ironically, our connotation of the ordinary is so ingrown that it prescribes that we must be ordinary even when we achieve extraordinary success. It is presumed that in popular culture a creation wins massive popularity simply because it is exceptionally ordinary. In this way, even success (which should elevate the ordinary person to an extraordinary position) is commonly viewed as fabulous popularity—a celebrity that results, paradoxically, from the exquisite accessibility of ordinariness.

Some time ago, I was a guest at a dinner party honoring an author who had just won a very prestigious literary award. I was seated on one side of the writer, while on his other side was the husband of the hostess, who had made great efforts to snag the honor of giving the party, though she and her husband apparently knew the author only by reputation and knew nothing about his remarkable novels.

Toward the end of the evening, during coffee, the husband, who had not said a word during the entire dinner, leaned toward the author and asked him with both innocence and concern: "Have you ever considered writing a really successful book?"

The author looked thoroughly dismayed.

I quickly changed the subject.

But there was something to be learned from the husband's

---

* "*Adult Literacy in America,* a 150-page survey conducted by the Princeton-based Educational Testing Service and released by the Department of Education, reported that roughly 90 million Americans over age 16—almost half that category's total population—are, as far as most workplaces are concerned, basically unfit for employment. . . . Perhaps the worst news from the survey was the hubris expressed by those who were tested: when asked if they read well or very well, 71% of those in the bottom grade said yes. If the ETS survey is accurate, the U.S. is not only significantly populated by people unprepared for current and advancing technologies, but most of them do not know that they do not know." (*Time,* September 20, 1993)

assumption that the celebrated author had deliberately refused to use his considerable talents to write a best-seller, the kind of book the husband would have considered a success because it would be fantastically popular and because it would make a lot of money. After all, reasoned the husband, why bother to write a book if it isn't going to be a best-seller?

For many people it is difficult to comprehend that most artists do not plot against the common good by producing works that are less than popular. The celebrated author at dinner does not choose the kind of books he writes any more than he chooses his sexual orientation or his nationality. He came by who he is by a long process that defies comprehension. By some quirk of fortune, popular success was not one of his aims or capacities. Perhaps he lacked an essential ordinariness, and so he had to be content with being extraordinary. Unfortunately, his host was unaware of what the author had achieved because the host had a very specific concept of success that had little appreciation for the kind of literary achievement the author had attained. Nor did the host grasp the fact that artists who achieve popular success possess a talent quite different from the talents of artists who achieve a more rarified success. Ignoring the highly debatable question of quality, it seems to me that the informing fact in this situation is one of difference in the creative lives of two very dissimilar kinds of artists whose works cannot and should not be compared.

In art and in society it has become progressively difficult to codify the qualities that make up an individual and an individual talent. The more we realize the impact of biology and biochemistry on what we once thought of as "human personality," the more we speculate about human beings as creatures largely formed and motivated in much the manner of other animals: by innate biochemical elements. The Faustian emphasis, so pronounced in the West, upon free will, mind, soul, and conscience, was once the ecclesiastical and romantic basis for considering people superior beings. That consensus is eroding at every turn, to such an extent that we begin to see the human being as an elaborate self-aggrandizing animal that is special and distinctive from other animals only in its unexcelled hubris.

"How are we to reconcile what [drugs like Prozac do] with our anti-deterministic notion of the continuous, autobiographical human self?" psychiatrist Peter D. Kramer asks. If a drug like Prozac can truly and fundamentally change a person's personality, then what is this entity we traditionally call the Self? Could it possibly be something as fundamentally biological as brain chemistry? "When one pill at breakfast makes you a new person," writes Kramer, "it's difficult to resist the . . . visceral certainty that who people are is largely biologically determined."

Our obsolescent notion of personality, derived largely from Freud, suggests that human mentality and sensibility are formed by experience—by nurture and not by nature. For two decades that concept of personality as the result of experience, education, and opportunity intermeshed, idealistically, with the tenets of egalitarian democracy. For instance, in the 1960s and 1970s, those who agreed with psychologist Arthur Jensen that intelligence is largely inherited were called racists, and the proposition that "biology is destiny" was unthinkable. Today, says Kramer, we are brought to a "frontier of contemporary thought" from which there seems to be no going back. Surrounded by "the material fruits of the new biology"—by the products of what Kramer calls "the new biological materialism" (such as genetically engineered plants and animals and recombinant-DNA probes)—the proposition that most of what we call personal attributes in human beings are largely innate, biochemical responses seems incontrovertible (Kramer).

This biochemical scenario sounds rather sinister, threatening us with all the negative potentials of mind and species control. But that scenario, for better or worse, will doubtlessly be the reality of the future.

For this essay, the implications of these revisions of our notion of human personality are important because they represent a drastic alteration in the conception of both the individual and the social group. The tenets of the new biology require me to clarify that when I speak of the individual as distinct from the group, I do not mean the staunch and self-created individual of either romanticist Rousseau or capitalist John Adams. What I have in mind is the view of an individual as a personality who combines the biochemical continuity of human evolution with the individuation that arises from both available experience and the assertion of will. In this way there is for all personalities an unquestionable biochemical link to the group—a biochemical reworking of the Jungian "collective unconscious" into something like a "collective biochemistry"— that creates those predispositions we call "humanness." At the same time there is the singular person whose experience and efforts and various uses of human predispositions produce an individuated being out of a set of highly structured biochemical possibilities. The exceptional individual of this sort does not exist in isolation but is part of the group and is capable of speaking in a singular voice from out of a collective vision. That voice is distinctly that of the individual. But what that voice says arises from the collective biochemical reservoir of humankind. As such, art is the act of an individual, but the expressive impact that art induces in the group is not created by the individual artist. It simply flows through the artist. It is not the work of art that is universally expressive. It is our *response* to art that is universal. Art gives us a sense of connection with a collective mentality, because what art expresses arises from and is recognized by that still mysterious and profoundly collective biochemical reservoir that animates our species.

There is no doubt that the exceptional person echoes the sensibility of an entire community, but there is also no doubt that he or she does so in a vigorous spirit of defiance that is bewildering to most people in the group. The defiance is the necessary act of "departure" that allows the hero to escape the constraints of the group and venture beyond what, for ordinary people, is understood as the known and knowable. It is a defiance that brings a boon to humankind, but it also causes the ostracism of those who create seminal ideas and social reforms: Nelson Mandela, Jesus Christ, Martin Luther King, Gautama the Buddha, Muhammad, and Karl Marx. Meanwhile, that enigmatic wisdom of ordinary people, which Green so greatly admires, turned Christ into Christianity, Gautama into Buddhism, Muhammad into Islam, and Marx into Stalinist communism, with all the obvious strengths and weakness of such popular movements.

Even today conservative populism sees the egalitarian movement not so much as the liberation of oppressed peoples, but as the subduing or dismissing of the social role of exceptional individuals, whatever their gender or ethnicity. We must remember that the unthinkable incursions upon the creative efforts of Soviet artists under socialist realism (the mandate to make "art for the people") was once touted as a populist edict, and the fundamentalist repulsion for "humanists" is also a populist stance. Yet, despite these and many other contradictions, populism persists today as a cultural phenomenon.

The populist battle to control education, government endowments, public art, and public opinion has greatly heated up since the 1960s, becoming a highly vocal contest between ever-increasing groups of oppositional lobbyists, coalitions, and independent activists. Yet, despite very considerable differences at both extremes of the debate, there has emerged a centralist position that acknowledges that both the community and the individual are essential elements in a truly inclusive society, and that the cultural elitism of the past was destructive because it encouraged cultural exclusivity and the exclusion of both individuals and groups on the basis of ethnicity and gender. A great many people have come to believe that it is the design of the wealthy and privileged elite to keep other groups on the outside, condemning them to live within the bounds of a neglected and depreciated "ethnic" culture. And yet the more "outsiders" insist that the doors of society open to alternative voices, the more resistant, and sometimes fearful, the elite culture becomes.

Some of this fear is understandable. The outsiders' quest for pluralism can easily change from an egalitarian ideal into a battle for dominance. It has happened many times before—between empowered and disempowered groups and also within the ranks of minorities themselves. The ascendant power often disposes of the old power in a terrible and pointless confrontation. This is the Bolshevik putsch and the French Revolution all over again. Libraries are burned; museums are devastated; schools are closed; intellectuals are assassinated; and war crime tribunals execute both the guilty and the innocent. When any group demands that populist culture *entirely replace* an elite culture of the past, it is actually forsaking pluralism and embracing the terrible exclusivity it originally repudiated.

In the case of populist art, if the movement is to achieve a valid status, it cannot simply reject traditional standards in art. Populist art will have to do something besides demolish the classics. It will have to affirm its own standards, its own model of cultural integration, and combine those ideas with mainstream concepts as well as the diverse concepts of all the world's cultures. If populist artists—who disdain "high culture"—nonetheless wish to present their works in galleries, concert halls, theaters, and urban marketplaces where "high art" is dominant, then it seems clear that they must introduce *inclusive* standards of merit based on their own measure of artistic achievement.

If anyone believes that artists who work outside the dominant culture do not need or have artistic standards, and if they believe that any form of artistic standard is elitist, then they don't know very much about the culture of outsiders. Jazz is such an outsider's music, yet it has evolved a unique set of standards by which jazz artists are judged—as distinct from the standards used for judging classical or folk musicians. In the American Indian Pueblo settlements, few of the old people may know much about Rodin or Picasso, but they are in touch with their own traditions and those unique cultural standards that allow them to recognize and praise the beauty and skillful construction of native pottery. Among older Japanese people there is also an instantaneous acknowledgment of a Kabuki actor of great merit with traditional chants of an actor's name voiced by the entire audience when he achieves a particularly excellent moment. This shouted adoration is interjected into the actual performance, becoming an exciting part of it, like the *"Olés"* at a bullfight. On the other hand, many young Japanese people have little or no comprehension of this bourgeois form of acting, which grew out of a seventeenth-century rebellion against the elitism of the Noh theater performed for the nobility. Ironically, to these youthful Japanese people the populist Kabuki theater is elitist.

Implicit in the word "culture" is the idea of a standard of merit. There is nothing elitist or exclusive about the idea of artistic standards. On the contrary, what pluralism really demands is not the abolition of "high culture," but the acceptance of the idea that there are many kinds of cultures that possess standards of equal significance and merit.

The old imperialist mentality saw itself as superior to outsiders, and it turned its arbitrary code of standards into a wall to keep the "barbarians" out. Today, the challenge for all of us is to evolve a sensibility capable of thriving in a diverse world in which there are many different and equally valid standards of merit and in which there are no walls and no barbarians.

Michel Foucault (1977) told us that "the moment when, together, the work of art and madness are born and fulfilled is the beginning of the time when the world finds itself arraigned by that work of art and responsible before it for what it is."

XXII.

The World

Triumph of Dreams

Every one of us is like a man who sees things in a dream and thinks that he knows them perfectly and then wakes up to find that he knows nothing.

Plato

A female figure, nearly nude except for a diaphanous scarf blown by the wind, stands within an elliptical wreath. She holds a wand and appears to be dancing. In the corners of the Tarot card appear the winged cherubim represented by a man, an eagle, a bull, and a lion. The symbol of this final Tarot card, which is called "The World," is most appropriate for this concluding chapter. It means completion and the end result of all efforts.

I will end as I started. You awaken from a dream. And what seemed so vivid and clear in your dream becomes the source of perplexity and uncertainty because you cannot express your experience in the words available to you in your waking life.

Taoist philosopher Chuang-tzu would intrigue us, though he would not comfort us, with one of his illustrious aphorisms: "Last night I dreamed that I was a butterfly, but today I do not know for certain if I am a man who dreamed he was a butterfly or a butterfly who is now dreaming that it is a man."

Plato would assure us that our experience of an unspeakable schism between the world of wakefulness and the world of sleep is an analogy of our entire relationship to that "exterior world" that we believe to be the ultimate reality, while we have no final proof that it is reality. He would likely remind us of his famous parable, in which he compares our world to a cave. We are prisoners of the cave and cannot look behind us into the source of the light streaming into the darkness. We see only the shadows of some distant but luminous reality we can never directly encounter.

Much of what passes as "reality"—what we innocently call politics and history and reportage—is nothing more or less than our dreams turned into banalities. Most of us are content with such a utilitarian fiction. We must live our lives in a political world of many practical dangers and few consolations. We must reconcile the vast diversity of our individual dreams with a homogeneous social mythology upon which we built our notions of justice and

317

equity. Yet no political philosophy or social system has ever explained death or joy or suffering. Even the prophets, whose voices have become remote and unbelievable for many of us, have been unable to quell Job's persistent outcry: "Why is light given to a man whose way is hid?"

For all the uncertainties about an ultimate reality, we still must forge governmental regulations and invent even the most commonplace laws. We must put up traffic signs and insist upon a collective consensus about the meanings of "Stop" and "Go." We must make the far more difficult decision about what children should be told about our own world and the worlds of others. And, despite the transitory and ambivalent nature of such practical decisions, we must somehow believe in them as realities with substance and context and permanence. As Sartre said: *We must imagine ourselves to be happy.* So urgent is our need to trust in our social and political parables that we sometimes forget that they are only the shadows of Plato's cave—unprovable doctrines, despite all of our passionate faith in them as facts.

Our dedication to reality leaves us so little time for our dreams. We neglect them. We dismiss them as nonsense. Many of us even repudiate them. We sometimes forget that we use the word *dreams* not only to describe the visions of sleep but also to describe our fondest hopes and aspirations—our fancies.

In turning our backs on the illumination of dreams we are left with nothing but the shadows of a world we can only know through banalities, relinquishing our unrelenting human desire to encounter the ultimate experience of ourselves.

Yet, happily, there are also people who refuse to abandon their dreams. Instead, they live between the worlds of flesh and fantasy. They change their languages in an effort to speak the unspeakable. And they undertake this complicated transformation of expression as an act of passion, driven by the hope of somehow capturing the illusive power of their visions that allude, momentarily, to that mysterious fire that casts the shadows that we call "our world."

Painters do just that when they abandon or rethink conventional concepts of visual representation. Composers reimagine the sounds and the forms they use to make music. Choreographers reinvent the human body. Writers destroy the ordinary language of daily life and use words "poetically"—as metaphors capable of describing the indescribable.

We have followed the paths of such visionary artists, winding our way through the labyrinth of dreams. And we have discovered the fragile trails that countless artists have imprinted upon the darkness of the labyrinth—luminous recollections of who we have been and what we are becoming. It is a mythic trail that helps us find our way through the vast interior of ourselves.

What the arts preserve is a world of sounds, words, images, and movements invented by those who have gone into the labyrinth before us. By those who have ventured to the center where ideas become acts. Where myths are transformed into rituals. By those who have risked a journey into the cavern of the heart, where art is born and where we dream ourselves into existence.

The trail leads to the world of art, myth, and metaphor—those intuitive and imaginal effervescences of the mind that coax us into the infinite darkness of things unknown and unnamed. Mythic tales that transform the unreal into a new reality. Metaphors born out of the dreamtime that mysteriously change the ineffable into something that is finally spoken. And, by such ancient acts of the imagination, the mythic and metaphoric elements of art are capable of changing forever the way we see ourselves and the way we see our world.

Bibliography

Allende, Isabel. *New York Times Book Review* (February 7, 1993).

Arnheim, Rudolf. *Visual Thinking.* University of California Press, 1969.

Artaud, Antonin. *Selected Writings.* Farrar, Straus & Giroux, 1976.

———. *Theatre and Its Double.* Grove Press, 1958.

Bachofen, J. J. *Myth, Religion, and Mother Right.* Routledge and Kegan Paul, 1967.

Baring, Anne and Jules Cashford. *The Myth of the Goddess.* Viking, 1991.

Barr, David. See Jamake Highwater, "Sacred Architecture."

Becker, Howard S. *Outsiders: Studies in the Sociology of Deviance.* Free Press/Macmillan, 1963.

Benedict, Ruth. *Patterns of Culture.* Houghton Mifflin, 1934.

Benson, Michael. "Is 'Quality' an Idea Whose Time Has Gone?" *New York Times,* Arts and Leisure Section (July 22, 1990).

Berger, John. *The Success and Failure of Picasso.* Penguin, 1965.

Bersani, Leo. "Is the Rectum a Grave?" *October* 43 (1985).

Bhabha, Homi K. "Of Mimicry and Man" in *Politics and Ideology,* edited by James Donald and Stuart Hall. Open University Press, 1986.

Burke, Kenneth. *Psychology and Form.* Macmillan, 1947.

Buruma, Ian. *A Japanese Mirror.* Penguin, 1984.

Butler, Judith. *Gender Trouble.* Routledge and Kegan Paul, 1990.

Campbell, Joseph. *The Hero with a Thousand Faces.* Princeton University Press, 1949.

———. *The Masks of God: Creative Mythology.* Penguin, 1968.

———. *Transformations of Myth Through Time.* Harper & Row, 1990.

Cardinal, Roger. *Outsider Art.* Praeger, 1972.

Cassirer, Ernst. *An Essay on Man*. Yale University Press, 1944a.

―――. *Language and Myth*. Cambridge University Press, 1944b.

Cassou, Jean. "Art and Confrontation" in *The Arts in an Age of Change*. New York Graphic Society, 1968.

Cousineau, Phil and Joseph Campbell. *The Hero's Journey: Joseph Campbell on His Life and Work*. Harper San Francisco, 1990.

Daiches, David. *The Novel and the Modern World*. University of Chicago Press, 1960.

Davies, Paul. *The Edge of Infinity*. Random House, 1988.

Deregowski, Jan B. "The Split Image," *Scientific American* (November 1972).

Dollimore, Jonathan. *Sexual Dissidence*. Oxford University Press, 1991.

Douglas, Mary. *Purity and Danger: An Analysis of the Concept of Pollution and Taboo*. Ark Paperbacks, 1984.

Douglas, William Lake. "A Garden Progress" in *Garden Design*. Simon and Schuster, 1984.

Dufrenne, Mikel. *The Phenomenology of Aesthetic Experience*. Northwestern University Press, 1973.

Dyer, Richard. "Getting Over the Rainbow" in *Silver Linings*, edited by George Bridges and Rosalind Brunt. Macmillan, 1987.

Edinger, Edward F. *Philosophical Papers, Quadrant*, vol. 11, no. 2 (Winter 1978).

Ehrenzweig, Anton. See Roger Cardinal.

Eiseley, Loren. *The Firmament of Time*. Atheneum, 1975.

Eliade, Mircea. *A History of Religious Ideas*. Two vols. University of Chicago Press, 1982.

Eliot, T. S. *Murder in the Cathedral: The Complete Poems and Plays, 1909–1950*. Harcourt, Brace & World, 1971.

―――. *Selected Essays*. Faber & Faber, 1932.

Feld, Eliot. From a National Public Radio interview, 1992.

Finkelstein, David. See Gary Zukav.

Foucault, Michel. *Language, Counter-Memory, Practice.* Cornell University Press, 1977.

———. *Madness and Civilization.* Random House, 1965.

———. *This Is Not a Pipe.* University of California Press, 1982.

Fowlie, Wallace. *Age of Surrealism.* Indiana University Press, 1960.

Friedenberg, Edgar A. *R. D. Laing.* Viking, 1973.

Fry, Roger. *Vision and Design.* Chatto & Windus, 1925.

Gardner, Helen. *Art Through the Ages.* Sixth edition, revised by Horst de la Croix and Riochard G. Tansey. Harcourt Brace Jovanovich, 1975.

Gates, Jr., Henry Louis. "The Weaning of America," *The New Yorker* (April 19, 1993).

Genet, Jean. *The Thief's Journal.* Penguin, 1967.

Gide, André. *Journals.* Alfred A. Knopf, 1931.

Graburn, Nelson H. H. *Ethnic and Tourist Arts.* University of California Press, 1976.

Green, Philip. *The Pursuit of Inequality.* Pantheon, 1981.

Hamilton, Edith. *The Greek Way to Western Civilization.* Mentor, 1948.

Hatch, Elvin. *Culture and Morality.* Columbia University Press, 1983.

Heisenberg, Werner. *Physics and Philosophy.* Harper & Row, 1958.

Hess, Hans. *How Pictures Mean.* Pantheon, 1974.

Highwater, Jamake. "Controversy in Native American Art" in *Arts of the North American Indian,* edited by Edwin Wade. Hudson Hills Press/Philbrook Art Center, 1986.

———. *Dance: Rituals of Experience.* Princeton, 1992.

———. *Myth and Sexuality.* New American Library, 1990.

———. *The Primal Mind.* Harper & Row, 1981.

———. "Sacred Architecture," *Omni* magazine, September, 1989.

———. *Song from the Earth.* New York Graphic Society, 1976.

Hoefer, Hans Johannes. *Bali.* APA Publications, 1991.

Hughes, Robert. *Culture of Complaint.* Oxford University Press, 1993.

———. *The Shock of the New.* Alfred A. Knopf, 1981.

Huizinga, Johan. *Homo Ludens: A Study of the Play Element in Culture.* Beacon, 1950.

Innes, Christopher. *Holy Theatre: Ritual and the Avant Garde.* Cambridge University Press, 1981.

Inverarity, Robert Bruce. *Art of the Northwest Coast Indians.* University of California Press, 1971.

Janson, H. W. *History of Art.* Prentice-Hall, 1962.

Joad, C. E. M. *Guide to Philosophy.* Random House, 1936.

Johanson, Patricia. See Lippard.

Joyce, James. *A Portrait of the Artist as a Young Man.* Penguin, 1916 (1963).

Jung, Carl. *Symbols of Transformation.* Princeton University Press, 1953.

Kaplan, Stuart R. *The Encyclopedia of Tarot.* U.S. Games Systems, 1978.

Kepes, Gyorgy. *Language of Vision.* Paul Theobald Company, 1951.

Kierkegaard. See Rollo May.

Knight, Christopher. "Multiculturalism in Art," *Los Angeles Times* (April 4, 1993).

Kramer, Peter D. *Listening to Prozac.* Viking, 1993.

Kubler, George. *The Art and Architecture of Ancient America.* Penguin, 1975.

Kuhn, Thomas S. *The Structure of Scientific Revolutions.* University of Chicago Press, 1962.

Lacan, Jacques. Quoted by Shoshana Felman in "Turning the Screw of Interpretation," *Yale French Studies* (1977).

Lahr, John. "Movable Feast," *The New Yorker* (April 26, 1993).

———. "The World's Most Sensational Absence," *New York Times Book Review* (June 24, 1990).

Laing, R. D. *The Divided Self.* Penguin, 1963.

Langer, Susanne K. *Mind: An Essay on Human Feeling,* vol 1. Johns Hopkins Press, 1967.

———. *Philosophy in a New Key.* Harvard University Press, 1942.

———. *Problems in Art.* Charles Scribner's Sons, 1957.

Lawlor, Robert. *Voices of the First Day: Awakening in the Aboriginal Dreamtime.* Inner Traditions International, 1991.

Le Goff, Jacques. *Time, Work, and Culture in the Middle Ages.* University of Chicago Press, 1980.

Leveson, Paul. See Lippard.

Levin, Harry. *James Joyce.* New Directions, 1941.

Lippard, Lucy. *Mixed Blessings.* Pantheon, 1990.

———. *Overlay: Contemporary Art and the Art of Prehistory.* Pantheon, 1983.

Maclagan, David. *Creation Myths.* Thames and Hudson, 1967.

Mallarmé, Stephane. Quoted in *Axel's Castle* by Edmund Wilson. Charles Scribner's Sons, 1969.

Malraux, André. *The Walnut Tree of Altenburg.* Alfred A. Knopf, 1946.

Mandell, Richard D. *Sport: A Cultural History.* Columbia University Press, 1984.

Mann, Thomas. *The Magic Mountain.* Alfred A. Knopf, 1960.

Marcel, Anthony. Quoted in *Discovery* magazine (February 1985).

Marien, Mary. "Cultural Literacy Isn't a Matter of A to Z," *Christian Science Monitor* (February 22, 1989).

Martin, John. *America Dancing.* Dance Horizons, 1968.

May, Rollo. *The Courage to Create.* W.W. Norton Co., 1975.

McLanathan, Richard. *Art in America.* Harcourt Brace Jovanovich, 1973.

Mead, Margaret. "Art and Reality," *Chicago Art Journal,* vol. 4 (May 1943).

Merleau-Ponty, Maurice. *The Primacy of Perception.* Northwestern University Press, 1964.

Mitchell, John. *The Earth Spirit.* Thames and Hudson, 1975.

Momaday, N. Scott. *House Made of Dawn.* Penguin, 1966.

Morgan, Barbara. Quoted from a conversation with the author, ca. 1980.

Morton, Kathryn. "If Billy Budd Had Been a Rat," *New York Times Book Review* (August 28, 1988).

Muller, Herbert J. *The Uses of the Past.* Oxford University Press, 1952.

Munsterberg, Hugo. *Film: A Psychological Study.* Macmillan, 1970.

Neumann, Erich. *The Archetypal World of Henry Moore.* R. F. C. Hull, 1954.

Nietzsche, Friedrich. *The Birth of Tragedy,* translated by Walter Kaufmann. Random House, 1968.

Paglia, Camille. *Sexual Personae.* Yale University Press, 1990.

Rahv, Philip. "Notes on the Decline of Naturalism" in *Imagination and Idea.* New Directions, 1949.

Read, Herbert. *Icon and Idea.* Harvard University Press, 1965.

Redfield, Robert. *The Primitive World and Its Transformations.* Cornell University Press, 1957.

Renfrew, Colin. *Before Civilization.* Alfred A. Knopf, 1973.

Rhode, Eric. *A History of the Cinema.* Hill and Wang, 1976.

Richardson, E. P. *Painting in America.* Thomas Y. Crowell, 1956.

Roberts, Richard, with Joseph Campbell. *Tarot Revelations.* Vernal Equinox, 1979.

Russell, Bertrand. *A History of Western Philosophy.* Simon and Schuster, 1945.

Sadoul, Georges. *Dictionary of Films.* University of California Press, 1972.

Scheler, Max. *The Nature of Sympathy.* Faber & Faber, 1954.

Schmidt, Paul. *Arthur Rimbaud: Complete Works.* Harper & Row, 1967.

Segal, Charles. *Dionysiac Poetics and Euripides' Bacchae.* Princeton University Press, 1982.

Slattum, Judy. *Masks of Bali: Spirits of an Ancient Drama.* Chronicle, 1992.

Smith, John Maynard. See *Time.*

Smithson, Robert. See Lippard.

Sontag, Susan. "Notes on Camp" in *Against Interpretation.* Farrar, Straus, 1966.

Sproul, Barbara C. *Primal Myths: Creating the World.* Harper & Row, 1979.

Starkie, Enid. *Arthur Rimbaud.* New Directions, 1961.

Steiner, George. "Eros and Idiom" in *On Difficulty and Other Essays.* Oxford University Press, 1978.

———. *Real Presences: Is There Anything in What We Say?* Faber and Faber, 1989.

Stevens, Wallace. "The Noble Rider and the Sound of Words" in *The Language of Poetry,* edited by Allen Tate. Princeton University Press, 1942.

Stewart, Hilary. *Looking at Indian Art of the Northwest Coast.* University of Washington Press, 1979.

Thompson, William Irwin. *The Time Falling Bodies Take to Light*. St. Martin's, 1981.

Thornberry, Neal. "In Search of Mediocrity," *The Christian Science Monitor* (February 1, 1989).

Time. "Adult Literacy in America" (September 20, 1993).

———. "The Church Search" (April 5, 1993).

———. "Science, God, and Man" (December 28, 1992).

Trilling, Lionel. *The Liberal Imagination*. Charles Scribner's Sons, 1950.

Vogel, Amos. *Film as a Subversive Art*. Random House, 1974.

Vonnegut, Kurt, Jr. Quoted in *The New Fiction* by Joe David Bellamy, University of Illinois Press, 1974.

Wentinck, Charles. *Modern and Primitive Art*. Phaidon, 1979.

Whyte, L. L. *The Next Development in Man*. Henry Holt, 1948.

Wilde, Oscar. *The Artist as Critic: Critical Writing of Oscar Wilde*, edited by Richard Ellmann. W. H. Allen Company, 1970.

Williamson, Ray. "Native Americans Were Continent's First Astronomers," *The Smithsonian* (October 1978).

Wingert, Paul S. *Primitive Art: Its Traditions and Styles*. Oxford University Press, 1962.

Woods, Gregory. "The Sweetness of the Unsavory." *Times Literary Supplement* (June 1, 1993).

Yates, Frances. *Giordano Bruno and the Hermetic Tradition*. Oxford University Press, 1964.

Yeats, William Butler. *Selected Poems and Plays*. Collier Books, 1982.

Zajonc, Arthur. *Catching the Light.* Bantam, 1993.

Zimmer, Heinrich. *The King and the Corpse.* Princeton University Press, 1948.

Zukav, Gary. *The Dancing Wu Li Masters.* William Morrow, 1979.

Zweig, Paul. *The Heresy of Self-Love.* Princeton University Press, 1968.

Index

Index